The Momma Puzzle was Shortlisted for the Santa Fe Writers Project Literary Awards and named a Finalist for the Wandering Aengus and Trail to Table Book Awards.

"Hilary Plattner has written a wonderful memoir, which reads more like a novel and detective story. In it, she works to solve the mystery of her mother's suicide, as well as Plattner's own obsession with it. She rummages through memories, interviews relatives, and reviews decades of letters that reveal 'momma's' perceptive and often life-affirming nature. Plattner is a skillful guide. She ultimately solves the mystery, at least to her own satisfaction, as to why her mother would choose to leave life and her young children behind."

— Alex Marshall, author, *How Cities Work* and *Beneath the Metropolis*

"Her mother was vibrant, complex, and gone too soon. Now, decades after her mother's suicide, Hilary Plattner is finally ready to confront the ultimate mystery: why? What follows is a daughter's relentless, decades-long investigation, leading her through forgotten letters and fading memories to piece together the life of the woman she called "Momma." Part detective story, part lyrical memoir, *The Momma Puzzle* is an unforgettable journey into grief, legacy, and the enduring love that finally brings peace."

— Kathryn Dare, *City Book Review*

"If you've ever felt like you didn't quite finish the puzzle of a loved one's life, or if you simply appreciate a beautifully told story of complexity and resilience, this book is a must-read. It's a comforting, affirming reminder that seeking understanding is a crucial part of healing..."

— *Los Angeles Book Review*

"The book's archival method—reproducing letters, Christmas cards, newspaper clippings—creates a feeling of intimacy while foregrounding what cannot be known. A painter's business card, dress designs clipped from magazines…accumulate texture, but the most powerful passages acknowledge the limits of documentation. Suicide, the author writes, makes people 'disappear'…"

— *Kirkus Reviews*

"Plattner pieces together her mother's life story in this moving memoir, tackling loss, grief, and the aftershocks of generational trauma... Plattner's early memories of her mother provide a respite from the memoir's heavy subject matter, and, in appreciating the quiet moments of their time together...she derives much-needed meaning, reconciling her anger, guilt, and resentment with lingering feelings of love for a mother lost to her long ago. "

— *Publishers Weekly's* Booklife Reviews

"Hilary Plattner felt wrenchingly alone in the wake of her mother's 1968 suicide. At the time, suicide was rarely talked about—it's still not talked about enough, and this silence perpetuates stigma, which in turn perpetuates shame. Plattner's deep longing and determination to understand her mother will help others navigating suicide loss feel not only less alone, but be more ready to release the shame they've carried themselves. A moving, illuminating, necessary memoir."

— Gayle Brandeis, author, *The Art of Misdiagnosis*

The Momma Puzzle

The Momma Puzzle

A Memoir

Hilary Plattner

First Edition

Library of Congress Control Number (application pending)

Casebound ISBN: 978-1-62720-653-2
Paperback ISBN: 978-1-62720-654-9
Ebook ISBN: 978-1-62720-655-6

Design by Apprentice House Press & Charlie Quick
Editorial Development by Caroline Drennen
Promotional Development by Caroline Drennen
Cover photograph by Jason Leung, Unsplash

Published by Apprentice House Press

Loyola University Maryland
4501 N. Charles Street, Baltimore, MD 21210
410.617.5265
www.ApprenticeHouse.com / info@ApprenticeHouse.com

For my family—past, present and future.

Contents

Author's Note

This is a work of nonfiction, yet everything contained in this book—aside from the letters and other documents of my mother's—is reconstructed from my memory. I have tried to write with compassion and respect. I do not claim that my version of the events contained in these pages is the final version or the only true version of what happened. Since this book centers around the private lives of my family members and others, most of whom were still alive at the time of writing, many names and some identifying details have been changed.

Prologue

One afternoon, soon after Momma died, I was playing alone in the living room. Nearby stood the record cabinet where I'd soon find her folder marked "Personal," and the bookshelves that still held all those books of hers. That day, I twirled around on the colorful carpet. Either it was the weekend, or it was summer, because Dad was home. When he passed through the room, he asked what I was doing.

"Trying to decide what to be when I grow up."

"And what's that?" He paused beside me.

"I think I'll die when I grow up," I answered, sharing my thought of the moment, not intending to worry or shock him. I didn't mean I had a suicide wish; I didn't even know what that was yet. In my six-year-old mind, I couldn't envision a job I wanted when I grew up. I'd mentally examined all the possibilities, but nothing appealed to me. The adults I knew—Dad, Nana, babysitters who came and went, my kindergarten teacher, a few others, and Momma, of course, but she was dead—didn't seem happy with their lives. Dad put a lot of effort into acting cheerful. He often had a goofy, Jimmy Stewart smile. Did he force himself to whistle "When the red, red robin comes bob, bob bobbin' along" during those years right after Momma died?

Despite his raised-eyebrow expression, as he knelt beside me on the carpet, he managed to say something sensible and reassuring like, "You're too young to worry so much about what you're going to do when you grow up."

His look of surprised concern set up a guardrail in my brain, though, a sort of warning that stayed with me years afterward, forever really. I didn't want to make him more miserable. I knew I didn't want my life to end like Momma's.

CHAPTER 1

Monster

Spring 1968. A weekend afternoon. The phone rang. I was in our kitchen in Amherst. Momma and Dad were avid antique hunters, amateur furniture refinishers. Our phone was a heavy black box made of hard plastic. Dad motioned for me to answer. My sister wasn't around to help. Cautiously, I lifted the receiver.

"Hello?" I mimicked how adults did this.

A woman's voice reached out to me: "Hello?" Strangely intimate, speaking right in my ear. "Is your mother there?"

This hadn't happened before. I didn't know how to answer. Momma recently died by suicide. In the bedroom she shared with Dad. The next morning, I was sent to kindergarten, told not to say anything to anyone. No further guidance.

Momma: that's what she wanted to be called. She didn't want any of those more common names for mother: mom, or mama, or mommy. Even the spelling she was particular about. Momma with an o. I'm not sure why that was the name she picked: not a run-of-the-mill label. She didn't choose the name for her role casually, which gave our family—me, Dad, Sydney—the impression she meant to stay, that she was taking her job as mother seriously. Maybe she was trying too hard, was too unforgiving of herself, holding herself to some impossible standard of perfection.

There's something about suicide. You're never supposed to talk about it. It's always a secret, always shameful. Suicide makes the person who commits it disappear. Even more than ordinary death.

Momma left no note. No last words. I didn't wonder about that until I was in grad school in my late twenties, trying to write down her story. I called my uncle Reid several times, trying to coax information out of him. Reid described his sister as a faithful correspondent, deflecting my questions with offers to send letters of Momma's. If he could find them.

On the phone in the kitchen, when the strange woman asked to speak to my mother, I froze. The pause, as I figured out what to say, went on for what felt like forever. Dad came to my rescue, plucked the receiver from my hand, and answered for me. I sensed his pain and rage, brought to the surface like a sudden rash. "There is no Mrs. Plattner," he blurted out, his words making it sound like she never existed.

• • •

Before she died, Momma made an elaborate party for my older sister's seventh birthday. The theme: the sea. Decades pre-*Little Mermaid.* Setting: our basement, previously and conveniently painted blue courtesy of home handyman Dad. Cake: thickly frosted in pink, homemade by Momma. Games: fishing for handmade paper fish. Guests: a few friends of Sydney's. Decorations: more paper fish adorning the walls, cut by Momma from colored construction paper, festooned with sequins, transforming the dim basement into a sparkling underwater kingdom. Despite that best birthday party ever, when Sydney grew up, she always seemed angry at Momma, as if she blamed her for abandoning us.

The rest of the world was also quick to look down on my mother, to condemn her for what she did. A man or woman with no children who dies by suicide is judged as merely sad, depressed, misunderstood, or even pathetic. But a mother who kills herself has committed a heinous crime, has turned herself into a monster.

• • •

The room was quiet except for the sound of her voice reading aloud. The ceiling sloped low over us in my parents' second-floor bedroom, cocooning us in that protected time alone together. Momma was reading to me from *Charlotte's Web*. She did the different voices: sweet, smart Charlotte; energetic, funny Wilbur; nasal, slimy Templeton. It was my naptime, and Momma was trying to get me to fall asleep, but that agenda slipped aside when the story had us both captivated. I lay at her side on top of the quilt, tucked under her arm while she read, and for a short while, she was mine.

The house beyond the closed door of the bedroom was quiet, the air cool, dim, smelling of clean sheets, the cotton quilt. On the wall behind us, two windows looked out over the garage, shaded by a line of cedar trees; another half-open window across the room opened onto the green backyard. White lace curtains hung at the windows. The bed we lay on was an antique my parents found at some furniture sale, the headboard and baseboard made of iron, a design of curling vines painted a creamy white by Momma. The wallpaper in the room was pretty, too, willow trees, white on slate blue. Under the windows stood a low wooden bureau, another antique refinished by Momma and Dad. Everything in the room was carefully chosen, creating the life they built together.

At the base of the bed was a small wooden door to the eaves, a crawl space used for storage under the roof along the front of the house, a space where Sydney and I sometimes played. This was the room where Momma would die, in those eaves. This was also the room Dad moved out of soon after Momma died there. Instead, he made a new bedroom for himself in the space beside our kitchen. When I asked why, he said, "I can't sleep up there anymore. This room was too small for a dining room anyway." Their old bedroom sat empty for years, used only for guests, which often meant Nana since Dad's parents rarely visited.

In high school, I decided to move my bedroom up there, abandoning the room in the addition that Dad had built onto our house after Momma's death. He didn't object to me taking over the bedroom he used to share with Momma, even suggesting a sunny shade of yellow for the walls, helping me repaint them, letting me use the same antique iron bedframe that was still there.

I can't remember if it was Dad or I who moved the box of Momma's old clothes from the basement to her old bedroom closet. I continued my habit of sometimes going through that box of her things, but I started doing it more often, a process that might be called growing up. I tried to sweep the sadness out of that unused room, but it lingered along with the dust.

While Momma read to me, we lay on the bed together. We got to the part where Charlotte is going to die. I don't know how many afternoons it took, but Momma must have read the whole book to me. She loved to read. The afternoon when she read to me in bed, of course I didn't know that she was going to die. Maybe she already decided though. I don't remember how close that day was to her suicide, possibly within a few months. Maybe she was designing a web of words to ensure I would be safe when she was gone, like Charlotte. Like a mother should. Or maybe that's my wishful thinking and she just left. We didn't discuss her much after what happened. No one in our family ever lightheartedly said: Oh, I miss Momma.

• • •

I have a lot of papers about her. Tons of documents. I still have her driver's license. I know she was short, five feet two. Documents alone don't give you back the person. I also have a miscellaneous collection of facts, details told to me by Dad, Nana, Reid, mixed together with memories, stories, photographs. Some photos I've kept, some I've already gotten rid of but half-remember. There once existed at least one Kodak print of Sydney's underwater-theme birthday party, a bunch of small girls dressed in pink, candles lit on a pink cake, sequined fish on the walls.

Facts: Momma liked cats and was a terrible speller. In college, she majored in French and became fluent. She studied in Paris and worked for the State Department in Vietnam before the war. She had dark hair, pixie cut, like mine until mine turned gray. She was pretty, with pale skin, freckles, and a lot of moles. For years I thought her hair really was black. That story didn't come out until years later. Another story no one talked about: Momma wasn't the first one in our family to die by suicide. Her father, Henry, also did, when Momma was ten: a grandfather I never knew. I don't want to accept that my mother was a monster. But she did make the decision to end her life as a mother with two young children, one of whom was me.

• • •

I live in an apartment in a small brick building in Brooklyn. I'm sixty already, with my own children who are both grown or almost grown. The building where I live is new. I'm not like my parents; I don't like antiques or fixer-uppers. I don't like saving old things. I work at a desk in the small bedroom that I share with my husband. The desk is new and tiny, snugged into one corner.

The papers I've saved about Momma, her father, other family members, I've purposefully collected over the years. But sometimes it seems these documents have been drawn to me, pages and pages. Collecting around me with an almost magnetic force, willing me to tell her story. But her story is hard to tell. I was told never to talk about her.

Lately I'm starting to think about getting rid of my papers about her. I've been thinking of having a farewell ceremony. I've gotten rid of so much already: pictures, letters. The last time we moved pushed me to perform a satisfying downsizing. The box of her old clothes that I saved for years is long gone, everything either given away or worn out by all my years of wearing them.

Momma is buried in the family cemetery plot in Sharon, north of Pittsburgh, along with Nana and Reid. If Momma were still alive, she'd be in her nineties by now, so there's a good chance she'd be dead already anyway, even if she didn't die by suicide. Momma wasn't the only woman who died by suicide in 1968. In the United States, the number of women who died by suicide that year is approximately 7,000. Not a small number. I don't know how many of those women were mothers.

I always felt alone with my mother's terrible death that we rarely talked about. The messages from people around me pointed to one possible conclusion: my family and I were strange and different. Momma's suicide meant there was something wrong with our family.

In the winter of 1967-1968, news of the Vietnam War was broadcast every night on television into homes across the country. Starting at the end of January, the Tet Offensive unfolded in vivid, violent news reports. For the first time, it appeared the

United States was losing the war. The battles dragged on until late September 1968, after Momma was already dead. The Tet Offensive was eventually seen as a victory for this country, but the loss for North Vietnam turned the war in their favor. The winter of 1967-1968 marked a low point in morale for the United States. Amid that context came my mother's suicide.

I still wonder who Momma was. Did she enjoy being a mother? Was she happily married? What about the family rumor of an affair she had with a married man in Saigon, before Dad—did that really happen? Was that connected to her death? I know her father's suicide was part of her death. I still have a lot of questions. I want to do more than find out what she was like or understand her death though. I'm hoping to say goodbye to her and her suicide story that's been an unspoken part of my family history. I'm asking my writing to assert its special ability to bring people and events to life. If I can have her again even briefly, if only in my own mind, I hope I can let her and her story go.

Everyone has a mother story, something at least. Some memories, anecdotes, names. My mother story was always too complicated to tell. When anyone asked me about her, I tried to answer, but inside I panicked. Stiff sentences fell from my lips, a mix of truth and lies. I wished I had a straightforward dead mother story, something more familiar, less shocking. Cancer. Car accident. Plane crash. Any of those would've been better. Even more, I wished I could say: Yes, she's still alive. Often, I said nothing.

Rites Held for Wife of UMass Asst. Professor,
Thursday, February 29, 1968

> Private funeral services have been held for Mrs. Ann Plattner, 35. She was found dead at 6 p.m.

Sunday in her home by her husband. Dr. Papp, medical examiner, ruled the death a suicide.

The Douglass Funeral Home was in charge of arrangements.

She was born in Sharon, PA, July 22, 1932, the daughter of Mrs. Eleanor Evans Baker and the late Henry Baker Jr. She was educated in the Sharon schools and graduated from Denison University in Columbus, Ohio. Following graduation, she worked for one year with an export and import firm in New York City and then associated with the State Department in Saigon, Vietnam. On March 28, 1959, she was married in Sharon to Robert Plattner. Their married life was spent in Columbus, Ohio and Ann Arbor, Mich. They came to Amherst in September 1966.

Besides her husband, and her mother, she leaves two daughters, and a brother, Reid E. Baker of Meadville, PA.

CHAPTER 2

Reid

At my desk in the bedroom of my small Brooklyn apartment, I begin going through her papers. First, a faded Xerox from my file of musty family pages:

> **J. Reid Evans Fatally Stricken on Visit to West,**
> *Sharon Herald. November 7, 1942*
>
> *Treasurer of Sharon Steel Corp. and Well-Known Churchman Dies Suddenly at Tucson*
>
> J. Reid Evans, 74, treasurer of the Sharon Steel Corp. and a former member of the board of directors of the corporation died suddenly late Saturday while visiting Tucson, Ariz.

J. R. was in poor health for some time, the obituary says, not specifying the illness. His wife, Maude, drove with him to Tucson for an extended visit. Probably for his health. After his death, J. R.'s body was shipped home to Sharon. The photo accompanying the newspaper obituary shows a scholarly-looking gentleman with a domed forehead, neatly trimmed mustache and goatee, wire-rimmed spectacles, a piercing gaze. He looks no older than fifty; they must have used a younger picture for his death notice in the paper. J. R. and Maude were Nana's parents.

The fat, worn folder sits in front of me on the crowded desk. The papers are jumbled together, out of order. From all the times I've rummaged through them, quickly trying to find an answer to something. In the sequence of deaths on my mother's side of the family, Nana's father was the first one who died. J. Reid Evans, or J. R., Momma and Reid's maternal grandfather, my great-grandfather. In the story of how events unfolded, first Nana lost her father. Her overprotective, doting father, treasurer of Sharon Steel. In December 1941, Pearl Harbor was bombed. Soon after that, the United States entered World War II.

November 1942. In poor health, for a recuperative visit, J. R. drove to Arizona with his wife, Maude, Momma and Reid's grandmother. Those two grandparents who lived next door to Momma and Reid on Linden Street. When J. R. and Maude got to Tucson, J. R. died abruptly, and Maude had to ship his body home to Sharon. That was the death of Nana's beloved father. The man in the obituary photo. Scholarly looking, piercing gaze. Two months later, Nana's husband of eighteen years died by suicide with a rifle shot to his head. Nana had two children: Reid, age twelve, and Momma, who was ten.

• • •

New York City, 1990. I was in graduate school, trying to write about Momma, the story of her suicide. I called Reid with a few general questions. What was his sister like? What did he remember about her? I wrote to my uncle ahead of time, arranged a time to speak.

My bedroom in a shared student apartment on Claremont Ave. near 125th Street was a long, narrow box with two windows looking out on an airshaft. I perched cross-legged on my hard futon bed, the phone pressed against my ear, scribbling notes, struggling to capture everything Reid was telling me, along with everything he didn't say. My uncle and I didn't know each other well. He rarely visited my family while I was growing up. On the phone, he sounded hesitant. Slightly uneasy to be talking to me, to be speaking about Ann. His sister who died by suicide years before.

I sensed that he managed his discomfort by talking a lot, not rapid fire, but in a slow, gentle drawl, a near continuous stream of words. He wasn't giving me much room to speak. That was fine; I didn't feel super comfortable talking to him either, didn't want to immediately confide a lot of personal information to an uncle I barely knew. Reid began by apologizing for not being able to remember Ann, for not having much to tell me.

I didn't realize I remembered Nana's voice so clearly until I heard Reid on the phone. My uncle sounded so much like his mother. I felt especially close to Nana when I was young. She made frequent visits to our house. Every summer we drove to Pennsylvania to stay with her for at least a week. Until my junior year of high school when she suddenly died. At seventy-two, Nana wasn't in great health, but her death was unexpected.

"Ann was always very quiet," he murmured. "She talked very softly. Like you."

I was just settling into this call, though still conscious of the difficult subject matter, and here was Reid, telling me my mother had been overly quiet, commenting that I was speaking softly too. I felt annoyed. I was trying to speak loudly so Reid could hear me, although he barely paused to listen.

Reid asked if I remembered the time he visited when I was young, soon after my mother died. He couldn't stop staring at me during that visit, he said, I resembled my mother so much. He could tell his gaze made me uncomfortable; he recalled that I made a face at him, stuck out my tongue or something.

"No, I don't remember," I said, raising my voice to be heard. When I was younger, people often told me how much I looked like my mother. Anyone who saw a picture of Momma, even if they never met her, would say that. Still, it was an uncomfortable comparison. It was as if I was being told that since I *looked* like her, I must *be* like her too. Since she died by suicide, that meant the unspoken question frequently floated in the air around me: was I going to die by suicide? I didn't think so, but other people seemed worried. "Other people" mostly meant my dad and Nana, who expressed their unspoken concern with worried looks they seemed to think I never noticed. Maybe this concern about suicide contagion now also included my unfamiliar uncle.

Reid continued speaking in his gentle voice. "Ann had difficulty talking to people. She was very shy, very withdrawn. No, I'm creating the wrong impression. She wasn't antisocial."

Reid's words about Momma continued to surprise me, jumping out from his continuous flow. He described my mother as almost a social misfit, then took it back. Was she really *that* quiet? Or was she quiet around her family, her brother in particular?

"I have to tell you this," Reid continued. "Your grandfather committed suicide. I think it affected her much more so than me. I never talked with her about it." I heard the tension in his voice as he spoke those words: committed suicide. I didn't respond, continued taking notes.

"I think it was a difficult situation working in a company where his father-in-law was a high official," Reid added in his meandering near-monologue.

"Looking back on it," he paused. "It wasn't something I was aware of at the time. My father was drinking a lot during those years before he killed himself."

I already knew from Dad the story that Momma's father also died by suicide. Dad had told me and Sydney when we were young, even though it was something we hardly talked about.

But no one ever previously mentioned that drinking was part of the picture of my grandfather's problems.

I had to get off the phone, run to a class, then hop on the subway, go to work: a part-time tutoring job downtown in the Village. I said goodbye quickly, making a vague plan about when to speak to Reid again.

Hours later, back in my room at bedtime, stretched out on the hard futon again, I had time to mull over the things Reid had told me. He'd sounded as if he'd been fond of his younger sister. But he claimed he couldn't remember much about her, describing her as soft-spoken, calling me quiet too. Did Reid fail to hear and see his sister when she was alive? I didn't dislike my uncle, but I felt protective of my mother, although she was already dead. What struck me most about the call was the number of times Reid said he and Momma talked to each other about their father's suicide: zero.

CHAPTER 3

Henry

From my file of family papers. Another yellowed photocopy: *Sharon Herald*, January 12, 1943. The notice printed in the town paper the day after he died:

Henry Baker Jr. Dies of Gun Wound

> Henry Baker Jr., 48, of 940 Linden St., died at 11:30 o'clock last night from gunshot wounds which were inflicted while he was examining the weapon at his home.
>
> Mr. Baker, a veteran of World War I, was with the Sales department of the Sharon Steel Corp. for the past 20 years.

There's a bit more to the obituary. The usual info about the survivors. His mother-in-law, Maude. Wife: Eleanor, my nana. Two children: Reid and Ann. The funeral and burial arrangements. The language is ambiguous. The word "suicide" notably missing. Leaving room to interpret the death as an accident, while not directly claiming accidental death either. Eventually Dad told me it was Nana who got the newspaper to print this sanitized version of the death of her husband.

• • •

New York City, 1990. I called Uncle Reid a second time. From my bedroom in the fifth-floor apartment of that elevator building on Claremont Avenue. It was already almost a month since my last call to Reid. I still felt awkward speaking to him on the phone, but less so this time. I got ready to yell into the phone so he could hear me. My mother's older brother, her only sibling. Even if I didn't regard him as a completely reliable source of information about my mother, I didn't have many other people I could ask about her. And I still hoped Reid would tell me something about her I didn't already know.

Again, he started out by apologizing that he couldn't remember more about his sister. In the same gentle drawl that reminded me of Nana, still not coming up with any actual memories. Instead, he began to relate a collection of facts.

"Ann liked cats," Reid announced in his soft voice.

I remembered getting cats when we lived in Amherst. I guess I never put it together before that those pets were Momma's idea.

"She was a bad speller," he added, something I remembered Nana also told me. That detail was more interesting later, after my uncle sent me the package of Momma's letters and I read some of her misspelled words.

Still talking, giving me little room to say much, Reid told me more facts, things I didn't know, or half-remembered. My mother went to Denison University. She studied in Paris for her junior year. After graduating, she lived in Washington for two years, working for the State Department. Then she was posted to Saigon, in the foreign service. Two years later, she came home, traveling through Burma, India, Afghanistan, Turkey, Iran. She returned in time to attend Reid's wedding, in the fall of 1958. My uncle was marrying Jean, my mother's best friend; not the first marriage for either. I took notes, listening. Reid was talking,

talking. Trying at least to tell me something about my mother. I liked hearing about her, about her life. As I struggled to follow his monologue, I wondered what it was like for Momma, seeing her brother marry her best friend.

In 1963, soon after I was born, after a brief marriage and two children together, Reid and Jean's relationship fell apart. Jean took Cliff, her oldest child from a previous marriage, plus her and Reid's two offspring, and moved to England. My uncle didn't mention any of that on the phone, and I didn't ask. Later, I read some of Reid's story in Momma's letters. Dad and Nana had leaked some of those details too. Uncle Reid's unhappy life was like the plot of one of the television soap operas Nana used to watch when I visited her as a child.

Before I hung up, I made a plan to talk with my uncle again soon. He mentioned Momma's letters that he wanted to send me. Letters she wrote to him from Saigon. I felt a bond with Reid, even though there was so much he didn't say, and I still wished he could remember more about Momma.

• • •

New York City, 1990. I called Reid a third time that year. What he talked about by this point was not Momma at all. Instead, in his now familiar, lilting flow of words, he told me about Wheatland. A childhood paradise in his mind. The old family house in West Virginia where he and my mother spent their childhood summer vacations. With Nana and their father, Henry, before his suicide. Maybe Reid talked so much about Wheatland because he loved the place and loved remembering it. But maybe he also felt guilty that he couldn't give me what I was looking for: my mother. More than just the facts: that she was quiet, liked cats, studied French. He couldn't conjure up any memories of her. Instead, he rambled on about Wheatland.

Reid was only two years older than my mother. They must have spent a great deal of time together while they were growing up, with no other siblings. He must have known her. I wanted him to tell me something more, something surprising that would make her come to life for me. I wished I could reach through the phone and shake him, snap him out of his foggy, soft-focus infatuation with this place he couldn't stop talking about, Wheatland.

I felt frustrated and disappointed by his inability to remember my mother. But somehow his blank mind didn't surprise me. I chalked up his absent memories to the painful subject always in the background: her suicide. Perhaps he felt guilty about that too. After their father's death, Momma was the one who also died by suicide, in the middle of her life, while Reid continued to live. As soap-opera-ish and full of imperfection as his life was.

• • •

Brooklyn, New York, fall 2021. In my cozy apartment, I search for and bring out another page from my thick, worn manilla folder of family papers. Henry Baker Jr.: Certificate of Death. The stamped date at the top of the page: June 1990. I must have ordered this document after one of my calls to Reid, when I wanted to find out more.

I study the form closely, knowing I've looked at this page before, though that was years ago. I'm not expecting to find any new solutions to these old mysteries, only wanting to refresh my memory, then lay these facts to rest, hopefully for the last time. When I study my grandfather's death certificate, I notice something I already knew, but had long slipped my mind. Two decades separated my grandfather's exit and my entrance. But the date he died and the date I was born were the same: January 11. Now I have a new thought: was my mother always depressed on my birthday?

The form is filled with facts, most already covered in that public obituary. Their Linden Street address, Henry's parents' names, the places of his birth, employment, and burial. His age is listed as well: "48 years, 8 months, 9 days." The time of death, as in the newspaper, is given: "11:30 P.M." Place of death: "Home." Nana is listed as Eleanor Evans Baker. But the line provided for her age is blank. I quickly do the math: when her husband died, she was forty-five. They were married eighteen years. Nana's signature is there, her name in neat black cursive. She had to sign the certificate as informant regarding her husband's suicide.

There's a coroner's signature as well, the word "acting" typed in. I can't read the name scrawled in black fountain pen, something like "Bigelow." Cause of death is clearly listed: "Gunshot wound of head through mouth, self-inflicted." Brutal words, hard to skip over. No ambiguity or smoothing out of the story as in the newspaper account. The line "Due to " is completed with the typed description: "Probable acute mania due to mental and physical strain of his occupation." Interesting that the word "mania" was used. Maybe in today's terms, my grandfather would be diagnosed as bipolar, rather than depressed. Next to that is the line "Other conditions," completed with the single word: "No." Then a mysterious code written in pen: "164c." Perhaps this unidentified code represents another lost piece about the already sad death of Henry Baker.

I put away the file, pushing inside all the fading papers, attempting to settle them into some sort of order. These generations of Momma's family. My family. The Evanses and Bakers. That great-grandfather J. R., who died after the car trip to Arizona with his wife, Maude. My grandfather Henry Baker Jr., who shot himself in their house on Linden Street. I have a separate, slimmer folder of papers for Dad's side of the family, a whole other story. This thick manilla file contains papers about Nana's family, the Evanses. And Henry's side, the Bakers. I try to separate the two sets of papers, the two families. Evanses on top, Bakers in a layer below. A lot of papers.

The fat folder slips. My newly reorganized pages, somewhat separated, move in a slow-motion slide, fanning out in a mess of papers at my feet on the floor by my small, crowded desk. So much for trying to organize all these saved pages. A photo slips out from the pile, tumbling onto the floor directly at my feet as I sit at my desk in the corner. One black-and-white photograph. I lean down to pick it up. The only picture I have saved of Momma's father, Henry Baker. My grandfather, who shot himself. Died by suicide on my birthday, almost exactly twenty years before I was born.

What are you doing here? I find myself thinking as I stare at his small photograph. Leaping out in front of me, where I can't ignore him. A slender man. Middle-aged. White skin, high, square forehead. Wearing a white shirt, standing, leaning forward in the picture. His prominent forehead looming toward the top edge of the photo as if he's about to step out of the image. Not quite smiling, a thin-lipped, straight-mouthed look—of what? Determination? Resignation? Sadness? Both hands shoved casually in his pants pockets. Momma's father who died. Not just died but shot himself. In that brick house on Linden Street. The house that was built by his father-in-law for his wife when they married in the spring of 1924. Then, on January 11, 1943, Henry shot himself in the head with a gun. "Gunshot wound of head through mouth, self inflicted," as his death certificate says. At 11:30 on a Sunday night, while Nana and Reid and Ann were at home, most likely asleep. Before Henry had to go to work the next day. Salesman at the Steel Corporation, always away during the week, traveling. Only two weeks together as a family at Wheatland during the summers. Henry Baker Jr., the grandfather I never knew. The man in this photo, still a young man there.

Why is his photograph here in my messy file of family papers? I must have shoved it in at some point instead of returning it to my box of photos. I have one bin of photographs left, a small, clear plastic container. A lot of other pictures I got rid of already, gladly downsizing, the last time we moved into this smaller place.

Should I put my grandfather's picture back with all my other family members in that crowded bin of photographs? I wonder, holding Henry's image between my fingers. No, as usual, I can't be bothered. Despite my good intentions to get all these documents organized as I go through them, I'm in a rush today. I need to call my daughter.

I push Henry's photograph into the file with the family papers about his relations and in-laws. Evanses and Bakers mixed together. Soon I'll get that done, get those pages in order, I promise myself. Another time, I'll move this picture of Henry to the box with the rest of my photos.

• • •

Almost every week I call my daughter, who's away in college at a SUNY upstate. On Zoom, I try to help her complete her graduate school applications; she's a senior, due to graduate next semester, in the spring. I'm trying to help her complete a goal she set for herself: applying to graduate programs for next year, for an advanced degree in psychology. But she seems to hate school! Why sign up for more? Why rack up debt with more school? Slowly, she looks at the applications with me, trying to finish them. Every week or so, we plug on. At this stage of her life, I think she would only say kind things about me to be polite. I'm mostly her annoying mother.

Our relationship is kind of tomato versus toe-MAH-toe. She's easygoing and confident, if a bit shy. I'm easily anxious, a star worrier, also shy. I like yoga, she's a dancer. I'm neat, she's… well, not a slob, just messy. I'm bookish. She hasn't enjoyed reading since she was in middle school and the arrival of cell phones revolutionized human existence. I'm average to her gorgeous. These days, post-Momma's treasure chest of stylish clothes, I'm most comfortable wearing stretchy athletic wear, the same few tops and pants rotated day after day, week after week, how you'd affordably dress an active kindergartner. With little help from me, since she was three, my daughter's known how to find a leopard-print winter coat in Target for a few bucks that made her appear like a movie star, a talent she's held onto long since the famous coat was retired. Around that same time, she got her aunts, my husband's two sisters, to give her lessons in makeup application using her pink Barbie makeup box, a toy another mom-neighbor-criminal-defense-lawyer-type gifted us to eject it as fast as possible from her own house.

My daughter and I are not genetically linked. I'm white, she's Asian, we don't look alike, except we're both short (she's shorter), and we're both females. But we are bound forever by destiny, luck, love. Like most mothers, I've tried to protect her from as many of the hardships of my life as I can. She wasn't much older than three, wearing her beloved leopard coat at the breakfast table, when I first told her a shorter version of what happened to her missing grandmother, Momma. I must have said my mother killed herself. I didn't know the better way to say it yet then: died by suicide, which lightens the heavy blame and stigma. I think the appetizer to that discussion was a short course on the

Vietnam War, followed by a sprinkling of words on the Korean War, because a picture on the back of some natural breakfast cereal box about saving the rain forests prompted her to start asking a lot of questions. I don't know what words I used. Not global capitalism or military-industrial complex. She was always super-smart, first inquiring about Heaven and God around that time too. I'm certain she would still say we were closer before her younger brother came, that everything was better back then, that his arrival cast a blight that destroyed her childhood, which she may continue to believe for as long as she lives. She is the shining star of my life, one of the universe's best blessings: a daughter. Even if we don't always get along.

CHAPTER 4

Mother

Along with rambling about Wheatland and apologizing for not telling me more about my mother, Reid kept mentioning her letters. Those few times I called him, he kept saying he was sure he had some letters saved somewhere that Momma wrote to him. His description of the letters kept shifting. First, he mentioned letters of Ann's from Saigon. Later, he said they were letters she wrote to him from Paris, when she was in college. What he finally sent me wasn't anything he mentioned before.

What arrived at that fifth-floor apartment on Claremont Ave., when I was still in grad school: a shoebox. Inside, it was packed full of letters. This was all he could find, Reid wrote in the note he included inside the box. He'd looked and looked. But these weren't letters Momma wrote to him from Paris or from Saigon, and they weren't to him at all. Instead, these were letters Momma wrote to Nana.

Reid's enclosed note explained that Ann was a faithful correspondent, ever thoughtful and mindful of Nana's great thirst for knowledge about me and my sister. Ann kept her diary through her letters, my uncle wrote.

Seated on the hard futon bed covered with my quilt, I unwrapped the bundle of papers inside the shoebox. Each letter was still in its original envelope, making them easy to sort into chronological order. I didn't struggle to organize them. The letters were carefully arranged, already in the right sequence. Preserved like a museum exhibit. A historian's or archivist's beloved project. Carefully saved by Nana and then Reid. Each one was a letter from Momma. They were the diary of a young mother. Written to her mother. All beginning with the same words: Dear Mother.

I laid them out on my faded quilt and started to read. In front of me were over twenty letters. Starting in 1961, a year before I was born, ending almost exactly two years later. If anyone had tried to talk to me right then, I would have led them out of my room, down the long hallway, pushed them firmly out the front door, and locked them outside by the elevator. I was finally alone with a piece of my mother, her voice on the page, and right then I didn't want to be interrupted. Thankfully, there was no one else home in the apartment. I was alone, listening in as Momma spoke to Nana.

> February 26, 1961
>
> Dear Mother,
>
> Sydney carries the doll around with her constantly on her rounds from kitchen to playpen to stairs, etc. She'll stop to look in the wastebasket, pull open a drawer, or tamper with the TV dial, then pick up 'her friend' and be on her way again—usually lugging it along by an arm or a leg. Priceless!

Momma's letters to Nana contain ordinary details. Momma writing about my sister when she was a toddler. This was the world I would soon be born into. Even if these mundane letters wouldn't capture everyone's interest, they captured mine. I read all of Momma's letters to my grandmother in one sitting. As I read, I felt sad, but also excited, sometimes puzzled. When

I finished going through the pile, I was tired, overwhelmed. I folded all the letters carefully back into their envelopes, placed the envelopes inside the protective shell of the box.

Later, I almost lost those letters. In the end, I only lost part of them. First, I typed them all. I was trying to do the opposite of losing them, I was trying to save them. I typed them into a single, long transcript. Then I started trying to write about them, to write about Momma. My story of losing her, looking for her, trying to find her. For a class on memoir writing, at the prestigious graduate program I was attending when I made those calls to my uncle.

I shared an early draft of my work, part of that lengthy transcript of letters, along with what I wrote about them. The teacher, a famous female writer, didn't react positively to my manuscript; mostly, she seemed to resent the length of what I'd submitted. In the writing world of New York at the time, that teacher had made a name for herself writing about an iconic male writer who for a time had been her boyfriend, but she didn't have children, wasn't a mother. She wanted me to cut, cut, cut. Her tone, especially her verbal critique in front of the class, was angry.

Looking back on that time from the distance of decades, I still don't know exactly why that teacher spoke to me so harshly in front of her class that afternoon. I imagine that whatever she was going through in her life that day or week or semester had nothing to do with me or my writing. For a long time, decades after that class, I never went back to those letters.

I kept the letters inside their original envelopes inside the shoebox Reid mailed me. Later, I moved to a house in Brooklyn where I lived for years with the man I married, and I kept the letters in the shoebox on a shelf of books in the room I used for my office, and I didn't take the letters out or reread them. For years

I saved the box of letters. Somewhere, I also kept that transcript of the letters, although I didn't reread that either.

When I recently moved, downsizing and gladly getting rid of so many things I didn't need anymore, I made the mistake of throwing out Reid's shoebox of Momma's letters. I donated boxes of books and used clothes, threw out papers. Carelessly, I must have held that shoebox, glanced at it. Asked myself: do I still need these old letters of my mother's? Then I tossed them out.

The memory of being sharply criticized by that teacher was still associated in my mind with those letters of Momma's. Who did I think I was, imagining anyone would ever want to read about my mother, her letters to her mother, after the way the famous writer reacted to my manuscript about them? I wish I still had all the letters Momma wrote to Nana, all those pages she typed or wrote by hand, the envelopes addressed to Nana in Momma's handwriting.

• • •

At the desk in my bedroom, on a rainy, gray fall afternoon, I open an old manilla file. This is another folder I did manage to save and not discard during that recent move into this smaller Brooklyn apartment, this new place where I now love living. I searched and searched for this folder after I moved, after I unpacked. Finally, I found the file inside my one remaining filing cabinet, stuffed full of all the papers I kept. Inside the file is a copy of the typed transcript of Momma's letters. This copy even contains the comments by that teacher. Thankfully, I can't read her scribbled notes on this faded, photocopied version from years ago.

Inside the folder, on top of the copied pages, is a small picture. Did I tuck this in here when I was packing for that move? For safekeeping? A photograph. I must have put this here. This small black-and-white picture is of my mother as a little girl. She stands by herself in a grassy yard against a background of dark trees. She looks maybe five or six years old in the photo. Close to the age I was when she died. In the photograph, she's a picture of charm and innocence. Short cotton summer dress, bare legs in white socks and feet in leather buckle shoes, one big white bow on each side of her chin-length hair, her head tilted thoughtfully to one side, hands clasped behind her back. Slight smile on her soft, round face. A pose of quiet reflection for the camera. The picture perhaps taken at their Linden Street home. The lawn marked by the line of a driveway, another line of a stone walkway.

When I see this picture of Momma as a girl, I want to lean my forehead on my desk and sob. Along with this familiar sadness, I wonder: am I kidding myself that I'm not angry at her? Suicide survivors often get told by others what we must be feeling. With those unhelpful messages imbedded in my mind, in the past I've searched myself for the recommended rage. When I haven't successfully located that prescribed emotion, I've worried I must be deficient in some way. As in: if I'd loved Momma more, would I mourn her death in some different, angrier way? But I've begun to realize maybe I've already worked through some of those harder emotions tied to her death: desolate longing, shame, suicidal thoughts. Maybe I'm ready to put things in order in my life's suitcase. It's not that I'm so old I worry I'm going to die tomorrow, but I want this last section of my life to be as lighthearted and productive as possible. I'd like to be released from the past: how does anyone accomplish that?

And maybe, just maybe, I think now, even though Momma is long dead, there's a way she can still help me. Maybe I can ask her to be a guide as I go through these letters and papers. She left when I still needed a mother. Maybe there's something that can be salvaged here, a way she can help me make sense of her story.

Instead of sliding her back in the folder with my typed transcript of those Nana letters, I place the small photo of Momma as a girl up on the shelf over my corner desk, tucking her picture behind the base of my lamp.

CHAPTER 5

Junior

After grad school, I stopped calling Reid. Sometimes he wrote to me; I don't remember writing back. I wasn't a faithful correspondent like Momma. At least once, Reid mentioned the family history he was working on. Almost a decade passed before he mailed me a copy: "Our Family History." Like in our earlier phone calls, Wheatland was what he recalled most vividly in those forty pages. A heaven where he fished with his grandfather, Dad Baker. Father of Henry, my dead grandfather.

Tied to a tree on the bank of the Shenandoah, ten miles from Wheatland, was a flat-bottomed boat Dad Baker used to take Reid fishing. Wheatland had no central heating, no electricity, no phone, no running water or indoor plumbing. When he visited as a boy, Reid helped with chores like cleaning and refilling the oil lamps. The main house, outbuildings, and surrounding land, everything was described in loving detail by Reid in his family history. Jean, his ex-wife, was never mentioned in those pages; even Momma barely made an appearance.

With his current wife, Reid had retired to the woods of southeastern Ohio, where they built a cabin together. "To me it was Wheatland all over again," he wrote, "…primitive cooking, dishwashing and bathing; sitting on the porch in the evening until it got dark, then lighting the kerosene lamps; and the night with its millions of icy stars and its profound silence, broken only by the cry of an owl or the whip-poor-will."

Every summer, Reid and Momma traveled to Wheatland in the family car, Nana in front, their father behind the wheel, a trip that took two full days. In 1940, when Momma was eight, the new Pennsylvania Turnpike was completed, reducing the drive to a single day. Despite her poor eyesight, after her husband's death, Nana became the driver.

According to Reid, Nana's father, J. R., worked as a bookkeeper for the Crucible Steel Company of Pittsburgh in his twenties. As a young man, J. R. rose quickly through the ranks of the company. In 1896, he married Maude Adams, a stunning beauty with light blond hair and eyes so blue they were almost violet. A year later, their daughter was born. That girl became my grandmother Nana. After Eleanor's birth, the family moved to Sharon, where J. R. joined the Sharon Steel Hoop Company, always called "The Steel Hoop" by J. R. He continued to rise to the position of treasurer, the job he held until his death out in Tucson. The Hoop grew into The Sharon Steel Corp., a major US industry, making J. R. a wealthy man with a Packard limousine and a large house on Linden Street.

Maude and J. R.'s only child, Eleanor, was born with eye problems. Years later, I remember Nana always wore glasses so thick her eyes appeared to bulge like a fish. Eleanor's girlhood dream was to become a concert pianist. But she grew up to be only five feet tall, with fingers that didn't span the chords of many piano compositions. Maude told Eleanor to forget a career as a pianist: she had to get married. In her twenties, Eleanor, daughter of the treasurer, met a young man who recently joined the steel company as a lowly trainee. Despite their difference in social rank, their meeting was inevitable. Henry Baker Jr. stood a mere five feet six inches tall, a diminutive stature that matched Eleanor's. Their wedding in the spring of 1924 was the social event of the season.

J. R. built a brick house for his daughter next door to his matching brick mansion on Linden Street. Christmas Day 1926, Henry and Eleanor's first baby, David, arrived: stillborn. Probably a shock on that family holiday. Following that, Eleanor suffered several miscarriages. In 1930, with the best possible medical care procured by J. R., Reid was born. Two years later, my mother, Ann, was welcomed into the Baker household on Linden Street.

My uncle wrote in his memoir that he never liked his name, Reid, given to him by his father, Henry Baker Jr., my grandfather who died by suicide. My grandfather was given *his* name by *his* father, Henry Baker Sr. According to Reid, his father resented the diminutive Junior tag on the end of his name so much that he refused to carry on the family tradition by giving his son the name Henry III. Instead, Henry Baker Jr. named Reid after his wife's father, J. Reid Evans, or J. R., the successful steel company treasurer. Reid said he spent much of life wishing he was Henry III.

Henry Jr. spent his life working as a traveling salesman for the company where J. R. was treasurer, living in the house built for him by that same father-in-law. I wonder if all that plus dragging around that Junior after him like a demeaning tail all his life was related to Henry's unhappiness and suicide, something I never had the chance to ask Reid.

• • •

Brooklyn, November 2021. A gray, rainy day, not at all cheery. I'm sitting at the small desk in my bedroom. When I'm done reading my uncle's history, I feel tired. Before getting up to return Reid's booklet to the bookshelf in the living room, I have the thought again that when I'm done with this project, maybe

I'll celebrate the final farewell with a ceremony. Maybe I'll have a bonfire of these family papers. Not the pictures; I don't have that many left. Probably not the letters, what I have left of them. Not Reid's family history, which I enjoy reading. But at least I could burn some of the other papers: the obituaries, Grandfather Henry's death certificate. I'm tired of carrying this heavy history of suicide around with me.

Maybe it will be a small fire, just a few papers. There's no fireplace in this compact apartment. No yard either. Some of our friends have portable backyard firepits. A sort of bulky metal bowl on feet that makes me think of a modern witch's cauldron. Maybe we could get one of those, set it up in our rear parking lot. But where would we keep it the rest of the time? I can't imagine dragging a smoking firepit downstairs to our storage closet.

I'm thinking about this, still intending to put away the family history booklet, when I notice Momma's picture tucked half behind the lamp on the shelf over my desk. That picture of Momma as a girl. When I catch a glimpse of her, I feel a stab of longing. She's been dead for so long, but I still miss her. I should return her picture safely to my plastic photo bin, also on the bookshelf in the living room. What about that other photo I still need to put away too? Grandfather Henry, my other family suicide? I stuck him in the folder of Momma's family papers. The fat folder that's still stuffed inside this overcrowded corner desk where I sit. I promised myself I'd store Henry's picture with the photos in the bin.

I go looking for Henry, fish him out of my file of family papers where I left him. Henry Jr., my grandfather. My mother, who died by suicide as well. I hold their pictures, one photo in each hand. They both died on a Sunday. 1943. 1968. Twenty-five years apart. He was forty-eight. She was thirty-five. They each had two children. Both ended their time on this earth early, midway through their lives. I never got to know either of them. Henry died before I was born, and I was six when Momma did it. They didn't get to have each other either, I think, looking at them. Momma was ten when her father died, not much older than the girl in this picture.

My mother, hands clasped behind her back, head tilted thoughtfully to the side. Her father, Henry, staring, serious. Instead of carrying them back to my photo box in the living room, I set the two pictures beside each other by the lamp on the shelf over my desk, these two black-and-white photos.

Hey, you two, I say to them silently, picking up Reid's booklet to take it back to the other room. Maybe you can both help me out. I had a similar thought the other day when I was looking at only Momma's picture. Maybe her father can be part of this project too.

OK, you two, I repeat silently to these family members who are no longer here. They're both quiet, of course, being just old photographs. They could be watching. They could still help me. Here's my idea, I tell them silently. I have all these separate pieces of paper. What if I go through everything and put it all together? Put all my different pages, papers, pictures, and letters into a single chronological sequence, a single story.

The desk in the corner of the bedroom where I work is too small for this project. But this is my available workspace now. Instead of finding somewhere else, somewhere with more room, I can recruit the wide bed into another work surface. I can bring out my papers, spread them across the flat expanse of the bed. On weekdays, when no one else is home.

OK, Momma? Henry? You ready to help with this project?

I'm still talking to them silently inside my head. Trying to talk to them; they're so quiet. In a way, quiet is good though. They're not interrupting me. I have a lot to figure out about how to fit these different papers together into one story. When I'm done though, then what? Will I be able to figure out what to save and what to throw out? Will I be able to find a sense of closure after Momma's sad death, even all these years later?

CHAPTER 6

Jean

New York City, 1998. Jean visited. Several years out of grad school, I was married by then, living in Brooklyn, no children yet. Working. Teaching writing, along with at least one other part-time job. How did my aunt find me? Ex-aunt. I almost never thought of her in those terms, as my aunt. Maybe Reid gave her my phone number; he still wrote to me sometimes. They had all those kids together, although their children were grown by then. I thought of her as my mother's friend. I didn't know the story yet of how they stopped being friends. Jean was passing through New York, staying with someone in the city. She must have called me. She said she had some letters from my mother she wanted to give me.

I must have met Jean at least once when Momma was still alive. But I was a baby and had no memories of Jean from then. One time, Dad took Sydney and me to meet Jean and her children, a few years after Momma died. I didn't remember Jean from that long-ago trip either.

The vaguely remembered edges of the person in my mind barely matched up with the woman who materialized that spring day in Soho. Momma's friend since they were in high school. A thin, sixty-ish woman with short, salt-and-pepper hair. Close to the same age Momma would have been if she were alive, while

I was midway through my thirties. Jean struck me as intense, almost high-strung, the opposite of happy and relaxed.

We were polite with each other, drinking mugs of herb tea in a cluttered loft living room, the apartment of the woman Jean was visiting. Jean recently went through the papers stuffed in the drawers under her bed at home, she said, apologizing for not giving me Momma's letters sooner. She talked nonstop—about nothing, about a mass of details not relevant to me. How she once lived in Prague with the woman whose loft this was, not stopping to ask me about my own life. Finally, I brought myself to ask a question that was on my mind. Something I never got myself to ask Reid.

"Did you know anything…was my mother having an affair with a married man in Vietnam?"

"No." Jean shook her head, no pause to try to remember. If my question surprised her, she didn't say so. She said she didn't know about a married man, pursing her thin, darkly painted lips. "The other man your mother was taken with, besides your father, was Bill. You'll see, he's mentioned in the letters."

Jean was on her way to Vermont, someplace far north. Vague about where and how long. She struck me as rootless. Going somewhere on her own after packing up her apartment, wanting to spend some time in Vermont was all she said. I don't remember where she'd been living, or if she was planning to return there. She spoke longingly about Vermont. At last, she handed me the bundle of letters.

"I tried to sort these into order for you." She passed me a plain manilla envelope. "But in case something's not in the right place, I think you'll be able to figure it out."

I left quickly, thanking my mother's old friend on my way out the door, impatient to get home and read the letters.

Not sure what I would discover about my mother. Jean hadn't said much, and I hadn't known how to get her to reveal more. Something about the letters starting when my mother was in college. It didn't register yet, Jean's answer to my question about Momma's rumored affair. Bill: I hung onto that name. I would look for him in the letters.

Inside my house, before eating dinner, I went to my desk with the letters. I had an entire office to work in on the ground floor of that house where I lived with my husband. It was still a few years before we adopted our daughter and turned that space into her bedroom; long before our son also joined our family and our apartment, and our lives grew even more crowded. The light in that ground-floor room was dim and cool. My desk, long against one wall, made from a piece of varnished plywood.

I felt excited to look at the letters Jean had handed me. I still kept the shoebox from Reid, containing Momma's letters to Nana, shoved on an upper shelf filled with books, gathering dust. I knew they were there, but I hadn't taken them down to reread in ages. I didn't think about those Nana letters that evening or try to figure out how that part of Momma's life fit together with this new piece from Jean. The Nana letters were still tainted with the impression given to me by that teacher that they'd never be of interest to anyone.

Inside the manilla envelope, the letters to Jean were wrapped in a single white sheet of paper. Handwritten on the outside of the page: "Ann's letters." When I unwrapped the paper, I saw on the reverse side something else was written. I could just make out beneath a scratched-out blot of pen: "Anne's letters." My mother's name with an extra e on the end. Jean must have written that first, then corrected herself. Had she really almost forgotten the spelling of my mother's name? Her old best friend.

Sitting at my desk, I started reading, as if I was gorging on a box of chocolates. These letters from my mother to Jean were written on many different kinds of paper, sometimes typed, sometimes handwritten in pen or pencil. Sometimes Momma's writing was neat, her graceful script adorned with small, decorative flourishes. Often her words were a messy scrawl, carrying an urgency to get her message down. Sprinkled among the sentences were occasional words or expressions in French: *eh bien*, *les enfants*, *voici*. My mother, the student and lover of French. There were almost always references to whatever she was reading, reading, reading. But for these letters, there were no envelopes and usually no dates.

As Jean had mentioned, the first letter began when Momma was in college. 1954. She was twenty-one, already much younger than I was the evening I first read this pile of past correspondence. Here was my mother, her voice.

> Thursday
>
> Jean—
>
> Am I interested?! Do you happen, just happen
> to know when our spring vacation is – exact
> dates are from April 9th to 19th. 'Magine
> that. I'd given up all plans of going to Florida
> must admit…

Each letter drew me in. Like eavesdropping on a private, one-sided conversation: my mother talking to her best friend. I was searching, listening for clues or answers to my questions. Who was this mother I used to have, what was she like? What made her happy? And more importantly, what later made her so unhappy? Was there anything here I didn't already know? And what about the story of that possible affair, the married man? Here in the letters, Momma was alive, rattling on and on in words.

As promised, Jean had tried to sort the letters into chronological order. After college, Momma traveled by ship to Southeast Asia for a job with the State Department, arriving in Vietnam in 1956. I saw the name Bill. He came and went in several letters. He wasn't married though. How could he be the one with whom my mother had an affair? In the stack of letters, she referred to several boyfriends, or possible boyfriends, including my father, who came and went in the pages. My father eventually reappeared when Momma returned home to Sharon in 1958, followed pretty quickly by their marriage.

I was still reading when my husband arrived home, poking his head in the door of my office to ask if I'd eaten. I must have reminded him about my visit with Jean. "A friend of my mother's," I mumbled, adding something about these old letters Jean gave me. Indicating I was busy by the way I remained hunched over the papers splayed across my desk. Later, my husband brought me food on a plate. I barely noticed what I was eating.

As I read, I felt curious about what I was learning, along with what remained unsaid. As usual, I also felt sad. I already knew that at the end Momma still wouldn't be here. But was there anything in the letters I didn't already know? The last letter to Jean came in 1962, soon after I was born. Momma was thirty. Six years before the end of her life

The house was quiet; my husband had cleared away my dinner dishes and gone to bed. My eyes felt like heavy chunks of cement. I counted twenty-one letters spread across my desk, covering almost a decade. Before folding and bundling them into their envelope, I sat briefly with the papers, the protective wrapper labeled "Ann's letters," and her misspelled name scratched out on the back. I felt as if I had just spent several hours with my mother. I was still trying to take in that she had been a real person. Now the pain of her absence was sharper.

Along with everything the letters contained, there were also the unanswered questions. As Jean said, there was no mention of an affair Momma had in Vietnam. There was Bill, one of a few men with whom Momma sounded infatuated, but he wasn't married. He almost married her but then didn't. While she didn't sound as head-over-heels infatuated with Dad the way she did with Bill, in the letters, she sounded happy about marrying Bob, as she called him.

Too exhausted for the moment to stand and walk through the house to the bedroom, I laid my head on my folded arms next to the letters on my desk. I thought of more questions I could have asked Jean, prodded her with, if I could have gotten her to stop chattering. Was Jean telling me the truth, that she knew nothing about Momma's obsession with a married man? Was this an edited version of my mother's letters? Had Jean taken out any correspondence she didn't want me to see? Jean hadn't looked like she was hiding or making anything up though. Her head shake of denial had appeared definitive. But I didn't know my ex-aunt well enough to judge if she was concealing anything. If Jean was telling the truth and as far as she knew, Momma wasn't seeing a married man in Vietnam, then the story I remembered from my childhood—the man in Saigon who promised he would leave his wife, but returned to his marriage instead—that story was what? A mistake of my childhood imagination? A misunderstanding of the facts by Dad?

Careful to keep the letters in order, I placed them in the outer wrapper, then inside the envelope, and tucked them safely away, high on my bookshelf. Not next to the shoebox of Nana's letters, but on a less crowded neighboring shelf.

After that single meeting, I didn't stay in touch with my ex-aunt. Jean never contacted me again or gave me her permanent address, and likewise, I didn't look for her. I did go through that packet of letters again, hoping to digest them more slowly, not long after the spring day when my mother's old friend handed them over. But it was many years before I was ready to study them more closely and ask myself again what the letters could and couldn't tell me.

• • •

Brooklyn, December 2021. At the corner desk in my small bedroom, I hesitate to begin, even dread, the task of trying to make sense of all these letters. Glancing up, I see the two tiny pictures I've placed on the shelf above my desk. Wedged upright by the base of the lamp, like two friends: my grandfather, my mother. Henry and Ann.

OK, guys, I continue silently addressing my two photographs. This may not be the job you chose for yourselves, but do you think you could help me?

I open the folder I've labeled "Momma's Letters." On top lies the sheet of paper that I still have from Jean, her spiky writing, my mother's name. Crossed out on the back: Anne, my mother's misspelled name with the extra "e." The pages smell heavy with dust. Many of these letters, the handwritten ones at least, have become difficult to decipher: my mother's writing on the pages is fading with age. I barely remember reading these letters before, yet I know I did, when I lived in that house in Brooklyn where I had my own office, before I had children, but it has been years since I looked through these pages.

The first letter is a single page, handwritten front and back. A small sheet of yellowed graph paper, something torn from a notebook, the even grid covered by lines of words. Momma's cursive handwriting is neat here, reminding me that she was still young, almost twenty-two.

Like a detective, I see something new this time when I read. Near the bottom left corner of the page: a tiny, circular hole, brown edges. A cigarette burn. I forgot. Momma smoked cigarettes. When I was a child, she preferred Pall Malls. Those square, red packs with white letters and logo. A popular 1960s brand, when everyone still believed cigarettes didn't hurt you. She must have already smoked in college.

There's her voice again, just like all those years ago when I first read this letter and the ones that follow. Saying "'magine" and "Cinci." Planning a trip with Jean to Florida over spring break. Sneaking away from college for the weekend to Columbus—the city where I'd eventually be born—with her high school flame, Mike, a match disapproved of by Jean and Nana. Kissy: Jean's first child, otherwise known as Cliff, from Jean's first marriage, possibly age two or three then. My future mother was a lively, cigarette-smoking, lying, likely sexually active, average young woman. This was her senior year.

> Jean—
>
> ...Kissy's devotion appalls me. Since he's been good ever since I left, though, it only substantiates my frightening conclusion: that children sense instinctively that I'm some sort of natural enemy. Lord, what will I ever do with 5 of my own?
>
> I really did expect that you'd be at Denison before this—I'd counted on it. As planned, I went

home the weekend after I was in Cinci & stayed over three extra days "recuperating from a tooth extraction," supposedly. Yes, Mike was home. When I got back Mrs. Mac, who is overbearingly house-motherly, was practically insistant [sic] that I have the tooth checked at the infirmary. I've never been so petrified in my life. I avoided her for days until everything died down, but she still keeps asking me how I feel.

Also as luck would have it Mike got a pass last weekend so Jan M., from here at school, & I met he & friend in Columbus! They also may be up this weekend, and so with Spring in the offing, studying has been & is, a totally degenerated concept of mass regimentation. You asked about Mike. I just wish you could see him now, be with him for a little bit to see if you'd reversed your hung-over impressions from high school. Maybe you'd feel the same way now, and wouldn't be able to understand how I was in such a haze—but truth is I am just that. Mother is still the great skeptic, so I'm fighting it out on the home front, too. Just might elope, but I guess if you're really going to you don't tell people so. Mike's not sure he wants to be anything else but a Cape Cod beachcomber, but even that has possibilities. Please don't think of it as the insipid "home-town idyll," Jean, it's just that I can't imagine ever marrying anyone else, & I'll be darned if I'll wait two years just for the sake of expediency.

Forgive the rush, but have an appt. in 5 min—Senior Comprehensive review—so must dash—love to y'all—

Ann

What she meant by needing to wait two years to marry if she didn't elope, I'm not sure. Also, what did she mean that children instinctively saw her as some sort of natural enemy, followed by that rhetorical supplication regarding what she'd ever do with her imagined passel of five offspring? As if motherhood was a destiny that would befall her, not a choice she deserved any say in. Near the end of college, her letter already expressed so much conflict about the prospect of being a mother, eerily prescient since she ended up seeming so dissatisfied with the domestic life she eventually created.

There in the middle of that first letter to Jean is one of her misspelled words: "insistant." I especially notice Momma's misspellings on this reading. Her errors grow to be an endearing tic as I continue reading her correspondence. She was a bad speller: one of the few things both Nana and Reid told me about her. She was human, imperfect.

• • •

I have so many papers about Momma, I didn't think I wanted any more. I thought I wanted to sort through everything, put it in some sort of order, decide what it meant, what I could discard and what I needed to keep, and be done with it. I really want to be done with all these papers.

Instead, I find myself searching for more information about her. I poke around online and find her Denison yearbook from 1954, the year she graduated, the year of that first Jean letter. After discovering the old college yearbook for sale, I buy it. Am I caught in a fantasy of making sense of her life? Trying to answer an impossible question: why did she do *it*?

The volume that arrives in the mail a few weeks later looks strangely familiar. Instantly, I detest the book's mildewy smell. I must have seen a copy of this black hardback before. Maybe we kept one on the living room bookshelf in Amherst. There was probably a copy at Nana's house.

I'm sitting at the small desk in the corner of my bedroom in Brooklyn when I do a thorough search of the yearbook. Just as I vaguely remember, there's almost nothing about Momma here. Along with lists and pictures of each year's class members, there's an alphabetical list of seniors. With Baker as her last name, there's Momma in the top row of one glossy page: a mini, square, black-and-white photo. Her name and hometown. Her major: French.

At the back of the smelly volume, I see another list of clubs and activities for each graduating senior. Following Momma's name are listed eight organizations that she supposedly joined during college. But when I scour the pages of the entire volume, Momma's not pictured in any group in which she claimed membership. The sorority with a name of Greek letters: not there. The multiple honor societies she belonged to: Phi Society, etc., etc. She's not shown with any of them. The other four clubs listed after her name: Yearbook, French Club, and a couple more. Not there.

The Young Republican Club catches my eye. I didn't know she was a Republican, then or ever. But that made sense given her family background: landowning father's side and the steel industry on Nana's side. As a child, I remember being dragged along to at least one anti-war protest, so my mother's beliefs may have shifted during the Vietnam War. Dad was always a Democrat. Political beliefs were possibly a source of disagreement between my parents.

I return to the single picture of her in the yearbook. Her senior photo. This postage stamp-sized black-and-white image. Level gaze, wide, high forehead, similar to her father's face in the photo of him that sits over my desk, beside that one of Momma as a girl.

In the yearbook photo, Momma's short, dark bangs are carefully curled. White Peter Pan collar. Her smile looks stiff. Très 1950s, as is everyone in that 1954 yearbook. My mother attended college and graduated. Yet she evaded being included in any of the photos for the groups listed after her senior picture. Was most of her life a disappearing act? Even as early as college, was my mother already on a trajectory toward erasing herself, or being erased? Or did she simply dislike being photographed?

Feeling sad and unsatisfied but also relieved at being done looking through her old yearbook, I shove the musty hardback onto the bookshelf in our living room. Maybe this smelly yearbook will be one of the first things I toss on a farewell bonfire. Even though I paid for this volume and had it mailed to my Brooklyn apartment. This dusty book is an empty shell, not containing anything about Momma that I need to keep.

Briefly, I allow myself to again entertain the fantasy of a bonfire, picturing a portable firepit. Maybe I can borrow one from a friend. I could set it up in our parking lot. Bring some papers outside and burn them one evening when the weather gets warmer. I let the plan melt into the future; not something I need to figure out right now.

• • •

On other days, to counterbalance work at my desk, I try to spend time with my son. He's an October baby, a teenager already. A basketball player. After school, if he's not busy, I let him order takeout and pick it up for him. Or I schedule a doctor or dentist appointment he needs, to get him out of school early, and afterward we order food together at one of his favorite places. Or I cook for him at home. Often, he wants toast with soft-boiled eggs. He likes them medium runny with salt, lots of pepper. After playing basketball, he can easily devour three or four eggs and three pieces of toast. I make them the way Nana fixed soft-boiled eggs for me. Tearing the buttered toast into bite-sized pieces, scooping innards of slippery, cooked egg free of the shells, mixing everything in a bowl. I enjoy feeding him; it's also probably a way of mothering myself.

My son hasn't ever asked me about my mother, so I haven't told him much yet. Once when he was younger, I made sure to mention what happened to his other grandmother, that she died by suicide when I was in kindergarten. The reason he has only one grandmother who lives in Florida. But when he didn't act interested in knowing more, I didn't force-feed him more of Momma's story. I hope that if I continue to mention occasional details about her, he'll ask more questions as he's ready. Lately, he likes to tell me that he is nothing like me. We are both particular and strong-willed and too often we get into verbal arguments. He's not the type of son who ever clung to me, either physically or emotionally, and since he started high school, it's been almost longer than I can remember since he said something as vulnerable as, "I love you, Mommy." But whenever he's sick or needs anything at all, clothes, food, money—the last two especially—he comes directly to me first. Although we don't look alike and he was not created out of my genes or my body, we are as close as my two hands when I clasp them together.

• • •

Returning to my desk in the bedroom on another cloudy winter day, I find my two picture companions perched on the top shelf. The photo of Momma as a child, those big bows in her hair, standing beside the second picture, her father, Henry. His serious gaze. Even if they are only sitting there, these pictures, not alive, not speaking, I imagine they would want to help me; I feel they are helping me.

Another issue though: I don't really know how to address both of you together, since, well, I never knew you together, and I never knew you at all, Grandfather. I'll just keep addressing you both as "guys" as in "you guys."

There are twenty more letters in the packet. I need to keep reading to see what, if anything, I can still learn. What about the lingering mystery of my mother's possible affair with a married man in Vietnam? Was that failed relationship related to her suicide?

CHAPTER 7

Personal

The folder is labeled "ANN BAKER." Her name in caps. Under that, the single word: Personal. Black pen. Her writing. That word makes it seem as if there will be something significant revealed in the folder's contents. A secret message. Something to explain *her*. Who she was. Or what led to her sad, violent end. Possibly something about that affair in Vietnam, if that even happened. I came across the folder by accident one summer, a few years after Momma died, when I was eight or nine. After Dad already built the addition on our old house, all those new rooms we didn't need.

I found the folder tucked away in our living room in Amherst, in the wooden cabinet that Dad built. His home fix-it projects were usually rougher: painting; plastering; repairing car engines; assembling that swing set in our backyard from old pipes, parts scavenged at the town dump. Dad didn't normally make things that required the delicate finesse of furniture.

The top section of the waist-high cabinet had a flat lid that lifted up. Inside was the rectangular space that contained our family record player. In the section below the turntable were two doors that opened outward. That bottom cupboard held vinyl records, incredibly old-fashioned now, everyday middle-class luxuries of the time, each in its own cardboard sleeve, stored upright and packed together. If I crouched down, I could see into that dark space. Between the records on the far right was the spot where I discovered Momma's folder.

As soon as I found it, I sat down to examine the contents. Marked with my mother's name, this person we barely spoke about, along with that word: Personal. I felt as if I'd found a secret treasure. Inside were a bunch of papers. Folded neatly, tossed together, in no obvious order. Even then, the pages smelled dusty and old. One by one, I opened slips of paper. I was a good reader, but this was too much for me. Some newspaper articles, something about bombs, the word "Saigon," that place where Momma once worked. A few comics, drawings from magazines, but I didn't get the jokes. Several Christmas cards. Pictures of dresses cut from magazines. So many papers. I couldn't make sense of them. The papers were like pieces of a jigsaw puzzle. But they seemed to belong to different puzzles; they didn't fit together. Except they were all papers Momma must have kept. In this folder with her name written on it, in her own writing. These papers must tell a story about her, and maybe she was the only person who could reveal their meaning, but she wasn't here.

I shoved everything back in the folder, brought it to Dad, asking if he knew what it was. All I received was a terse, mumbled response tinged with annoyance. "Just a bunch of old papers your mother was saving. From when she was in Vietnam."

Nana was visiting then as she often did. Not satisfied with Dad's answer, I showed the folder to her next, asking if she knew anything about it. Dad's usual undercurrent of anger and loss was added to and amplified by my grandmother's sadness. "Some papers she saved. I don't know why," Nana muttered, peering down at me through her thick glasses.

I put the folder back in the bottom of the stereo cabinet, wedged beside the vinyl records. I knew the folder meant something I couldn't yet put into words. Momma had lived another life before she was my mother. Even though she vanished, she was once a real person. She'd lived in another country that I knew was far away. I sensed that something about this larger world that had belonged to Momma was in this folder, and maybe Dad and Nana didn't know about that part of her. Or remembering her made them too sad to talk about her.

I already had the idea in my mind back then that Momma fell in love with someone in Vietnam, a man who promised to leave his wife for her. Maybe Nana or Dad told me some scrap of that story the day I found the folder and brought it to them. I don't remember either of them telling me though. I only know I got that idea in my head somehow, but it was something I was too young to hear or understand.

I still have Momma's folder. The tape holding the edges together is brittle, yellow, coming off in places. One whole side has broken open, no longer taped together at all. The smell is the same: dust, years gone by. I already know there is no answer contained in this folder; I've looked through the contents many times. For some reason Momma saved these papers. Put them in this folder, labeled it with her name and the word Personal.

Maybe Dad downplayed the significance of Momma's file because he felt threatened by her record of a time in her life when she wasn't thinking about him, was involved with people and events that didn't include him. That time when he must have been thinking about her, waiting for her return.

There's nothing left to do but go through the contents of the folder. Twenty-four bits of paper, including the envelopes. This time when I look at these papers, I don't want to rush. I want to read through the contents of the Personal file, try to make sense of what's here one more time. I want to put the contents of

Momma's Personal file in order, with my goal of making a single story, one chronology, including the different sets of letters: the ones to Jean, Dad, Nana.

First from this file, there's a slip of newsprint. A brief, undated article. The year penned in the top right corner, followed by a question mark: 1957? That could even be my own handwriting, from years ago. My own unanswered question from a previous time I tried to write this story.

Ann Baker in Foreign Service

In the top corner below the handwritten year is a photo of my mother. "Ann Baker," the typed caption states.

> Miss Baker is one of the many American girls who selected Foreign Service as her career, giving her the opportunity of a good living and interesting travel to far-away lands.

Then some details about her life. Her Linden Street address, mother's name, high school and college. Identifying her as a member of the United States Foreign Service, now working at the American Embassy in Saigon. When Vietnam was still written as Viet-Nam. The article goes on to plug those secretarial positions: available to girls aged twenty-one to thirty-five, single, American citizens, no dependents. Even as young as eighteen for positions in Washington, DC.

Back to the picture. Black and white on yellow newsprint. A head-and-shoulders portrait for the paper. Short, dark hair. A perfect curl swirled over her forehead, large and square like the forehead of her father in that picture of him that still sits over my desk, beside Momma as a girl with bows in her hair. Another portrait of my mother frozen on paper. In it, Momma gazes upward and to the right, smiling with lips closed, a Mona Lisa-esque half smile.

When I'm done reading, I leave the clipping briefly on my desk, trying to take in that this was really my mother. That young, serious-for-the-newspaper-photo face. When I think about her, I'm usually filled with deep sadness, even all these years later. Her father, Henry, died by suicide when she was ten. Yet from what I can tell from her saved papers, she seemed to live her early life with gusto. She had a loving but sickly, nearly blind mother who later became my nana. An older brother, Reid. Somehow my mother, the poor speller, managed to grow up, go off to college, live in Paris as a student for a year. Worked in Vietnam for the State Department at the start of the US involvement in the war there. A few years later, she returned home, got married, had a family, two kids. But then her life ended. That abrupt, violent end.

As I sift through her papers, I'm still trying to piece together the two ends of that story, to fill in the middle. Understand who she was, what happened to her. I have these papers about her. My folder of family papers that I've collected: obituaries, Grandfather Henry Jr.'s death certificate. The Jean letters. Some of the Nana letters. Reid's memoir. Momma's Personal file. So many papers.

There on the shelf above my desk are my two guides. Today, I don't feel hopeful about them helping me, two people who died so miserably. Ann and Henry.

Recently, I celebrated my sixtieth birthday. January 11. The anniversary of your January death, Grandfather. The day of your suicide, I think, still speaking to him silently inside my head. Eighty years ago is a long time. I'm still recovering from the cascade of events that followed your actions from that day.

I had a fantastic birthday, guys. We ate a simple dinner at home: me, my husband, my two almost-grown children. That's not all I have planned for my January birthday either, guys. This year, I decided to celebrate the entire month. I'll see friends; buy things for myself that I need. New old-lady walking shoes. New cell phone case. One night, we'll all go out for dinner too: husband, children, me. I might also see a play with my husband, like Momma used to do with Dad.

Maybe I can have that celebration bonfire I think about, burn everything I no longer need. Will burning the papers I'm done with finally help me be done with my unhappy family story? Will writing down this history of Momma help me find her, and release me from her? A bonfire could be like a big farewell bash.

Momma and Henry don't say anything about my bonfire idea. I don't know if they approve of bonfires. Maybe they're both afraid that would really be the end of them. After all, neither chose fire as the way to make their last exit. And all that's left of them now are these pictures and papers.

CHAPTER 8

Bon Voyage

Like most of the letters from Momma to her friend, the next Jean letter is not dated. I know the years my mother worked in Vietnam though, and from the other letters that follow, I can guess that this one was from 1956. I could have placed this letter in front of the previous PR article about foreign service positions, but putting that article first helps tell the story of where Momma was headed when she set out on this ship.

AMERICAN PRESIDENT LINES

On Board S.S. President Wilson

Saturday

Jean—

Sorry, am "indisposed" in cabin right now or would go get ink from steward. For moment docked in Los Angeles harbor. Didn't realize till left San Francisco that would be stopping here too. Don't leave tomorrow until 4:00 p.m. Keep thinking—"Can pack up everything, cancel reservations, go home, marry Bob." Know I won't but idea has much appeal. Not cold feet, you realize, over that long ago. Marriage, Bahamas—sounds good, though. Last night water very choppy cutting up along coast. Will be glad when we cut directly across Pacific—cancel both anarchistic and seasick tendencies. Actually I'm working myself into the—prior to home leave—"Asia First" fervor by reading Chester Bowles' Ambassador's Report.[1] I think you would enjoy it.

Just called room steward about 10 minutes ago. Very thirsty—don't want to bother him again this evening since almost midnight. So order two brandy alexanders. When he arrives I feel obliged to explain that both drinks are for me. He glances into cupboard anyway, pockets tip, and closes door discretely behind him. Very canny these ship hands! So now to try to condense what has happened in past few days.

First of anything I want you to know how really good to see you it was. For coffee for cigarettes for consolation (though you undoubtedly didn't think of it as such) I am eternally grateful. Until Chicago was not so much desolate as benumbed! Since this total venture has become a bit more concrete. Slept most of way in plane. Revived when voice over speaker announced Great Salt Lake, Rockies, and Reno below. Country from Wyoming on surprizingly [sic] like fantasy of moon country—very crater-ish. Sorry to say—very scant impressions. In San Francisco cocktails on the "Top of the Mark" where can look out over harbor—supper at Tarantino's on Fisherman's Wharf. Rode cable car on the outside. Very colorful—everyone very friendly—love San Francisco.

Late at pier next morning. Visitors ready to disembark. Chinese girls in native dress handing out flowers. Everyone throwing streamers. Even more color. Think this is better than Mauretania tourist. Make way to cocktail lounge. Much snapping of publicity pictures. People standing around in mink stoles, orchids, and dark glasses. People screaming “Have a nice trip” bon voyage and all that and hugging each other. Meet other foreign service girl who is sharing cabin. We discover that three quarters of passengers are employees of American President Lines, taking jaunt up to Los Angeles, who plan to return to work Monday. Very disillusioning. Anyway anxious to see who gets on tomorrow. So far the permanent list seems to be made up of old married couples (the retired polo player sort) and nouveau riche fizzler variety. Few interesting types at meal sitting however, —a wife of one of the steamship Company’s higher echelon traveling to Honolulu. Also a Standard Oil jaded world traveler on his way to Yokohama and just recuperating from a bout with malaria in Africa. Last night after absorbing all possible at bar of liquid and Shriners’ atmosphere, decided to go up on top. Think I will breathe great gusts of salt air—stamp around the deck—“one with nature, elements and all that”—meet only missionary on way to Hong Kong with similar purpose. Everyone else still partying in cocktail lounge or running the stateroom circuit below. Crushing anticlimax.

Today go into Los Angeles. Take bus out to Hollywood and Vine. Everyone looks like Moira Shearer with toreador pants and scarf tied around ponytail (in Red Shoes[2] that is). Hollywood, Los Angeles, not just appalling but downright awful. This is more a horrified than pseudo blasé analysis—believe me! Anyway bought Gibbons’

> Decline and Fall of Roman Empire,[3] went to movie, and came back to boat.
>
> As I've been meaning to say though, how would you like to be maid of honor about six months from now. Will you consider it—though of course things are dependent on a great many factors. That should be just about the time limit though. You know my favorite old French saying don't you—"la plus ca change, la plus c'est la meme chose."
>
> —Ann

Captured again on the page is my mother's voice as I don't remember it from life. Speaking in joking, confiding tones to her friend. Referring to books and movies, places she saw, people she met or observed, sprinkled here and there with a pretentious-sounding French word or expression, along with a dash of her signature misspellings, not that frequent given that this was one of the main idiosyncrasies both Nana and Reid related about her.

Momma's letters do bring her to life for me. I feel caught up in the adventure she's embarking on; so caught up that when she mentions Bob, my dad, half joking about dropping everything to go home and marry him, I feel surprised, almost forgetting that by that point they already met. I'm interested to hear that Momma and Jean met up briefly, maybe in Chicago, just as Momma was setting out on her trip.

I try to picture my mother as a young woman, exploring San Francisco on her own, riding on the outside of a cable car, sipping a cocktail while enjoying the view of the harbor from the Top of the Mark, an iconic spot that still exists atop the Mark Hopkins Hotel, known for its 360-degree city views, I learn online. Momma also dined at Tarantino's, another San Francisco landmark, one that's since vanished. In May 2020, during the COVID pandemic, the restaurant was wiped out in a fire that erased an entire warehouse at Fisherman's Wharf. Momma's letters are mini time capsules, containing glimpses of people and places sometimes long gone.

As much as she found to love about San Fran, Momma abhorred Hollywood, describing everyone in terms of starlet Moira Shearer from *The Red Shoes*. I wonder what movie she took in on her solo night out in Hollywood, maybe something not worth mentioning since she usually included the names of the movies and plays she saw, along with the many books she read.

Her favorite French expression translates roughly to, "The more things change, the more they stay the same," a familiar saying that I find reassuring. I wish that was actually the mantra she lived by. Instead, her byword was more like: expect the unexpected. But that's probably not a saying in French.

Both my mother's ship, the *President Wilson*, and the sister ship, the *President Cleveland*, belonged to the American President Lines, two-class ships sailing with express service to the Far East, I learned when I searched their names online. Their 1940s modern first-class public rooms and pool occupied the entire Promenade Deck, while economy had a lounge, veranda, and pool aft on the lower decks. The twin ocean liners were especially popular with tourists, government and military personnel, and other travelers sailing between the United States and Asia.

My mother was one of those government personnel traveling from the US to Asia. I'm sure she sailed economy class. It seems her port of debarkation was Yokohama. From looking up old sailing schedules, I can guess that the voyage took about two weeks. But how did she travel from that city in Japan to Saigon? Plane or smaller boat, or some combination that included a bus?

Momma sounds so alive in that first letter, but also as if she's trying to convince her friend what a fantastic time she's having, lightheartedly dropping references to sights and activities, possibly showing off for Jean, who may have been stuck at home with a kid somewhere near Chicago. Momma jokes about having cold feet about heading to Vietnam but doesn't admit how scared and lonely she may have felt.

However she traveled for the last leg of her journey, my mother's next letter to Jean did arrive from Vietnam, typed that time. But Momma didn't write the next letter to her best friend for another year. In the meantime, she sent four letters to Bob. The same Bob she mentioned to Jean in that first letter from the ship. The Bob my mother eventually married. Bob who became Dad.

• • •

My two picture guides? I crawl into bed, not up to facing them this evening. Instead, I stream a movie on my laptop, something I've never seen before: *The Red Shoes*. Moira Shearer: toreador pants, scarf tied around her ponytail just as Momma described her to Jean from the ship. I'm alone in bed, alone in our snug apartment. Everyone else is out doing their different things. I stretch out luxuriously under the covers. I find the movie silly, a melodramatic fairy tale that lulls me to sleep before the ending.

CHAPTER 9

Bob

AMERICAN PRESIDENT LINES

On Board S.S. President Wilson

Monday

Dear Bob,

What a desecrated crew aboard for this cruise—mostly retired polo player variety. One well lubricated one was 'buying' in the bar last night—this his third world jaunt—said his bar bill last trip ran $240. This time with much foresight has attempted to correct the situation with a private stock—2 cases apiece scotch, bourbon. Just beneath him in alcoholic prowess though with more of an international flair is a Standard Oil vet, a Hemingway type character, just recovering from a case of malaria in Africa—Mau-Mau country no less. And many more. They all sit up in the lounge and read "After You Marco Polo."[4] One woman at my table does this sort of thing as a hobby—she collects slides and data for lectures to Methodist women's clubs back home. Which you might consider at least constructive, but don't think you would say so if you met her. Awful! She threatened her husband—poor soul—that if he didn't take Dramamine he would get seasick. He did—at least he wasn't at breakfast this morning.

All of which I hope you won't think is pseudo-critical. Just a few bits salvaged from a whole conglomeration of impressions. No final judgements—rather quite a bit to think about for some time to come. Actually there are quite a few more than congenial people on this trip. In fact three quarters of the passengers didn't even appear today. Storm. Much rolling. Even guide ropes have been strung up. As yet I haven't 'defaulted.' This morning played bridge with a Canadian couple. She is originally French, he is to be Vice Consul to the Philippines—both very young. Anyway, practically everyone else was confined below. Then we had to hang on to bridge table—luckily chained down—to keep from sliding from one end of the lounge to the other. One dear little lady, who was kibitzing, toppled completely over backwards in her chair and had to give up her position as 'observer.' It's not that it's all that rough, but the ship is so tiny that the heave ho is much more evident.

Really this is our first day out too. I didn't realize till we had left San Francisco that we were to make an overnight stop in Los Angeles, too. So final sailing wasn't until 4:00 yesterday afternoon. Twice in three days went through the ordeal of flowers handed out, Hawaiian bands playing, streamers, bon voyage, sailors, all very colorful, all very anticlimactic. Especially so since up to deadline kept having a little parley with myself—"Can pack up, cancel reservations, fly home." I think the only thing that stopped me from doing so—and I hope you recognize the irony—was that it was so totally impractical. Oh, I'm getting back some of the original fervor reading Chester Bowles "Ambassador's Report" (by the way I think you would enjoy it—Asia first concept and all that) but for perhaps the first time I think I could actually stand to live without climbing the Matterhorn or going down the Zambesi [sic] in a dugout canoe. So good-bye to Richard Halliburton. I'll raise begonias yet—who knows? Zounds what a tantalizing proposition. All of which proves that I must love you very much to waver so much in something I've wanted for so long (How's that for analytical passion!)

Think I shall go 'upstairs' or 'up top' or however you approve saying it—for breath of fresh air. The other night—first night out I went up on deck very late—very rugged, love sea, love salt spray—think I will watch sea—all very nice—very exhilarating—meet only missionary with similar purpose on way to Hong Kong, 'jaded' international tourists still partying below. All of which is sheer nonsensical rambling.

Except for—much love,

Ann

There's my mother again, springing to life, writing this time to my future father, trying him out, perhaps, as her principal confidant and recipient of her diary-style correspondence. Telling him about the people she observed on the ship. By the time she first wrote to him, she'd already been on board longer than when she wrote to Jean, so he got to hear even more about fellow travelers, with one overlap: The Standard Oil vet. By that point in the voyage, it sounds like more alcohol was flowing. Future Dad was privy to the same self-deprecating anecdote as Jean though: Momma's trip "up top" to commune with nature, only to meet the Hong Kong-bound missionary seeking the same goal.

Future Dad gets the same *Ambassador's Report* book recommendation. But for him, she doesn't drop the second title mentioned to Jean, *Decline and Fall of the Roman Empire*, single volume, not the six-volume version. Did she already give up reading that dense tome by the time she wrote to him? Or was she doing the classic female dumbing down of her intelligence for a potential male mate?

Lying on my bed in the small Brooklyn bedroom or sitting at the tiny desk, I tried reading the single volume *Decline*, but like the 1950s anti-communist political analysis by Bowles, I found that ancient history with its lengthy, convoluted sentences tough going. For lighter enjoyment, I read the travelogue *After You, Marco Polo* instead.

For Future Dad, Momma mentions SF and LA, but without all the colorful details she shared with Jean. Similarly, Momma jokes about wanting to cancel everything, fly home. She doesn't directly confide to Future Dad her fantasy of marrying him, as she did with her girlfriend. Indirectly though, she alludes to a desire for a domestic life, while still asserting her primary aspiration for travel and adventure. Still, she addresses Bob as "dear," tells him she loves him, signs her letter "much love." If I were a young man receiving her letter, I might have felt confused about her intentions. I don't quite remember if I asked Dad what he felt when he received her letters. I think he told me he loved her, but that he didn't want to stand in the way of her plans.

From my small Brooklyn desk, rereading Momma's first letter to my future dad, I feel sadness, longing. For a mother I never got to keep. For both of my parents, the life they didn't get to enjoy for long together. I would never peruse this letter and be able to predict: this is a woman who in X years will die by suicide. Is it always that way with suicide? Someone is on a path: their life. Then they happen to turn left instead of right or vice versa, get stuck, pulled up short at a desperate dead end.

I look up Richard Halliburton whom Momma mentioned, read about the famed American travel writer, adventurer, author; known for swimming the forty-eight-mile length of the Panama Canal in 1928. It took him fifty hours over ten days. In March 1939, barely ten years later, he left Hong Kong aboard a motor-powered Chinese junk called the *Sea Dragon* en route to San Francisco. Some twelve hundred miles west of Midway Island, he and his boat encountered a typhoon, and disappeared. For me, it's an unhappy echo of my mother's fate.

• • •

When Dad gave me his letters from Momma, the pages were folded together inside a single airmail envelope. The letters she wrote to him soon after they met. Two from the ship on her way to Vietnam, two more mailed after she reached Saigon. After rereading and sorting them into the right order, I decide the envelope must belong to the last letter. The airmail envelope postmarked Dec. 20, 1956.

I don't remember exactly what Dad told me when he handed over his letters from Momma. I was always wondering about Momma, asking questions about her. I would go into Dad's room, the small room off the kitchen he turned into his new bedroom, after he stopped sleeping in the upstairs room he used to share with Momma. At night after dinner, I could always find him downstairs, working at his desk. If I perched nearby on his twin bed, he would stop what he was doing to talk.

It must have been soon after her death when Dad first explained to me and Sydney that Momma died by suicide. Already he'd moved downstairs to the room that used to barely hold the dining room table. That first time he talked to us about her suicide, Sydney and I sat together on his new narrow bed, with Dad hovering over us, looking desolate, worried. The details of Momma's suicide had been in the paper, so he had to share everything before someone else did. But it was too late. Children at school had already taunted Sydney with the details: the rope, the plastic bag.

"I have to tell you this," Dad said, or something equally blunt: "Your mother killed herself."

Later, at some point, I also remember him telling me, "I think your mother blamed herself for her father's suicide."

I was probably in high school when he entrusted me with the letters. When Dad gave me his letters from her, he also told me his story of how they first met. "It was at a picnic, at a lake outside Sharon," he said. By chance, he was brought along by a friend to even out the numbers for a double date. He never had a serious girlfriend before. He'd joined the Navy at eighteen straight out of high school, served two years in the Pacific at the tail end of the war, never seeing any combat. Afterward, he went directly to college on the GI Bill. The summer he met Momma, he was working at Westinghouse in Sharon. He was not quite thirty, she not quite twenty-five. Dad said they both already knew she was leaving in two weeks: the Foreign Service job in Saigon, working as a secretary in the embassy on the other side of the world.

"We went out together every night for two weeks," he confided. "I didn't ask her to marry me. I didn't want to stop her from going." Later, he regretted not telling her how much he wanted her to stay, he admitted.

"Your mother was the most alive person I ever knew," Dad once told me. Striking, since she was the first dead person I ever knew.

I used to have a photo of the picnic at the lake the day they met. A black-and-white snapshot. Momma smiling, laughing. Someone throwing water at someone else. My mother ducking, head thrown back, hair wet, a white shirt unbuttoned over her bathing suit.

Dad was in the shot, too, not snapping the picture. He looked goofy, with a half-embarrassed grin, tall with stooped shoulders, the black plastic-rimmed glasses he always wore; more like a college student than someone who already served in the Navy, graduated with that difficult electrical engineering degree, working a steady job as some kind of sales manager.

• • •

I pull out my small plastic bin of photos, empty it onto the double bed, my work surface. I'm searching for the picture I remember, the one of that day at the lake: someone throwing water, Momma looking relaxed, laughing. The beginning of my parents' relationship, which led to my existence. I can't find it anymore. I must not have saved that picture, but I wish I did.

The second letter to Dad. A sheet of crinkling onionskin, faded black fountain pen script, Momma's writing again. This time, below the ship's letterhead, in caps: my mother's full name. She was on the ship long enough to have personalized stationery printed.

AMERICAN PRESIDENT LINES

MISS ANN ELIZABETH BAKER

On Board S.S. President Wilson

Saturday

Dear Bob,

You did ask for a photo didn't you! This is the best I can do for the moment. Have not gone native. The very trite costume was last resort for ships' masquerade—with grass skirt borrowed from steward, flowers (wilted) pilfered from lounge, many layers of greasepaint. The next day we docked in Honolulu to see the real thing. Hula dancers on pier—compliments of Chamber of Commerce.

Tomorrow—arrival Yokohama. Feeling slightly mild case of sun poisoning—yes it has been a glorious cruise. Actually because the time element on shipboard is so nonexistent I still don't feel as if I've gone anywhere or am going anywhere—yet. To be perfectly frank my heart is no longer in this little venture…

I'm not going to be an infant and say right away 'don't like it here, want to go home'—but I will grant that you may have been very right all along—as usual. Not that you are always 100% correct—Ann

From between the crinkling pages, a tiny, black-and-white image slips out. Like the picture of her father that still watches over me at my small Brooklyn desk, along with the younger version of herself. Momma's grown-up shipboard image shimmies out from between the pages she wrote long ago to my future dad. This time, the photo is cut into an uneven shape, signaling that Momma's picture was manually edited, perhaps removing some other person. Perhaps an irrelevant person. Or someone Momma didn't want Bob—my future dad—to see. Someone she befriended on the voyage? The other foreign service girl mentioned in the shipboard letter to Jean?

In this thumbnail snapshot, Momma poses on the floor, bare legs folded under a Hawaiian fake-grass skirt, the costume she described to Dad: a necklace of flowers; her face looking too tan under layers of greasepaint. The unaware racism of the time makes me cringe. Even at that tiny scale, my mother appears slightly glazed with alcohol from the party.

These are things I can't get the young girl photo version of my mother, chaperoned as she is by her dad above my workspace, to answer: Who were you with in that snapshot on the *SS President Wilson*? What message did you mean to send to Future Dad: wait for me, please, until I return? Maybe that was something you didn't know how to ask, not after your own dad abandoned you. But Bob-Future-Dad did wait for you, even without you asking.

• • •

At the top of the third letter, following the day of the week, is a penciled-in date: "7/16." Dad's writing, or mine from an earlier time when I read this letter? I can no longer remember or recognize whose scribbled date that is.

Monday

Bob,

Greetings from Saigon! Cesspool of the Far East, vice capital of the Orient.

Actually I rather like it. How long have I been here though—four weeks. I hang my head in shame for not having written sooner. It's incredible the way time is almost non-existent. Strictly a phenomenon of "this part of the world." Which I hope you won't think is a too very feeble excuse.

I just must send you pictures of this place. Any other sort of description just couldn't do 'justice' to the local color. Suffice to say for now that it's a lot more primitive than exotic. Everyone says, though, that with mosquito netting and scotch in the drinking water that it is possible to survive! Of course there are quite a few civilized features—among them a golf course—which I haven't seen yet. However, I have heard that if you expect to get out of the rough, nothing less than a lawn mower is in order.

How is summer in Sharon though? Especially how is your summer? Seems so very very long ago—that is a year ago. When I sit on the sidewalk along Catinat—the main drag—eating rice out of a little bowl with chopsticks, I know it will be time to go home. Meanwhile, my dear, I've settled down into a reasonably native life.

Do write Bob, sooner than I have. Want to hear from you so very much—

Ann

The paper is tissue-thin, like old skin, the fountain-penned words fading away, all of it barely legible; time has been passing since I last looked at these pages, years ago already.

Momma persisted in writing to him instead of to Jean. But she didn't address her letter with "dear" this time. She didn't sign her letter "love" this time either. She did call him "my dear" in the letter though. Her tone is still entertaining, joking, calling Saigon a cesspool of the Far East. But the plot has taken a turn; she's no longer constantly homesick. She says she's starting to like it there.

I feel frustrated that she couldn't tell him what she wanted, that she didn't seem to know. She seems to know how to dangle bits of female allure to keep herself attractive to him; to keep him waiting in case she needed him, for whenever she would likely return home. Maybe she remembered in the back of her mind Nana's requirement of a suitable marriage. Or maybe Momma felt insecure if she hadn't yet received a return letter from him.

I cringe, too, at the background political plot: US government and military personnel, among whom she numbered in her humble secretarial role. The trajectory: colonization, war, mass destruction, death.

Aside from the romance and the politics, her timeline confuses me. She mentions already being away for four weeks, but also not seeing him since the *previous* summer—a year earlier. Her details in these letters don't match up with the story of their relationship that I remember hearing from Dad: that they met two weeks before her departure to her job. What about the extra intervening year she refers to in the letter? Either I misremembered, or Dad mixed up the chronology in his retelling; both things are equally possible and likely. Maybe she just meant it *felt* like a year ago. Or else she was really that confused about the passage of time, as she mentioned more than once in her letters.

Maybe after meeting him that summer in Sharon, she did not proceed directly to Vietnam. Perhaps the intervening time can be accounted for by a year she worked for the US Foreign Service in Washington, DC, as Reid mentioned in one of those past phone calls I made to him; the same secretarial positions in DC available to "American girls" touted by the PR article from Momma's Personal file.

Further confusing the picture, Momma's first obituary mentions that she lived after college for a year in New York City, not in DC. I always had it in my mind, probably from something Dad told me, that Momma worked for a year in New York. But is that even true? Was it my father who told that version of Momma's life to the paper for her obituary?

This possible scenario—that she lived and worked in DC for a year, after they met but before she went to Saigon—raises other questions though. Wouldn't there have been more letters, possibly more visits? If she was in DC and he was in Sharon, her hometown, for a year after they met? There's probably some simple explanation for this mismatch of time and place in the storyline that I'll never know. And why is this even important anymore? The point is that their relationship was stop-start, uneven, not straight ahead. Maybe the story of my parents getting together almost didn't happen.

This is not something my picture guides can help me with, standing guard above my desk. They do give small boosts to my mood and motivation, to balance out the sadness and loss in the story. About facts and logistics, they remain mute.

CHAPTER 10

Armpit of Winter

There is a fourth letter to Bob. But first, two more items from her Personal file. Not dated. These two papers could come here, marking the beginning of Momma's life in Vietnam.

• • •

The front of a card, thick paper, the back torn off, decorated with a circular design, dark blue raised ink. Vietnamese letters. I should ask someone to translate this for me. No names inside. Probably a generic greeting card message: "Peace," or something like that. Saved maybe because Momma liked the design, or it reminded her of a place she once went or the person who gave this to her.

• • •

Another slip of yellowed newsprint. No date but a scribble of pen on the upper right corner, difficult to read, possibly a year: "1956." A catchy headline:

U.S. Theme is Yes, We Have No Cabanas

A note in blue pen, bottom right:

SAVE

DALAT!!

That is Momma's writing, I'm certain. The word "Dalat" isn't mentioned in the article or in Momma's letters, but when I look up that name online, I confirm what I remember from reading this clipping in the past: Dalat, also spelled Da Lat, is the name of a small capital city of a province in southern Vietnam, known as the "city of flowers" as well as "city of eternal spring," due to the ubiquitous flowers, the temperate climate. A famous resort location developed by the French during the colonial era.

With a jokey tone, the article discusses budget cuts the US State Department was forced to make at the time. Cuts to programs at "hardship posts overseas." In a quoted interchange from a censored transcript, at the time recently released, one elected official, Representative Rooney, questioned another elected official. Rooney inquired how much of a million-dollar allowance for foreign service people the following year was for food, cocktails, and other such expenses.

"Mr. Chairman, luncheons and small dinners, I would say, are one of the most effective places to conduct business," replied Deputy Assistant Secretary Hall, parrying the question. Those words "small dinners," so decisively underlined, again in Momma's blue pen, possibly hint at the backstory of Momma's dating life in Saigon, while not revealing exactly who accompanied her. Or maybe I'm reading too much into this tiny detail, and Momma simply enjoyed the comedy of that scene, two elected officials sparring over government expenses.

Dalat was a well-known, popular destination in Vietnam, a place it doesn't seem Momma visited, but she probably heard about it when she worked in Saigon. The catchy headline about cabanas refers to the title of a popular song from 1922, "Yes! We Have No Bananas," about a shortage of that fruit resulting from a fungus known as the Panama disease. To put the article's budgetary haggling in perspective, a million dollars in 1956 would be worth ten times as much just over half a century later, in 2022.

Did someone back home send this article to Momma? Dad or Jean or even Reid? Or did Momma cut it out herself? Seeing what I'm certain is my mother's writing and underlining on this old slip of newspaper, I feel as if she just passed through the room, a ghost who nipped out again. I miss her. Her absence hangs heavily over all these papers.

• • •

It is late February, the armpit of winter, the time of year that drags on and on. Today is actually the anniversary of Momma's suicide, February 25. Not a date I usually remember or think about. These shortest days of the year seem to me the hardest time of the year, especially in this northern climate where we get so much gray weather and darkness. I don't think the timing of Momma's suicide was a coincidence. Happening at that low point of the war, also during the lingering darkness of late winter. Soon after the anniversary of her father's mid-January suicide.

February 25 was not a day we talked about or acknowledged when I was growing up. Lately, I sometimes think about inventing a holiday to commemorate the anniversary of Momma's death. Maybe I could have that bonfire I sometimes think about, possibly burn some of these papers when I'm finally done looking at them. Will doing that help me say goodbye to her?

My mother, the little girl in the picture on the shelf above my desk beside her father's image, does not look directly at me. I want to think if she did, she'd have a young version of that Mona Lisa-esque smile I noticed in the newspaper photo of her from before she departed on her Far East adventure. Maybe she went looking for part of herself in Vietnam, before she became entangled in the destruction of that country, something she possibly regretted.

CHAPTER 11

Practical Cats

The last letter to Dad from Momma is typed, this time on her work stationery, more yellowing tissue paper. This is the letter that must have originally arrived in the airmail envelope, the one postmarked Dec. 20, 1956. The envelope Dad used to hold his letters from Momma, until he handed them on to me.

THE FOREIGN SERVICE
OF THE
UNITED STATES OF AMERICA

Tuesday–December 18

Dear Bob—

The monsoon is ending, orchids in bloom, and Christmas is almost here. Never have I felt more un-Christmas in my life. I'm going to spend the holidays swimming in the South China Sea and try to forget that palm trees should be pines.

However, so much for nostalgia! As for the life, I do like it. So far I've acquired an opium pipe, a Chinese boyesse and a Siamese cat named 'Macavity.' I have been tiger hunting; I've met a local entrepreneur 'who knew Greene well;' learned to eat reasonably well with chopsticks (well enough to avoid starvation); in fact, the only thing I haven't been able to become accustomed to is the Vietnamese delicacy—Nouc Mam—fermented fish oil, just as bad as it sounds, but believe me the natives love it.

In the six months since I've been here, I haven't been out of Vietnam, although I have seen a great deal of the country around Saigon—rice paddies, jungles, northern mountainous terrain, rubber and tea plantations, refugee villages, as well as the MOI country. The MOI's are native tribesmen just ten years out of the headhunting stage. First reaction to all this before taking it for granted was 'just like the geography books,' National Geographic or what have you. Actually, it is beautiful country. I've sent home some photos, and just last week about 200 colored slides. I sincerely wish you would feel free to stop by the house to see them. Mostly I've just been experimenting wildly with film and camera, but it might give you a better idea of what it really is like here, if you're at all interested.

Also I'm enclosing an article that I just came across in Harper's, about Diem's reign. Practically the biggest attraction so far was the celebration of the country's first free elections in November (1st Anniversary). Like a great carnival with parades and Naval review competing with dragon dances in the streets and war canoe races—ever the oriental touch to the festivities. The article also mentions the Binh Xuyen bandit area south of Saigon. Well, before I even knew that such a spot existed, a group of us took a cross-country trip via sampan, native bus and oxcart, mainly just to see how far we could get on such an off the main route, 'primitive' venture. What we did was to come right to the brink of the territory mentionned [sic] (still a renegade stronghold) before being turned back by a Vietnamese military guard.

This last was the most exciting thing so far. You mention typhoon, revolution. Saigon itself has had few repercussions from the latter events. Mainly this is because communication system is just about nil here, except for daily USIA Bulletin and a few French journals. (I find out more about Vietnam from what people back home have seen on TV than anything). Of course the 'old hands' are constantly lording it over the newcomers with tales of what it was like during the war when things were really happening, before the casinos and dens closed down, etc. Right now though, it's a very mild, conservative existence. Sidewalk cafes offer the ultimate in adventure.

Surprisingly, I don't too much mind my job either. For the most part it's routine secretarial work. Since it's in the General Services Section though, much of what I do is on my own—reservations, correspondence, and so forth. (I've become an expert in calming temporarily maladjusted people sans electricity or plumbing. Needless to say, the Public utilities work very erratically, if, when, or at all). Also I've filled the gap on occasion doing everything from painting to filling fire extinguishers, from supervising coolie gang to being officer-in-charge of the Ambassador's Vichy water. Ludicrous perhaps, but not dull!

Merry Christmas. I've meant to write much sooner. Ann

"You mention typhoon, revolution…" she wrote to Bob-Future-Dad. It seems he did write back to her at least once, sounding worried. The same concerned, often protective father I later knew. He must have already understood something about her penchant for danger, for risk. She casually mentions a recent adventure, a cross-country group trip to the region of Binh Xuyen bandits south of Saigon via sampan, otherwise known as a rowboat, along with various other slow means of transport, to the point when they were turned back by military guards. No wonder Dad worried.

She also naively comments on the one-year anniversary of South Vietnam's "first free elections," which she witnessed in Saigon in November, referring to the fraudulent referendum in which Diem proclaimed himself president of the newly created Republic of Vietnam. On a more mundane note, Momma discusses her secretarial duties in the General Services Section of the embassy, sounding as if she enjoyed complaining about her varied and colorful duties.

If she'd lived until the current century, I'm hopeful she would have updated her vocabulary to include Indigenous people. Equally cringe-worthy is her use of the term *boyesse*, a French word for male servant, which sounds especially demeaning since in the same sentence she mentions her pet Siamese cat Macavity, named after one of the characters in Eliot's *Old Possum's Book of Practical Cats*, a reference Dad might have missed. *Cats* the musical wasn't a thing yet, and he was more the practical businessman type, never as big a reader as she was.

Then there are the two hundred colored slides she mentions sending home, pressing Future Dad to view them at her mother's. Once when I was about five, probably not long before her suicide, Momma tried to get Dad to help show me and Sydney her Vietnam slides. After dinner, Dad set up the projector on the table in the crowded dining room next to the kitchen, before that was his bedroom.

I felt excited and curious to see Momma's pictures. Then Dad said something to Momma I didn't hear. She stormed upstairs, slamming doors. Dad went upstairs after her. When he returned, she didn't come with him. Sydney and I waited nervously and obediently at the dining room table with the lights dimmed, rolling our eyes at each other. Since my older sister always enjoyed knowing more than I did, I knew she didn't understand what our parents were fighting about because she said nothing. Dad showed us Momma's slides himself, flipping through the colorful images that flashed on the wall in the dark, not saying much except to mutter angrily, "Bunch of pictures of water buffalo."

A lot of brown and green. Grass. Water. "Who are they?" I hesitantly inquired. Some pictures flashed on the wall, people wearing conical hats like upside-down straw ice cream cones, something I never saw before.

Dad shook his head, annoyed. "I don't know."

It was like watching a movie with the sound off. Without Momma's help, the pictures made no sense, didn't fit together into a story. I was too young to understand where Vietnam was. I only knew Momma took the pictures when she worked in that faraway land. Before she was our mother. Somehow these pictures made Dad say something to Momma that made her mad.

Why didn't Dad want to look at her pictures that day in 1967? Why, nearly a decade after she took those pictures, did he still resent any reminder of that place where she once lived and worked? Maybe their fight had something to do with the story about the man Dad believed she fell in love with there, that possibly married man. I didn't know about the story of Momma's love affair in Vietnam yet at the time my parents fought about her slides.

• • •

Accompanying Momma's 1956 Christmas letter to Dad is a gold Christmas card. Inside, her blue pen writing:

> Merry Merry
>
> Christmas—
>
> Ann

On the facing side, a preprinted greeting, "Merry Xmas From Saigon," and the words in phoneticized Vietnamese, "Cung Chuc Tan Xuan," which translates roughly to, "Happy New Year."

On the red-white-and-blue-edged airmail envelope is the typed address:

> To Mr. Robert Plattner, State Towers Apts.,
Sharon, Penna.

Her return address, also typed:

> Ann Baker, American Embassy—Box 31, Navy
150 c/o FPO, San Francisco, Calif.

FPO for Fleet Post Office, Momma's return address on that 1956 airmail envelope, her Christmas letter to Dad. The relay station where overseas government employees could send and receive mail.

A quick peek online brings up a picture of State Towers Apartments in Sharon. A dingy, tan building. The brief accompanying review tells me this older high-rise is still conveniently located on the main street heading into Sharon. A second reviewer asserts: "I would not live in these apartments, just like a big block cube, no amenities."

The building in the photo looks vaguely familiar, like something from a dream. Dad lived there before I was born, according to the address on the colorful but faded airmail envelope. I was probably driven past that place as a child, my parents pointing out where Dad lived before he got married. That dismal-looking building. His bachelor apartment when he received Momma's flirty, entertaining letters from Saigon.

• • •

While I've been rereading Momma's letters and papers, thinking about her more than I have in years, a new thought floats into my mind: what was it like for me when she first died? How did I get through the first day? What was it like being in our house in Amherst, walking through those rooms where she used to live with us, trying to take in that she was dead? I barely knew anything about death at age six. I didn't get to practice first with any easier deaths. A pet goldfish or hamster for example. Even a neighbor or grandparent. I did what anyone going through a traumatic shock does: my body and mind knew automatically how to make myself numb. Death is a cruel reality for anyone to adjust to, especially when it's your mother.

"OK, you two," I try speaking to my pictures aloud today, another day of gray, cold winter. "What can you do for me today? Any kind of small pep talk you can give me?"

CHAPTER 12

The Addition

Like hunting for pieces from a puzzle, in Momma's Personal file, I find the article from *Harper's* magazine, mentioned in her last letter to Dad, the article she enclosed for him. No longer with her letter that he saved and gave me. Instead, the *Harper's* piece is with her papers in her file. A small, unsolved mystery: who moved the article from the envelope with the letter to the Personal file? Momma or Dad? And why? Again, why does this even matter anymore? Also slightly curious though, the date of the article is from the beginning of the year, not the end: January, not December, 1956. In Saigon, Momma probably had access to mostly outdated magazines.

Reprieve in Viet Nam, by Senator Mike Mansfield. Harper's Magazine.

Quickly, I glance through the brittle, yellow pages. The subheading claims that the article, "...brings back a heartening report on our chances of saving Indochina—a key area which seemed almost sure to fall to the Communists only a year ago."

It's hard to get myself to read this "heartening report," delivered with the naïve optimism of 1956, knowing that millions of people would be killed in the Vietnam War, counting soldiers and civilians on both sides.

From her letters and those few saved papers, it seems my mother went to Saigon looking for adventure, swept up in the events and perspective of the United States at the time, and just plain needing a job, accepting a position doing what she knew how to do and what was available to someone of her age and background: college-educated, young, white, middle-class female. Given those conditions, secretary was the obvious answer, maybe the only answer. There were also her individual characteristics: her personal history that she was trying to overcome or escape—her father's suicide. All that plus her knowledge of French led her to the former French colony, where US involvement in a war was beginning to unfold.

I manage to drag myself through the *Harper's* article enough to digest the gist of its unapologetic sales pitch for Diem, then president of South Vietnam. According to Senator Mansfield, Diem was successfully working to build a free nation in South Vietnam and looking as if he had a chance at winning a free election. Instead, seven years later, in 1963, President Diem was assassinated in a US-supported military coup, a few weeks before President Kennedy was also shot and killed. By that time, Senator Mansfield had become a skeptic of Diem's leadership and of US involvement in the war.

These papers hold Momma's words, her handwriting, her typing. Her presence still hovers over everything. When I read through these papers of hers, a cloud of sadness settles down over me like a fog, not easy to disperse.

• • •

From Momma's Personal file, three more slips of paper: three cartoons. No dates, everything brittle, ancient. First, a political cartoon from *The New Yorker*: a crowd of men dressed in Arab robes run through a keyhole archway, carrying sticks and placards. The caption reads, "The United States Embassy? Just follow us. We're on our way there right now."

Also from *The New Yorker*, a line drawing of a tribal elder with a book in his outstretched hand, lecturing a band of youths, everyone in grass skirts, bare chests: "Young men, you've now reached the age when it is essential that you know the rites and rituals, the customs and taboos of our island. Rather than go into them in detail, however, I'm simply going to present each of you with a copy of this excellent book by Margaret Mead."

Last, a *Peanuts* comic strip, no political or current events commentary. The joke concerns Snoopy preferring Beethoven over Brahms or Bartok. What are these cartoons doing in Momma's Personal file?

When I was in my twenties, first living away from home—college, later that apartment on Claremont Ave. in upper Manhattan, followed by other apartments in the city—I remember Dad sometimes mailed me cartoons clipped from magazines and newspapers that he found amusing and thought I might enjoy. He wrote brief notes, never lengthy letters, to accompany these occasional clippings. His laconic yet consistent correspondence helped tether me to a sense of home during that itinerant period in my life. These cartoons saved by Momma in her Personal file could be the remainder of what Dad mailed her when she was away from home, since she didn't save any letters or notes from him.

• • •

In our kitchen in Amherst, on the wall by the door that led to the basement, a colorful poster appeared one day when I was in junior high. The poster was the kind popular in student dorm rooms in the late 1970s and early '80s: a picture of a cute, furry brown animal with a yellow daisy hanging from its mouth.

Above, in large letters, the kitschy slogan: "I eat problems for breakfast." Probably with an exclamation point. I think the animal was a gopher, with giant front teeth.

Dad found the poster at the university bookstore, thought it was funny, said it cheered him up. He hadn't yet handed over his letters from Momma. I wasn't quite a teenager, not yet completely embarrassed by everything he did. Even if I apologized about the dumb poster to my friends who came over, privately I enjoyed the silly animal picture.

After Momma died, Dad tried to mother my sister and me. Typical of men of his generation, he was never skilled at expressing his feelings. When he hugged me, the experience was more like being grabbed by a wild animal than receiving affection. He cooked, even bragged about his cooking. His food was simple, Depression-era survival nutrition. Milk was mixed with powdered milk to make it go further. Vegetables were canned or frozen. Fresh fruit was a luxury he reprimanded us for requesting. A special dessert was a gallon of Breyers ice cream. He only bought margarine, never butter.

Every year when I was growing up, after Momma died, after the addition was finished, Dad rented out the extra bedroom upstairs, the one that had belonged to me and Sydney. Not the smaller upstairs bedroom that used to be his and Momma's, which remained empty except when Nana visited. Syd and I had our own separate bedrooms downstairs in the new addition.

Every year Dad found female students who rented the larger upstairs bedroom in exchange for cooking and cleaning. Every year he got into arguments with the renters. "The girls," he called them. The fights were about unclear expectations and responsibilities. What housekeeping tasks and how much. He thought he was offering a good deal. Busy students, "the girls" usually left before the school year ended. Unpaid mothering in exchange for room and board was too much work. For me, it was fresh heartbreak if I liked "the girls" that year. Sometimes it was a relief when I didn't. Since the cooking kept changing, I learned not to be a picky eater. Even after years of arguments, I never succeeded in getting Dad to see that "girls" was a demeaning term for our adult female renters.

Even after Dad's new addition was finished, we continued to congregate in the kitchen in the original part of our house, a simple room of imitation brick linoleum floors, fake wood Formica counters. The kitchen in the old part of the house was where Dad put up that poster. The kitchen was where we ate and argued together: Dad and Sydney and me. It was Dad who did most of the cooking. Who would help him clean up after dinner? Who should clean the house, after "the girls" inevitably left? It was the gopher eating daisies, eating problems for breakfast, who watched over us during those meals and arguments.

Dad found a way to survive the disaster of Momma's suicide. He returned to work on Monday morning, the next day; sent my sister and me immediately back to school; acted as if nothing happened, defying anyone in our small town to carry on their negative gossip about us. He added those rooms onto the house, extra rooms we didn't need, almost never going in the room where Momma died. He put up that comic poster with its simplistic philosophy. How to deal with life's problems, like a beloved wife who died by suicide: swallow everything.

What would Momma and her father, my two family suicides, have thought about a picture of a gopher professing to eat problems for breakfast? The two separate photos, Henry and Momma as a girl, both appear so serious, their images gazing down at me from over my desk. I never got to meet Henry, that grandfather. I don't know how he'd respond to a kitschy animal poster. Would Momma, the young woman who lived in Saigon with Macavity, her Siamese cat, have smiled at a fat gopher gulping down a flower? I'm hopeful she might have enjoyed it, even if she wouldn't want that poster decorating her kitchen wall. Or would she have been too sad to laugh at that picture; or been alternately down and then overly wound up?

If I had one hour with either of my parents, now that Dad is also dead, is there anything I'd still want to ask them? Maybe I'd just sit quietly beside them, even when no more questions came to me. My two watching photos can't grant me that hour, can't make my feelings of loss go away. But my two photo guides continue to sit with me while I sift through these papers.

CHAPTER 13

Dad

Summer 1999. Dad visited. We were in the kitchen of my house in Brooklyn. Dad lived in California by then. He'd supposedly retired, rented out the house in Amherst, hadn't yet sold it. He moved to Los Angeles, found a new college teaching job, and continued working. In a few years, my husband and I would adopt a baby. Dad would meet someone, get married again—finally. But those things hadn't happened yet, both of us forming new families for ourselves. Still, every summer when I lived in Brooklyn, almost until he died, Dad visited for a few days at least, sometimes a week.

In my sunlit kitchen, across from each other on stools at the narrow island counter, we sat and talked. I don't remember exactly how we got into that conversation. Still, we were going over everything one more time. He was telling me about the day Momma died, suddenly bringing out another detail he never mentioned before.

"We fought that day," he said. The fight was about chores, how Momma wanted to pay me and my sister for setting the table before dinner every night, when I was six and Sydney was eight.

There was a chart on the inside of the pantry cupboard in the kitchen in Amherst. I remembered a red-and-blue diagram on the back of the tall door, something Momma must have made. That cupboard held our canned food and boxes of breakfast cereal. Later, Dad's liquor bottles filled the top shelf, along with his case of beer that always took up the bottom of the cupboard.

If Sydney and I set the table correctly, placing each item—plate, napkin, fork, knife, spoon, glass—at the four seats so they matched the picture inside the cupboard, then we each got to keep the coin Momma left under the placemat at our seat. That must not have happened many times because I don't remember ever getting to keep the coin.

Dad told me about that part, sitting across from the counter in my kitchen in Brooklyn. He said "no" to the coins under the placemats for me and Sydney, disagreeing with Momma. A common topic for a family fight: money; chores. An arbitrary last straw in the bigger picture of Momma's life. Her father's suicide; Nana changing the story to accidental death for the obituary in the paper; the end of Reid's marriage to Jean; the end of Momma's friendship with Jean; Momma's suicide attempt in Ann Arbor when I was three. Possibly another earlier suicide attempt before she married Dad—that story about a failed relationship with a man.

That winter, 1968, the long New England winter, the war in Vietnam constantly in the news. During the start of the Tet Offensive, the last day of January, the late-night news showed footage of the American Embassy in Saigon under attack, dead American soldiers and Vietnamese enemy fighters shot, images of American soldiers trying to contain what looked like chaos, a losing battle. I don't know if Momma watched the news that night or read about it in the paper the next day, but she could have. Pictures and descriptions of violent killings in the place she'd worked a decade earlier.

On February 1, 1968, another violent photograph from the war appeared around the world in newspapers and on television.

The photo of the South Vietnamese chief of national police putting a gun to the head of a Viet Cong officer, executing him in the street. Another image of a violent death that could have resonated for my mother, who'd worked in that country and whose father also died with a bullet to his head, even though it was his own hand and not another's that pulled the trigger.

On February 25, 1968, Sunday afternoon, Momma and Dad got into an argument. Even if Dad sensed something was wrong, he didn't go check on her; they were in the middle of arguing. Possibly while I was climbing to the top of the playhouse down the street with Sydney. Then that was it, Momma was dead, and Dad was left with that to regret and feel guilty about for the rest of his life. With his ongoing cascade of stories, everything never quite fitting together into one tidy version of what happened that explained everything.

Is that how it happened, Momma? Or would you tell your story a different way? I have your picture as a girl, before you knew how your life was going to turn out. Sitting on top of my desk next to a picture of your father, by my lamp and my cup of tea, growing cold. When this picture of you was taken, I think your father was still alive.

CHAPTER 14

Far East Splendor

More from Momma's Personal file: a business card with a name, no date: "Ho Tan Thuan." Followed by the words: "Artiste. Peintre." An address in Phu My, a cruise ship port approximately eighty miles from Saigon, now renamed Ho Chi Minh City. On the back of the card, a handwritten message in French:

"Vous presents ses Voeux pour le Nouvel An." A formal way of saying, "Wishing you a Happy New Year."

• • •

Connected to this business card because it features the same man, a painter by the name Thuan Ho, is another short news article, more brittle yellow newspaper, no date:

Salon de Beaux Arts Prizewinner Has New Showing at Alliance Francaise Hall.

The piece announces an exhibit of paintings and drawings at the Alliance Francaise headquarters on Rue Gia Long in Saigon, by Thuan Ho. Below the article is a picture. A young man in a white shirt and dark tie poses in front of one of his paintings. His favorite painting, the caption claims: *A Part of the Garden in the Country*. A romantic title. Also ironic, given the war there. The man appears thin to the point of starvation.

I google him. Thuan Ho (1920–2008). A painter who lived in Vietnam. One article says he won first prize for watercolor at the Alliance Francaise in 1955, and for oil painting in 1959, along with other facts: where in Vietnam he was born, where he went to school, other awards he received. This article announcing his show could have been from 1956 or 1957, when Momma lived in Saigon. She could have met him, probably went to the exhibit featured in the article she saved in her Personal file. She saved his business card with the handwritten New Year's greeting scrawled on the back. This painter could have been a friend or acquaintance. Someone, like her, no longer alive.

• • •

More from the Personal file. A short note typed on a rectangle of yellowed paper.

> To: Miss Ann BAKER,
>
> G.S. Office.
>
> Dear Miss,
>
> I have the honor and am very glad to wish you:
>
> A <u>MERRY CHRISTMAS</u> and
>
> A <u>HAPPY NEW YEAR DAY of 1957</u>
>
> Your supply-man:
>
> <u>NGUYEN</u>.

A slip of paper with a typed Christmas greeting. Quirky punctuation likely typed by someone not familiar with English or typewriters. Important enough that Momma saved this message. G.S. stood for General Services, the embassy department where she first worked, she told Dad in that 1956 Christmas letter, his last letter from her.

Her supply-man—was that the same man Momma referred to with the denigrating term *boyesse*? Or did she have both a *boyesse* and a supply-man? And what exactly did her supply-man supply her with? Groceries? Alcohol? Momma makes several references to drinks and alcohol in her letters: brandy Alexanders, other cocktails. Once she also mentions an opium pipe. I don't think she acquired a drug habit in Vietnam though. Later she wrote to Nana about the psychiatric medications her psychiatrist prescribed.

• • •

Another Christmas card, the front torn off, no date. Not the matching back to the other card front with the circular blue design; this one is larger with thinner paper. A preprinted, standard message in ornate type:

With Best Wishes

For a Merry Christmas

And a Happy and Prosperous

New Year

The penned signature is illegible. The second name may be Thuan, like the painter. But the first name here looks more like Yung. Yung Thuan. Probably not the painter. Another friend or acquaintance of Momma's?

• • •

A square brown envelope labeled in pencil: "Dress Designs." Inside: folded slips of faded paper. Ads for six dresses, each clipped from a different newspaper or magazine.

One from *The Diplomat*, the only one with a date: April 1957. An elegant evening gown in black and white, a giant white bow decorating the impossibly tiny waist, further adorned with a pair of white roses. Modeled by a Caucasian woman with a blond updo, drop earrings, elbow-length white gloves, heels; the full, formal treatment. An outfit for the theater?

Another picture of an evening dress with a poufy skirt. Plus, one of an evening coat, an ad for Lord & Taylor, from *The New Yorker*, aptly or ironically titled "Far East Splendor."

The other three clippings that slide out of this brown envelope picture practical, shirt-style dresses for everyday wear or the office. I'm not sure why Momma saved these pictures of formal and informal dresses during that period of her life, except she apparently loved clothes.

• • •

Amherst, 1966 or 1967. I'm with Sydney in the living room in the old part of the house. The addition isn't built yet. This memory is from before Momma dies, I'm pretty sure, because it's a happy memory, not yet tinged with loss. It's Christmas, and there's a feeling of excitement, of energy-charged particles in the air like the strings of colored lights on the fat evergreen standing in the corner, illuminating the darkened room. Along with blinking, colored lights, the tree is decorated with our familiar ornaments, some of them handed down from Nana. Colored metal and glass balls. One pale pink and one pale blue fairy angel ball, both made of Styrofoam decorated with felt, lace, and sequins, possibly handmade by Momma; the pink is mine, the blue is Sydney's. No matter how much I search my mind, I can't find my mother in this memory. If she was still there, maybe I was taking her for granted like the air, not knowing she'd soon be gone.

Sydney and I are hiding; she says she has something to show me. We crouch on the floor while people come in and out of the room, distracted, not noticing us. Dad, Nana, possibly Momma too. Nana must have recently arrived. A pile of presents crinkling in crisp, bright wrapping paper and bows has appeared under the sparkly tree. Sydney motions for me to follow her as she crawls across the floor, carefully dragging a stack of wrapped packages from under the tree to our hiding place under a table in the corner. Quickly, she shows me how to poke a tiny hole in the paper near the corner of each present.

"No one will see," she tells me, "if you do it right." She peers into the hole. "This one is yours. That one's mine."

"How do you know? What is it?"

"Yours is always red. Blue for me." Nightgowns. A Christmas gift we both expected every year from Nana.

Sydney uses her technique to announce the contents of the last package in our stack: "A book." Acting like she's doing me a big favor. "I can't tell what book it is, but I bet it's for us," she whispers.

I don't tell her that I don't want to know. I want to be surprised. I'm caught up in her bossy big sister way of doing things.

There's a scratchy carpet under us, a black lacquer coffee table nearby. The table is something Momma brought back from Vietnam. To the left is the couch, another old thing Momma and Dad found at an antique market and had reupholstered. To the right is the brick fireplace. A fire might have been burning there in this memory. Winter, people bustling in and out nearby. Momma must have been there. This might have been our first Christmas in that house. I would have been four, maybe five, possibly soon before Momma died. Maybe she was sad, depressed that Christmas, and that's why I can't find her in that memory.

Christmases after that were always sad, lonely. Dad, Sydney, and I always got a tree, decorated it the same way: colored lights, familiar ornaments. But the main person was always missing. Sydney and I didn't sneak under the tree together to tear a hole in the wrapping paper of each present to find out what was inside again.

• • •

OK, my friendly companions, you old pictures: what do you have to say about that Christmas memory, and the Christmases that followed? There's nothing you can do to make everything better. In fact, you're both part of the problem, you two whom I picked to guide me through these documents and memories. Your deaths, one after another, decades apart, your unhappy, desperate acts created this history for me. But how can I blame you for problems with which you clearly received no help, for your miseries and inner demons? And I'm not a child anymore; somehow I did survive all that.

I wish I still had some of those family Christmas decorations though. Dad threw them out when he left California, where he lived for almost a decade with his second wife. Near the end of their lives, they shifted their home to an Oregon retirement community where they both later died. Before leaving LA, out went the boxes of Christmas decorations. Knowing Dad, probably to Goodwill or someplace useful. I forgot to tell him in time that I wanted to keep some of those decorations.

CHAPTER 15

Suburbia Lost

The next letter to Jean from the sheaf of letters she gave me. This one typed on a sheet of pale pink tissue paper. No year, but I looked up the day and month Momma typed at the top, confirming it must have been 1957.

> Saturday–June 15
>
> Dear Jean—
>
> Eh bien, your letter arrived like a gust of fresh air into this torpid clime. So many times I've attempted to write, but tropical inertia on top of my normal sluggishness has made me just about "useless."
>
> At this point one awaits the monsoon! Just like Louis Bromfield says. The water shortage is frightful. It's possible to salvage about a basin of water a day before the tap runs dry to drink, scrub teeth, face and feet in (all or either-or, according to personal rationing preference). Ants are another bone of contention. Actually they're psychic: the kitchen shelf can be completely bare, but by the time you get bread or sugar out of the refrigerator and over to the sink, there's a whole swarm waiting there expectantly. Lizards and man-eating mosquitos round out the picture

of the seamier side of life in Saigon. Believe me, another year of this will just about complete the transformation to gaunt, hollow-eyed harpie [sic].

I work in political section now—for LD, the Embassy's Chinese Affairs Officer. About two years ago, LD took a Kon-Tiki like voyage across the Pacific from Taiwan to San Francisco in, no less, a Chinese Junk. A remarkable character. One of my favorites here. He sold movies of the trip to the "I Search for Adventure Series" and was much written up in Life Magazine at the time so you may even have seen or heard something about it.

Alas! I missed out completely on the Quiet American[5] – that is, except for watching various scenes being shot. To no avail parading through the Majestic or lounging for hours in the Continental bar. The wife of one of the producers that I met said that the film would probably be released about next October. A friend with USIS (the government information service here) suggested going to Tay Ninh for the shooting at the Cao Dai temple there, as extras. The Agency had been approached by the movie company for assorted types—americains), but impossible to get away at the time. The whole project livened up things here immensely. Friend with movie camera took pictures of the company taking pictures of Audie, so have already seen a sneak preview of sorts. Of course, the old hands who were here at the time consider Greene a sot and an opium addict and the Quiet American, sheer blasphemy.

Viet Nam has been hitting the news a bit, you must admit, what with the Nixon visit, the Ban-Me-Thuot shooting, Cannon's murder, Diem's

US visit and so on, at least enough to be jerked out of the backwoods atrophy as far as the "public" is concerned. Have been sort of off and on dating UP correspondent BN… more so when the Chinese situation is "good news" such as during the riots at the Legation. Filet mignon in exchange for non-informative hedging. I should complain; it's a fine arrangement. Journalists who have been banished to the Orient for years are surely a strange breed but that's a subject in itself.

Reid leaves for Middlebury this month; Paris in September. You know you asked about the "vie" there. I'm afraid I can't help you on budget estimates. All that I know is that Paris is expensive; the cost of living is but definitely not one of the advantages. I can't dissuade you any more than that; I'd be there myself this instant if it weren't more expedient to wait. Despite the differential, free housing, and nothing to spend money on except PX goodies, I somehow haven't managed to save a "sou". In any case, I'll be going home through Europe next June! Sometime I may even be stationned [sic] there myself. After all, there are continents and continents left to see. Plan to retire sometime age 40 with colored slides. Chalk talks to Presbyterian women's clubs back in the States—what a future.

Lord there's so much more to tell you…do let me know what developments there are in yours and Cliff's exodus. Reminds me of a favorite gem from Tennessee Williams' "El Camino Real"[6] that "there is a time for departure even when there is no certain place to go." (To by no means advocate roaming for the pure sake of roaming.) I imagine

> you may feel somewhat akin to what is meant by it, as I have in the past.
>
> In most ways I wish that I'd just been able to stay back home but I'm sure as hell glad that I didn't. If that makes any sense. Suburbia lost.
>
> Ann

No more letters to Dad but there is so much packed into this letter to Jean, Momma's first from Vietnam to her friend. Near the letter's start, Momma drops a name that means nothing to me until I look it up. Louis Bromfield: a bestselling American novelist from the 1920s who reinvented himself as a conservationist-farmer, an early proponent of organic agriculture. I suspect my mother enjoyed peppering her letters to Jean with colorful, cultural details.

Filming of *The Quiet American* began in Saigon on January 28, 1957. I wish Momma had succeeded in being hired as an extra. Then I could spot her in the background of a scene, like a ghost passing through. I scribble a reminder to myself: watch *The Quiet American.* Even if Momma is not in the movie, the world the movie inhabits—late 1950s Saigon—promises to hold her spirit somewhere within its black-and-white frames. Before I find a way to stream the film though, I read that novel. I vaguely remember reading it in college or grad school but not liking it much. This time, I enjoy it, but I don't read for any deep understanding; I consume for pleasure.

Momma mentions being transferred to the embassy's political section. I can't tell if that was a promotion, but she seemed to enjoy her new position. That her new boss, L. D., was the Chinese affairs officer was perhaps why Momma was being dated by the UP correspondent whom she brags to Jean about.

The riots at the Legation were anti-American riots that took place nearby, in Taiwan on May 24, 1957, not long before this letter. A member of the US Military Assistance Advisory Group (MAAG) shot and killed a Chinese man whom he accused of threatening his wife. Protests erupted in Taiwan following the shooter's acquittal—news events that Momma was probably aware of since she was dating the UP journalist, B. N. I learn about those riots by digging online. Momma doesn't mention the marital status of B. N., but I doubt he was the married man I searched for in her letters. Momma doesn't sound enamored with him; instead, she categorizes B. N. as a member of the strange breed of journalists who've been banished for years to the Orient, using a term for Asia now considered outdated and derogatory.

In a single line, she turns into a mini encyclopedia of Asian affairs, alluding to a slew of other current political events of that time. July 6, 1956: Vice President Nixon visited South Vietnam. February 22, 1957: Ngo Dinh Diem, president of South Vietnam, survived a communist shooting assassination attempt in Ban Me Thuot. On the night of April 11, 1957: Lucien Cannon, the head of the Canadian delegation of the International Control Commission (ICC), was murdered in his sleep. May 8–12, 1957: Diem visited the US and was hailed as the "miracle man" of Asian politics. Perhaps these were all news items Momma discussed during her dates with B. N. I sense she enjoyed flexing her intellect for effect with Jean.

I don't know what Reid was doing in Middlebury, probably a stint of college teaching, but it seems Jean's first marriage was on the rocks. She hoped to depart soon to travel, possibly to Paris, where Momma divulges Reid was also headed. All this hints at an outcome that none of them yet knew: the future union of Jean and Reid, another marriage that wouldn't end well.

In closing, Momma quotes a line from *Camino Real*. For her, the words sum up a feeling she called, with a mix of horror and longing, "suburbia lost." It seems she both longed for home, as far as she could picture what was being prescribed and allotted for her as home: life as a wife and mother. Simultaneously, it seems she refused to accept being limited and defined by that domestic destiny. In the end, maybe she never felt at home or satisfied anywhere. If that state of unresolved inner conflict was close to what she experienced as a wife and mother, it goes a long way toward explaining her unhappiness and death by suicide. I don't take it personally if she felt unfulfilled by motherhood. Too much time has passed, and I've accumulated too many experiences beyond being her child. But I feel sad thinking about her and her life; and as always, I miss her.

Momma's next letter to Jean was handwritten on her US Embassy stationery. This is the point in the correspondence when it begins to become clear how much of the two friends' relationship revolved around a shared love of reading and books. It seems the friends later mailed books back and forth while Momma was still across the globe in Vietnam.

**THE FOREIGN SERVICE
OF THE
UNITED STATES OF AMERICA**

Mon Aug 12

Dear Jean—

Clonk—there goes J. Arthur Rank again—with News & Sidelights from South Viet Nam, land of nuoc mam, the better fermented fish oil. Sorry about Greene—didn't mean to be an iconoclast pushing over cherished idols and that sort of thing. Incidentally he always has been one of mine, but in this case it's strictly repetition of local gossip. The Living Room,[7] The Power & the Glory[8]—these you might say are his most "penetrating" studies of sin, conscience so on. After all, the way I see it, his favorite "recherche" is good vs. evil—why not give the chap credit for knowing what he's talking about. The thing that does annoy me, however, is his anti-Americanism in Quiet American (the major cause of the outburst being that he had run into some visa trouble from the States.) Solid criticism is one thing, sheer pettiness, another—but then I suppose genius has as much right to—if not perhaps moreso [sic]—this sort of whim.

What I do in the political section is straight secretarial—steno shorthand phone files, with minor variations—crossword puzzles when things are dull. In General Services, was more of Girl Friday jack-of-all trades—all sorts of ridiculous errands cropping up—everything from messenger & supervising coolies & filling fire extinguishers to tracking down my boss (who was always out "checking on wake housing," in other words stationed in one of the many local cafes). What I do now is somewhat more routine, but at least know a bit more about South Viet Nam; you can be just so much interested in people's housing & plumbing problems.

No LD is definitely not grey flannel variety. We have a plot whereby I get info of the take on travel & representation requests successfully ok'd by the Budget & Fiscal Office. He is utterly immersed in the Chinese community here and

> seems to thrive more than nicely on cabbage and fish-head soup. About the best thing I can say about him is that he's completely interested in & involved in what he's doing & so few people are. Have you found it so? Vital is more what I'd like to describe—not dedicated, which is usually synonomous [sic] with dull. Anyway just mention it in passing because it strikes a note with me that seems to have been missing for a while back—the old citadel days "keep the faith" type of outlook. Refreshing, to run into occasionally. And you, my friend, have by the way always been of that variety, of indefatiguable [sic] esprit. Lord, I must be feeling more jaded than usual this evening, to advocate getting out & polishing off old aspirations. Heavens, I don't mean to sound grim—not really—just momentarily striking out against a state of mind where "le temps s'enfuit"—time passes and every cocktail party is bigger & better.
>
> And how have you spent your summer vacation? Essay please—Ann

J. Arthur Rank: another name dropped by Momma that I need to look up. The "clonk" must refer to the striking of the gong that heralded the opening credits for hundreds of films produced by the J. Arthur Rank Studio from the 1930s to the 1960s, including *The Red Shoes*. Momma mentioned that movie over a year earlier in her letter to Jean from the *SS President Wilson*. The movie that lulled me to sleep before the end.

Momma's phrase "News & Sidelights from South Viet Nam" baffles me until I decide she must mean her own letters to Jean from Saigon, in her joking tone that's becoming familiar to me. "Sorry about Greene," she writes, not sounding sorry. Apparently, Jean idolized Greene or at least *The Quiet American* and objected to some of Momma's comments about him. By this point of rereading these letters, I've started reading the titles she mentions. *The Living Room*, *The Power and the Glory*: neither play does much for me. Interestingly, the first one is about the death by suicide of a young woman following her affair with an older, married man.

L. D.: Momma goes on for a while about her boss. Is he the married man who lied to her, promising he'd leave his wife? Momma sounds in awe of him, in a schoolgirl-crush sort of way, even comparing him to Jean.

The terms "old citadel days" and "'keep the faith' type of outlook" are opaque to me. Similarly, when Momma writes about the plot with L. D., "whereby I get info of the take on travel & representation requests successfully ok'd by the Budget & Fiscal Office," I'm mystified. Her words make me think of that article from her Personal file: "U.S. Theme is Yes, We Have No Cabanas." The one with the words "small dinners" underlined in blue pen.

I pull out Momma's Personal file again, sift through the ancient papers to find that slip of yellowed newspaper, rereading that quoted interchange, Subcommittee Chairman Rooney questioning Deputy Assistant Secretary Hall about the million-dollar budget of the time for food and cocktails:

> "Mr. Hall, do you find you get much work done at these soirees and parties?" Mr. Rooney asked.
>
> "Mr. Chairman, luncheons and small dinners, I would say, are one of the most effective places to conduct business," Mr. Hall said.

It sounds like dialogue from a play. Maybe not Graham Greene or Tennessee Williams, but a drama. But it's not; it was news. Whatever the relationship between these two pieces of paper—that letter to Jean and the Cabana article—the letter allows a glimpse into the type of relationship Momma had with her boss, one that possibly involved joking about bribes to get travel expenses approved. Despite a possibly comfortable work relationship, L. D. doesn't sound like the man with whom Momma became romantically involved. After this letter, she doesn't mention her boss again. And there in the middle of this letter is another of Momma's characteristic misspellings, "indefatigable," along with the showy French word, "esprit." Both meant to describe Jean. Someone with a tireless spirit. Someone who didn't give up. Unlike Momma, who, in some way, did give up.

This letter doesn't show it, but Momma and Jean's friendship will later split apart. Jean also gave up, in her own way. She turned against Momma, years after this. Although, in the very end, Jean never completely gave up on her friend, even after Momma died. Jean kept my mother's letters and eventually passed them on to me.

Here in this letter, Momma is still alive. She mentions feeling jaded by too many cocktail parties, even sounding a bit down. Homesick possibly. Missing Jean. Missing the element that was the opposite of travel and adventure, the element with which she always seemed to struggle: home.

And what about Momma's boss at the embassy, L. D.? He must have been older than her, probably married. Even though he only appeared briefly in her letters, was I right in guessing they were never romantically involved? What if I tried locating L. D., even contacted him? What would I learn? He'd be quite old, if I could even find him, if he was alive. Would he remember a young woman who worked in his department as a secretary that long ago, for only a year? If he did remember my mother, what would he be willing to say, to a stranger? I would have to tell him she was dead, even if I didn't mention her suicide.

If he was the one she had an affair with, which seems unlikely, I doubt he would tell me anything. He wouldn't reveal anything about something as illicit and private as an extramarital affair. He would know, or would figure out, who I was: the daughter of one of his former secretaries.

Finally, I succumb to my curiosity and search online for both Momma's former boss at the embassy and the journalist, B. N. They were both well-known enough to bring up multiple results, but it's too late to contact either one. Both men have already gotten too old and died.

• • •

To Jean, Momma wrote: "And how have you spent your summer vacation? Essay please—Ann."

I've been keeping those two pictures, my guides, in an envelope lately. To protect them. Maybe also to protect myself from their unwavering gaze. I have to dig around to find the envelope. It's buried under the piles of papers that keep building up around my small corner desk.

Grandfather Henry Baker Jr. Sunlight falling on half of your face. Hands clasped behind your back. Tie, vest, jacket unbuttoned. High forehead, receding hairline. You died at age forty-eight. I've already lived longer than you. Sadly, your suicide, even if it wasn't your fault and was the best you could come up with in the face of whatever problems you were carrying, also seems to have set in motion the subsequent suicide of your daughter. There she is beside you in her own separate picture. Looking thoughtful, her hair in those two giant bows on both sides of her head. Hands similarly clasped behind her back, standing on the grass in some yard that could be either Wheatland or one of those twin houses on Linden Street.

I watched the old black-and-white version of *The Quiet American* on my laptop. Of course you were not in it, Momma. Miss you guys. Essay please.

CHAPTER 16

Scars

Summer 2001. Dad's annual visit. Again, we sat in the kitchen in Brooklyn, across the counter from each other. Late at night this time, after my husband and the baby were asleep. My husband and I had adopted a baby, a girl. That summer she was already one year old. I felt exhausted most of the time. I was almost done asking Dad all my questions; I didn't have extra energy for that anymore. Still, Dad came to visit in the summer. Maybe only the summer before, he didn't come, when my husband and I were first home with the baby. Already, I could barely remember the blur of those first few days, weeks, months with the new baby.

This visit, talking in the kitchen late at night, I had some family pictures on the counter. I asked Dad something about one of the pictures of Momma.

"When was this one taken?"

He glanced at the photo, picked it up. "I forgot about this one." He made a face. "That was when she started dyeing her hair black." He brought out the words like he'd bitten into a dead insect.

The mother I remembered had black hair. I never heard anything before about her dyeing it. "Her hair wasn't black?"

"She started dyeing it," he repeated, his lips twisting downward, practically spitting out those unexpected, bitter words. "When she came home from the hospital…the mental hospital."

He said something else about a bottle of hair dye, black like shoe polish. How horrible she looked, her hair like a helmet. He said he hated it when her hair was black. She came home and changed her appearance overnight. He never understood why, he claimed. By then, I'd heard those words from him already: mental hospital. Dad looked angry, like he could have taken the picture and ripped it in half on the counter.

"But her hair wasn't really black?" I repeated. While I was trying to digest that new fact, I happened to ask something else, something like, "Was that after the first time she tried to kill herself? In Ann Arbor?"

Dad looked upset, hurt, as if we were going over an event from a week earlier. He shook his head slightly. He was almost seventy-five that summer. Still teaching full-time, business classes at a public college in a suburb of LA. Every summer, he drove across the country to New York and back, visiting family and friends along the way. That summer, he hadn't remarried yet.

"But you know that wasn't the first time," he said. He was leaning down, staring at the photo on the counter, Momma with her black hair. "The first time was in Vietnam. Over that stupid bastard. That man she—well, he left her, and then she cut herself. That's when she first tried to—"

He held both his hands palms up on the counter. "You know, she had slits on both her wrists. Here on the inside."

"No," I said quickly. "I don't remember any marks."

I remembered the story about a married man in Vietnam. The story I'd asked Jean about in that Soho loft a few years earlier when she handed over Momma's letters; the story Jean said she didn't know about. But I never heard that my mother tried to kill herself because of that affair, before she married Dad, or that she had scars on her wrists.

"It's not the kind of thing you notice about someone," Dad said. "Watchbands, jewelry, long sleeves. People keep their arms covered. You don't always notice things about people." He said he first noticed marks on her wrists only after they were married.

"You never noticed before that?"

"She always wore bracelets," he added. "To hide the marks."

Now I was the one to shake my head, disoriented. "How long were you married before you noticed the scars?"

He said he didn't remember. "A year at least." When he saw the scars, he asked her about them. She told him she cut her wrists, before they were married. Dad was almost bending over the counter, looking like he was in pain, like he was the one who'd been cut. Even all those years later.

She dyed her hair black when she came home from the hospital in Ann Arbor, when I was three. But that wasn't her first attempt, that time we almost never talked about. Behind that silence lay another silence. An earlier suicide attempt, something Dad never told me about before. When she cut her wrists. Because a man promised to marry her but then didn't. And she hid the scars from Dad by wearing bracelets until after they were married.

"She never told me about her father's suicide until after we were married," Dad added.

• • •

I remember once riding in the front seat of our car beside Momma. Fall, a crisp, sunny morning, probably not long before she died. Momma was driving Old Blue, our Chevy that always smelled of sour milk from the time she backed into a delivery truck in the supermarket parking lot, spilling a gallon of milk in the back seat.

On this morning, Momma was driving me to kindergarten. I rarely got to sit in the front seat beside her. While she drove, holding the steering wheel with her left hand, she didn't talk to me and I didn't look at her much, my familiar mother: short, dark hair; black sunglasses; red lipstick. I focused on the wrist of her hand that I held and the object on her wrist.

Once I asked, "What's this?" and she answered, "My wristwatch."

She didn't explain how to tell time with it or say I could have a watch like that, too, when I grew up. The watch on her right wrist was gold-colored with a stretchy band. I played with the segmented, metal band, stretching it and letting it snap back against her wrist.

"Stop, you'll break it," she reprimanded me, continuing to face forward as she drove. The skin on the underside of her wrist was soft and silky.

I think I would have noticed marks. I don't think she would have let me study her wrist or her watch for so long if she had something to hide. Even though she was curt and distracted, I wasn't afraid of her. I felt I could ask her if I saw something I was curious about or didn't understand. Is my memory reliable? Did I revise this scene in my mind, erasing any scar on that one wrist of hers that I touched, studied? Do I trust my memory? Not quite 100 percent, but I have to go with what I remember. My mother's right wrist: no scar.

• • •

At my desk in Brooklyn, a cold day, sunny at least, still not quite spring, remembering the visit from Dad that summer years ago, I try to think of something to say to my two pictures, propped at eye level on the shelf by my lamp.

Did you have scars on your wrists, Momma? Did you cut your wrists? I ask her silently. I speak to them both in my head: Did you know, Grandfather and Momma, that I've struggled with suicidal thoughts?

In a silent exhale, I confess to them: once I ate rhubarb leaves from our garden in Amherst when I wasn't quite twenty after I read somewhere that they were poisonous. Before I went to college, before graduate school and my calls to Reid. Also, once or twice I took too much aspirin, but only enough to make me sleepy, sometime in my thirties after I was married, during those miscarriage years. A few times I went running alone late at night in the park near our house in Brooklyn, even after the children came. At least once I walked along the beach at Coney Island and thought of jumping in the ocean, but the water was too cold. Sometimes I still think about walking into oncoming traffic, but I just think about it, I don't do it; it seems too messy and painful.

It's a lot to tell them at one time. But I feel like they can take it in and understand. They're quiet, listening. Not worrying about me. Not judging.

CHAPTER 17

Girls

Next from Momma's Personal file:

U.S. Offices Damaged, 18 Hurt in Saigon Blasts, Saigon, Oct. 22.

A bombing. I look up the event to confirm the year: 1957. Three bombs exploded in a single day. The news clipping from Momma's file is taped to a sheet of pink tissue paper. The same pink tissue paper that Momma used to type that letter to Jean in June, two letters ago.

Attaching the article to another sheet of paper allowed Momma to piece together the front and shorter last sections. But what was the significance of the news story to her? Why go to this length to save it? Was this pink tissue the only kind of paper she had? Did she want to make the article stand out somehow, to highlight it, and this was the only colorful paper she had? The faded type also makes the long article difficult to read. The tape is extremely yellow and cracked. The story details three bombings that happened on a single day in October 1957. The first two bombs went off outside hotels used to house American military. Thirteen American personnel were injured, plus five Vietnamese and Chinese civilians, including one child. Eight of the US military were seriously hurt and evacuated to Clark Field in the Philippines. The rest of the US injured were treated at a nearby dispensary. None of the five Chinese and Vietnamese civilians were seriously injured, although one man was knocked off his bicycle.

• • •

What do I feel as I handle these papers that Momma also touched, held? It's not as simple as: oh, I feel sad; I miss her. I feel a combination of curiosity and urgency, as if the piece of paper must contain some clues about who she was, what happened to her. As if I'm a detective on the trail of an important detail, and she must have been here, a person who passed by moments or hours ago. If I search carefully enough, I may catch a glimpse of her before she vanishes completely. But no, this piece of newsprint is seventy-five years old. I've looked at it many times throughout my life. I'm not going to learn anything new about my mother from these typed words.

I also feel the opposite of intense interest: it's hard to get myself to look at this paper or any of these papers of my mother's. I move lethargically. I drink several cups of black tea with milk before I can settle at my small desk and concentrate.

I also feel protective of the papers that I simultaneously wish to be done with. By this point, I've had the foresight to make copies of everything. All her letters. All the items from her Personal file. Even that short family history written by my deceased uncle. If I'm going to look multiple times at each aging document, I don't want to get oil from my hands on them. Or tea either. And often I write notes on my copies of the papers. So, most of the time, unless some detail makes me consult the original, I'm handling copies.

The originals of the papers reside in folders in my one filing cabinet in this compact Brooklyn apartment. Maybe I'm both protecting the papers and also protecting myself from them.

From the smells and memories these old documents contain. And yes, I'm both preserving these papers and simultaneously wanting to throw them out or possibly burn some of them. Wanting to be done with them and move on.

The connection between the papers from two different files, both using the same pink paper, interests me. For this, I bring out the especially fragile originals. That June letter to Jean from 1957, typed directly on pink tissue paper, the one where she uses the term "suburbia lost." And the newspaper article about the three bombs going off in October 1957. The third bomb exploded later the same day inside the USIS library after it was closed:

> Nobody was in the library and nobody was hurt although about 30 American Embassy employees, mostly single women, live in apartments above the library...Embassy girls, awakened from their siesta, poured into the street from their apartments over the library.

Was my mother one of those "girls," disturbed from an afternoon nap, rushing into the street when a bomb exploded? Was this why she saved the article? Did she clip the news story, or did someone see it in a paper back home and mail it to her, Nana, or Reid maybe? It doesn't seem Momma was still corresponding with Dad by this point.

Communists were blamed for the bombs, trying to embarrass the South Vietnamese government during the American-backed Colombo Plan Conference for Asian Economic Cooperation taking place that week in Saigon. After the bombs, the approximately two thousand Americans in Saigon were told to restrict their movements around the city to necessary business. The casualties caused that day were the first injuries to Americans in the Vietnam War. By the end of 1957, the number of terrorist attacks rose to thirty incidents, with seventy-five local officials assassinated or kidnapped in the last quarter of that year alone.

Is there nothing in the end that ties together these two different papers? The June 1957 letter to Jean when Momma worked in Saigon, typed on pale pink tissue paper; a letter Jean handed over to me together with that sheaf of my mother's letters, the one time I met Jean as an adult, in a Soho loft on a spring afternoon, 1998. And this article about three bombs exploding in Saigon on October 22, 1957, saved by Momma in the file she kept of her miscellaneous papers, mostly from Vietnam. The news article taped to the same pink tissue paper. No connection except that they were papers related to Momma. A letter she wrote to her friend about her life in Saigon, wanting to go home, yet simultaneously repelled by the idea of home. And a news story about three bombs exploding, the third one detonating in the USIS library, sending the "girls" who lived upstairs running into the street. Embassy employees, possibly including Momma. A matter of chance that no one was injured or even killed by that third bomb. Two pieces of paper. Both using the same pink tissue paper.

• • •

Daytime. In the kitchen in Amherst. Sitting on the floor; red-black-and-gray brick pattern linoleum. My legs crossed, crisp newspaper spread out beneath me. Momma hovering over me.

"Be still. Don't move," she has to tell me over and over as she snips my hair, bits of my dark, wet hair dropping, flicking, raining down on my lap, my shoulders, onto the crinkly newspaper, tickling, making my nose itchy, prickling the back of my neck.

"Sit still. Stop moving."

I'm alone with her. She snips with the cold, hard tips of the scissors in as straight a line as she can across my forehead, making me look nice, a girl, the little girl who she wanted me to be, who I wanted to be for her, to please her. Quiet, motionless.

"Close your eyes," she says. If I can do that, my haircut will turn out looking perfect. I say nothing, enjoying having her attention focused on me, her scissors pressing a line across my forehead.

We must have enacted that cost-saving home haircut ritual many times. I have one clear memory of Momma cutting my hair. I wasn't aware it was something she probably did to save money; probably many parents didn't pay for a child's haircut in the 1960s in the United States.

It's something I never attempted with my own children: daring to cut their hair myself. My children were strong, willful, active. Never motionless or docile. My mother was adventurous, creative, had an eye for style, a steady hand and the small household budget of the wife of a grad student, later college professor. She was thrifty, careful. Shaping my crooked bangs, my short bowl cut into something easy to care for. Similar to her own more stylish look; similar to how I still wear my hair—a lifetime later.

• • •

Cutting: she cut out the article, taped it to the sheet of delicate tissue paper. Kept it in her file marked Personal, with her name: Ann Baker. Who else would have taped that article to the pink tissue paper? The pink paper was hers, possibly from the embassy. She typed a letter to Jean on the same paper, four months earlier the same year.

Dad said that in her first suicide attempt, Momma cut her wrists. It's a slip of a story, almost nonexistent, like tissue paper. Pale pink paper like thinned blood. Something hard to put into words makes me connect this pink tissue paper and the story I know barely anything about, that Momma possibly first almost died by suicide around the time she returned from Vietnam because of a man who promised to marry her and then left her before she married Dad.

• • •

Now, what do you feel, guys, my two photo friends? Momma as the little girl, Ann. Grandfather Henry. My two suicides. Watching over me as I struggle to find—what? Answers to my questions that remain after your deaths? Why did you save those papers, Momma? Why the pink tissue paper? Why did you die the way you did? Such a complicated question to answer. And Grandfather, you started it, why? Momma, I think you liked pink. As a teenager, I started wearing those old clothes of yours that Dad saved, noting that you had multiple pieces of clothes that were pink. Was that all the pink paper meant to you, a color you liked?

CHAPTER 18

Goddamn Jewel

Dear Jean—

How did you know I've been on a Faulkner binge—and would appreciate The Town[9] more than anything. In the past few months have read The Unvanquished,[10] Intruder in the Dust,[11] Big Woods,[12] Sartoris[13] & a biography – The Life of…,[14] Knight's Gambit.[15] All except A Fable[16] which I couldn't get interested in and which sort of made me want to throw up even though I set about reading it with a real passion—ready to be convinced at least 10 times.

In fact, I've been reading a great deal—besides Saroyan (Rock Wagram,[17] have you?) Mann, Dostoyevsky (filling in the gaps, with these) Robert Penn Warren—one of the few latter day literary saints worth apostolizing. Besides these, Agatha Christie, pulp magazines, thank heaven an occasional New Yorker, travel folders, political & economic surveys (really desperate), books on chess & cryptography, the Herald Trib (funnies, Bankwald [sic]—how do you spell it—especially, whom I love madly), and from cover to cover the August Sears & Roebuck catalogue [sic]. That's actually the best edition—if you're interested in reading it that's the one I suggest. The Summer sales make it much more interesting.

Boredom is legion in Saigon at this point. The cocktail parties become more and more the same thing, actually until it's the same one big party—the warm-up, the party itself, the finishing up party & the tapering off party—all in time for a new or the next one which is actually only a continuation of the last. Some of my best friends are alcoholics. The sober ones discuss amoebic dysentery or the Colombo Plan Conference, so it's really preferable that way.

Are you still working in the hospital? When are you going—are you—to Europe? In other words where shall I get in touch with you in the future—keep me posted. Please.

Over Labor Day, was planning on going to Burma, but the flight (special) was cancelled. So went to Nhatrang which is more or less the Riviera of Viet Nam. Really wonderful beach-comber beaches. Miles & miles. Coral reeves [sic]—fantastic little fish. Took a junk out to one of the islands off the coast, skin-diving. Like 20-Thousand Leagues…" only "you are there." For lunch, sea urchins, raw, bread dipped in salt-water, and mangoes.

Jean, do write. I'll just be sitting here with the overhead ceiling fan going with my boyesse padding silently in and out with gin & tonics, meditating on the lizards chasing mosquitos on the ceiling.

> Sorry to cut it short, but we've just been descended on by MAAG with a not too uncommon routine "gripe" about life in Saigon. They arrive in Bermuda shorts, pith helmets & swizzle sticks or whatever you call those little pseudo-Gendarme clubs—Quelle Splendor—the age of Kipling is not o'er! Sometime I'll really try to write something sane—
>
> Ann

No date on that one. Momma mentions a holiday trip over Labor Day weekend, as well as the Columbo Plan Conference, which places that letter sometime after October 1957.

My mother certainly had sophisticated literary tastes. I've been trying to read along with her, but her reading takes off here; there's no way I can keep up. Seven books by Faulkner, including one she didn't like, plus some early biography about him. Add to that Saroyan, Mann, Dostoevsky, Robert Penn Warren, Agatha Christie, magazines, newspapers, clothing catalogs, books on chess and cryptography. To say I admire her voracious reading appetite, her intellect, is an understatement. I try the first title from her Faulkner binge; *The Town* is a challenging spot to launch into that author's works. In college, I read at least one of his novels; probably *As I Lay Dying*. I decide to begin there even though that's not on her list.

Never as literary as Momma, my father rarely read fiction, never poetry. He told me once it was Momma who got him to see plays when they were married. I think they loved watching movies together, too, on their small black-and-white TV set more often than in theaters. As a professor, Dad read and wrote articles and books related to his field: business; real estate. He regularly read the *Boston Globe*, the *Wall Street Journal*, *Newsweek*,

BusinessWeek. After Momma died, he continued their habit of bedtime reading to my sister and me. The *Little House* series, a yearly hardback sent to us by Nana at Christmas. *The Wind in the Willows*. And so on.

As a child, I was an avid reader. After Dad became a single parent, he shopped for the weekly groceries on Friday evenings, dragging Sydney and me along to the supermarket in Old Blue, buying McDonald's takeout for dinner, adding a stop at the discount bookstore in the same shopping plaza. I chose a weekly book from the shelves, cheap paperbacks that I consumed like fast food; titles Momma might have choked on. Book versions of the latest Disney movie junk: *The Love Bug*, *Million Dollar Duck*.

When I moved into my new bedroom in the addition, I inherited Sydney's rock-hard, wooden bed. The antique bed, updated from ropes to plywood supporting the double mattress, was so uncomfortable my sister was glad to get rid of it. This was the same bed where Dad, Sydney, and I huddled together in our new family configuration when Dad delivered the news about Momma's death. Despite the negative associations carried by that bed, I gladly became its new owner, a rare time I liked one of Momma and Dad's antique projects.

The space below the bed became my perfect reading spot. A sleeping bag, pillows, and a lamp transformed the private place into a cozy cave where I could curl up with a book for hours. I started doing my homework there too. Dad, Sydney, and Nana all knew where to find me, and they knew not to bother me when I was reading under my bed.

• • •

That last letter from Momma was from late fall 1957. She had a *boyesse* padding silently in and out with gin and tonics. Maybe she lived in an apartment over the USIS library. MAAG, or

Military Assistance Advisory Group, were the US military personnel sent to other countries to assist in training armed forces and facilitating military aid.

"Quelle Splendor": another of Momma's French expressions. Among numerous titles, Rudyard Kipling, the British author, in 1899 wrote a poem called "The White Man's Burden," urging the United States to take control of the Philippines. The ideology asserted the duty of white people to manage the affairs of non-white, native people, believed to be less developed. In Vietnam, the justification for taking over the country was a battle against communism, but the underlying racist ideology was the same.

Momma's holiday trip over Labor Day weekend to Nhatrang, the Riviera of Vietnam: coral reefs, skin-diving, meals of raw sea urchins, bread dipped in saltwater, mangoes. Sounds super sensual. Did she travel alone, with a group, or with someone in particular? The journalist? Her boss? Neither of those men have been mentioned again since her previous letters.

> Jean—Just got your letter and am amazed, envious with what you're doing it's so downright unique. I wrote you last week via Henderson, New York. Mr. H's address—rather hard keeping track of you, you know, like pulling the proverbial rabbit out of the hat to decide where to try to corner you. Will they forward?
>
> Anyway I loved the Faulkner—I've been reading & reading him & trying to forge an oasis of civil war grandeur here in the "jungle." Merely pioneer pretensions. Actually every morning I get up & first thing check to see if my eyeballs have turned yellow yet. Jaundice means two months at Clark Field in the Philippines, but no luck yet.

> In August I read in the Times Overseas Edition of a Britisher who organized a bus trip from Calcutta to London—through Kashmir, the Near East & Europe—three months—and who might be doing it again. I got his name from the Times & have just written him in the hope that I can go home this way & figuratively thumb my nose at Pan-American & the well-travelled route. Everyone here says it's mad but at least I'm mad about the idea tho hardly dare hope it will materialize. Much more to write & I will. I think I'm going back to Mike.
>
> Prosaic? Ann

The above is handwritten on a petite white notecard, thick paper, no date. Musty smell. For this, I consult my file of originals. Careful not to spill tea on these documents. I'm guessing at the order of some of these undated letters, trying to piece them together from Momma's references to what she was reading, among other clues.

Henderson, I learn, was a global investment management company with headquarters in London. A place Jean probably parked some money; meaning she had funds to park, a monetary ticket that possibly helped her escape from that first unhappy marriage, possibly also later from Reid when that marriage came apart. Seems Jean recently departed on the trip she'd been planning. Momma also mentions a trip she was dreaming about, researching. Her route home soon took her through parts of Asia and Europe. Whether or not that trip was organized by the British man she contacted from the paper, I don't know.

In the last line of her note, Momma abruptly refers to her old high school boyfriend, Mike, a name she hasn't mentioned since that first letter to Jean, her senior year of college. Yet here

Momma is claiming, whether joking or not, that she wants to "go back" to Mike.

For Momma, the idea of adventure and travel always seemed closely linked to her idea of home. Like reverse sides of a coin, escape and entrapment: she flips quickly from one to the other. Wanting to flout the traditional means of homeward travel, a flight on Pan Am, her plan involved an adventurous route through more than one distant region of the world. This time more clearly than before, she reveals what might have been for her the connecting link, the catalyst that was supposed to resolve these two conflicting ideas: travel and home. Adventure versus suburbia. Freedom versus marriage. The link, the means of getting from one to the other: a potential mate; a husband who's simultaneously a wild, "bad boy." For example, the type Momma seemed attracted to: Mike. The high school sweetheart who Momma hoped Jean would reverse her former, hungover impressions of: beachcomber Mike.

• • •

Today, bright, clear, still chilly, a hint of spring, I feel happy reading this card written years ago by Momma. Fortified with cups of tea, I even enjoy handling copies of her original papers. How can I think of discarding her original letters when I'm done? Will I ever be done?

> January 10 Friday
>
> Dear Jean—
>
> For the first time since I've been here I'm actually missing the States. Tonight anyway I have a most unholy yen to be sitting someplace cool—brisk shall we say—in slacks & turtleneck sweater, sneakers preferably. Anyway you know

the feeling don't you. Munching apples in front of a big fire. Thinking nice brisk uncluttered thoughts. What an improbable reverie, there's nothing in the atmosphere or life here to even "humor" it along—must have arisen like sheer spontaneous combustion.

The Tennessee Williams—poems especially. Since didn't dream he had anything like that & plays—thank you, thank you. "Zooey"[18] I liked. I've been meaning to write for a long time to say so. Nothing I'd read for a long time has hit me so—just right (the "Buddy"—"listen to this buddy..." particularly). It was a sort of a pleasant surprise since I'd developed an almost condesending [sic] (pseudo) attitude toward Salinger. Taking too much to heart what the "critics" said—you know, the "slick" categorizing patter as well as the way so many people just sort of brushed him aside in discussing "literature" as a mere child, & schizophrenic at that. I'd like to read "Carpenter Raise High the Roof."[19] What an orgy of reading lately—all in a matter of days your Williams, Schweitzer (who is sort of my Billie [sic] Graham—spiritual faith healer, though even Lambaréné after several scattered doses of "saving souls" enthusiasm is becoming a bit tiresome), Dostoyevsky—"The Idiot",[20] Joyce's "Dubliners",[21] Steinbeck, Bernanos' "Diary of a Country Priest",[22] Eliot's essays,[23] & Sean O'Casey.[24]

Went to Cambodia—Siem Reap—just before Christmas. Where "famous" Khmer Dynasty ruins are. Didn't expect to be particularly awed, but was. & enchanted. Walked & hiked &

climbed & saw so many temples & statues & bas-relief & Buddhas that was ready to light a few josh-sticks myself by the time were ready to leave. Even rode on an elephant. Of course, I have to qualify that by saying that it was a very domesticated elephant at the hotel. Had a big 10-foot platform-hitching post to climb up & get on (until then I always thought the elephant swung you up on its back with its trunk). With a sign in English & French: "Rides for Tourists 2:00–3:00). Anyway it didn't detract too much from the adventure. Ah, wilderness.

Jean, the bit about Dick is about the vilest thing I've heard in a long time. Incredible. What's the point—what sort of "terms" or concessions does he hope for—Cliff? Or support? Gad—at least one good thing I imagine is that it will leave a sordid enough impression to counteract any pangs (or regrets?). Who would have expected the "and now my proud beauty," twirling moustaches, approach from "good old Rich."

I kind of think I'll get married when I get back to the States. At least it's so far in the future that I can be reasonbly [sic] sure that I want to now. This one is a "country boy" from Alabama. He's back in the States now—left in November. Just about the time I was checking for him in the obituary columns he sent me a telegram (followed by another a few days later; otherwise I would have thought he was on a binge) asking me & more from shock than anything I wired back "when?" He's son of a Baptist preacher—the usual, from that purview, hell-raiser, flunked out of his last year at military school, then was

> in Korea, then State Department, doesn't read anything. Rather "likeable" though. The usual decadent Southern mule-driving background. Anyway, he evolved at a convenient time last summer and in conjunction with my interest in Faulkner. His Aunt Bill (whom he was named after, not William) was the town character—had the main street built around her Magnolia tree rather than cut it down.
>
> Will write soon again. When I feel less phlegmatic. Strange how days just seem to "happen" here, you sort of get into the habit of letting them be that way—even liking it. But will try to overcome this lax tendency.
>
> Ann

January 10, 1958: the date on that letter. One day before the anniversary of her father's suicide and my own birthday, still four years to go before I was born. Momma's homesick fantasy includes being somewhere with cool weather, dressed for fall, munching apples in front of a fire. All ingredients of a life that was, ironically, what she was living in Amherst ten years later when she felt so miserable that she died by suicide.

It sounds as if, not for the first time, Jean sent Momma books. Tennessee Williams, both poems and plays, plus a Salinger story from *The New Yorker*. Like her Faulkner binge from the previous letter, Momma mentions an orgy of reading. It's quite a reading list. A matter of days—really?

Lambaréné is a city in Gabon, Africa where, in 1913, Schweitzer and his wife established a hospital. In 1954, shortly before this letter, that work won Schweitzer, but notably not his wife, a Nobel prize. A quick look online tells me the hospital is still there.

Momma describes another recent trip, just before Christmas. This time to Cambodia: Siem Reap, the famous Khmer Dynasty ruins. An adventure she manages in a few lines to make exciting and humorous, with a description of her domesticated elephant ride. Again, she omits subjects from her sentences, avoiding saying who she traveled with.

She reveals a bit more about Jean's messy breakup. Dick, aka Rich, was Jean's ex. When she's barely done commiserating with her friend about her terrible divorce, Momma mentions planning to get married herself. For the first time, she tells Jean about Bill, sharing a lot of details. A country boy from Alabama, named after an eccentric aunt. He's not a reader, he is likable, and he does fit the "bill" for her "bad boy" type: binge-drinking, hell-raising military school dropout. He's even associated in her mind with her adored Faulkner. Also, it seems he already proposed, twice actually, via telegram. He already returned home to the States two months earlier, in November, and Momma claimed she was actually wondering if he was dead when she received his wired marriage proposal, so she must not have heard anything from him recently. She wasn't sure whether to take his proposal seriously at first since she wondered if he was sober when he sent it. It also sounds as if she still wasn't sure whether to take him seriously even after the second telegram since she mentions being shocked, and her response wasn't "yes"; it was "when?" It sounds like they had a sort of joking relationship; probably also a "drinking together" relationship.

I wonder if Bill was Momma's traveling companion, to Nhatrang over Labor Day, the trip mentioned in her previous letter. Maybe also to Cambodia before Christmas, if by "November when he left," she meant the very end of November. And if by "before Christmas" she meant way before Christmas. Sounds unlikely for the recent Cambodia trip. Was Bill the man she was upset enough about when he dumped her that she tried to kill herself? She doesn't sound that "in love" with Bill. It sounds more like she thought of marrying him as a joking adventure.

Before reading her next letter, I return to her description of that trip before Christmas 1957. Cambodia, Siem Reap, the famous Khmer Dynasty ruins. I do some poking around online. There are approximately fifty Buddhist and Hindu temples dating back to the twelfth century located in the city of Siem Reap. The online pictures of the ancient, crumbling temples look vaguely familiar, especially a few of the famous, perfect photo-op ones: bas-relief Buddha heads; Buddha faces; moss-covered, ornate stone structures encased with thick vines like snakes descending from the sky or rising from the earth. I think some of these stone structures may have been pictured in Momma's slides. The slides Dad and Momma later fought over, that time she tried to get him to help show them to me and Sydney, not long before she died.

She wrote to Dad about her slides previously in her last letter to him from Vietnam. Christmas 1956. The trip to Cambodia came a year later. These pictures couldn't have been part of the collection of two hundred slides she mailed home to Nana, urging Bob to visit her mother's house in Sharon to view them. But when she traveled to Cambodia a year later, she must have still been taking photographs, adding to her collection of slides. I'm certain that some of these iconic images of the temples at Siem Reap are ones I remember seeing somewhere before, maybe in that slideshow in Amherst that my parents fought about.

In closing, Momma mentions feeling phlegmatic, as in apathetic. This sounds like a downswing following her recent, possibly manic binge-reading phase. This reminds me of Momma's father, my grandfather Henry. The man in my picture, hands clasped behind his back, gazing straight into the camera, face half in shadow. My first family suicide: one of my two family suicides that I know about. One of my two picture guides. I also consider what I'm learning about Momma. She seemed to have these periods of concentrated intellectual activity, intense reading binges. This one in the winter, just before the anniversary of her father's suicide; close to the same time of year when she also later died by suicide. Maybe her suicide was connected to one of her intense manic phases. Overall, I keep in mind that the letter was written on the eve of the anniversary of her father's suicide, although she didn't tell Jean that.

THE FOREIGN SERVICE
OF THE
UNITED STATES OF AMERICA

Monday May 26

Dear Jean—

Do you have or have you listened ever to Sibelius' Symphony No. 1–E Minor (preferably Sir Thomas Beecham).[25] I don't know why I just must ask you this today since for at least the past year every time I've played it I've thought that I must mention it to you & see what you think of it. I don't mean this as a sort of "if not—run to your nearest record shop"—just that I've always thought of it as "hope music." Which I know sounds silly but it's the best way I can describe it, i.e. as being "excruciatingly right," somehow.

Another thing I've liked especially is Saroyan's "Human Comedy."[26] Or Steinbeck's "The Pastures of Heaven."[27] Or Gide's "New Fruits."[28]

I would have written much sooner except for 2-week vacation in Japan & the Philippines via MATS. Got back last week. Unfortunately work again. Except for today which is another holiday: Buddha's Birthday.

Of course, I'll be home for the wedding. Let me know the "for sure date." When you said that I probably had meaningful-to-me plans I'm sorry but I almost had mild hysterics.

The last thing I have are plans. If anything—I'd thought about wending my way home at a leisurely pace—perhaps getting a job on the way—at least staying till my money ran out. Because I don't expect to get back to Europe. But that's about as definite as I've gotten. I kid you not—if it weren't for your marrying Reid—there'd be no reason for me to—and I wouldn't plan to get home soon.

Why don't you get married at our house, Jean? That is, if you are married in Sharon. When I read your last letter that struck me as the thing to do—under the circumstances of Reid's now-wavering Catholicism & all that. I think that should be very nice and work out well. And compromise as much as you want to—without letting it really bother you—with mother's viewpoint that "getting" married is more important than "being" married.

And good luck!

Gad! You have more guts than I do. I've always thought eloping or living-in-sin was the easiest

> thing to do, or the only thing to do, faced with her ultimatums.
>
> Write please do. And forgive my scanty correspondence. It is not that I don't think of you almost always & wish you well.
>
> Ann

A letter from May 1958. Springtime. Sibelius. I find a version of his Symphony No. 1 on Spotify. "Hope music," Momma called it. I don't hear anything in this music that I would call hope; I find the symphony full of longing, sadness, disturbing even. And another word I'm searching for: remorseful? Maybe those are all ingredients of hope.

Momma lists more books she's reading. I'm no longer trying to keep up. I'm not planning to follow her full Faulkner protocol. I want to try some of her other recommended titles. I'm way behind though.

Another vacation trip, this time two weeks in Japan and the Philippines via MATS (Military Air Transport), a perk of the embassy job apparently. Again, no mention of who she was with, though I suspect she wasn't alone. What would she be more inclined to omit: tour group, friend, solo trip? Or another lover? Bill, the country boy from Alabama, had left for the States in November. Bob, Future Dad, had fallen out of the picture.

In the letter, suddenly Momma mentions Jean marrying Reid. It was only a matter of months since Momma's note to Jean via Henderson when she discussed Jean's departure on a trip. Then came that January letter's reference to Jean fighting with Dick. Now this quick turnaround: Jean jumping into a new marriage. To Reid no less, becoming Momma's sister-in-law, with Momma urging her to get married "at our house" in Sharon, meaning at

Nana's on Linden Street. The home where Reid and Momma grew up, the same house where their father shot himself.

At the end of the letter, Momma mentions Nana's ultimatums. The pressure to get married must have been constantly in the background for Momma, something handed down along the maternal line. From Nana's mother, Maude, who quashed Nana's dream of becoming a concert pianist. It sounds as if Nana let Momma know that nothing less than a husband would suffice.

I put Sibelius on, turn it up loud.

> Dear Jean—
>
> So you want to know what I think about your marrying Reid. Apparently, you do need the reassurance more than I need not to sound "corny." So voici.
>
> In the simplest terms possible, when mum wrote me that Reid was engaged to Melanie, I said quote but there's someone else I always hoped he'd marry unquote.
>
> It's certainly not the sort of thing I'd ever actively considered before much less verbalized. (I did mean you. I hope you realize that "sans la dire"). Fantastic and contrived as it may sound at this point!—that's particularly why I didn't mention it to Reid when he finally told me "the news." Because it might have sounded too much like pulling a Mme. Sosostris sleight of hand leaving a "why of course, I've known it all along" phoney [sic] effect.
>
> But I did say it. In one of Saigon's crustier little bars after work when I finally got around to reading my mail. I just skimmed through and came

out with a "My god, my brother's engaged." And everyone went right on talking except for a few "that's nice" 's. And I said "Yeah." And Bill said, "What's the matter, aren't you glad about it?" or something to that effect and I said "Yes, it's a fine idea, but…"

Anyway, that evening turned into a big party, and I gave the letter to Bill to keep for me and he eventually remembered to return it a few weeks later. And in due course, after absorbing the details (I had only skimmed for content before) I wrote mother that I thought it was a fine idea and Reid that it was a fine idea and Melanie that it was a fine idea.

In fact it <u>might</u> have been a fine idea. I mean it certainly wasn't any business of mine to be disappointed. If I've come to any conclusion in the past few years—one of them is that no one has any priority over anyone else's life—anyone that is, who <u>should</u> just have the role of disinterested spectator. And still with all this rationale I couldn't even try to be enthusiastic to myself: I mean, if I had any picture of Reid's future it was of some character with a prince [sic] nez pouring over books on the inquisition with his wife (a Melanie) out plowing through endless fields of wheat (Mother said she could drive a tractor) with callouses on her hands & wearing a babushka. I know I'm not being fair to anyone concerned, and I'm not trying to be flip, but that's about the only picture I could come up with. And tried to say "so what, what's wrong with that—so be it."

As for you & Reid—you can imagine what I may have thought, felt—when I did finally hear about it. Gad! It's sort of akin to someone saying "Yes, Virginia, there is a Santa Claus,"—or—"We have just recounted the election returns and…" If you know what I mean. To use an old biblical phrase "My cup runneth over."

I've tried to think in the past few weeks about what first gave me the idea about the two of you that I didn't know I had myself. As I said it's certainly nothing I "anticipated" or hoped for in the sense of "bringing about in any concrete way." Even if I'd known I'd thought it was a "good thing" I never could or would have said "Bake, don't you think Jean's a goddamn jewel" or vice versa.

So much more the miracle!

From a self-centered (that is my own) point of view, I suppose it's the satisfaction of having the two people perhaps that I think the most of—reach out and recognize each other. And however it is, or came about—I can hardly stand it, I'm so glad of it.

So much for my reaction. Advice—why the hell do you need it? You'll only do what you have to do.

In any case—I do have or would like to say much more—I will continue "opinions"—tomorrow—if not advice. At least I'll try—Ann

The last word from Momma in Vietnam was sometime around June 1958. A few catchy French expressions. A few more characteristic misspellings. One of the few times Momma refers to Nana as "mum." "Bake": the only time Momma uses this nickname for her brother. The one time she directly mentions writing letters to them, along with a letter to Melanie, tractor-driving, babushka-wearing fiancée with calloused hands, an unsuitable match for Reid.

Surprisingly, there's Bill again, too, the country boy who already returned to the States, making a cameo appearance in Momma's story of a night in a crusty Saigon bar, back in November when she perused the letter announcing Reid's match that wasn't meant to be, although she tried to go along with it.

She gives a peek into her Saigon life outside work, the ever-bigger parties that left her forgetting for weeks an important letter left in her boyfriend's pocket, making me recall her previous descriptions of feeling jaded, phlegmatic, fantasizing about crisp fall weather, a fireside, sneaker-wearing, apple-munching life that never made her happy in real-time.

Madame Sosostris is the clairvoyant character in Eliot's "Waste Land." A reference I imagine that Jean, unlike Dad, probably did get. There's sadness mixed surprisingly with satisfaction for me as I sift through these details, these letters of Momma's that she once touched, handled, annotated. Even with my unanswered questions, I feel like I'm finding her, finding out what she was like. Lively, binge-reading, cocktails-in-a-crusty-bar drinking, mood-swinging, witty, deceptive, sensual. Even though she remains irretrievable. My French-speaking, misspelling, cat-loving mother. Who was also a weak and selfish mother because she left. And there at last, I think with satisfaction, is one piece of that rage I'm recommended to feel by miscellaneous suicide experts, like a distilled tonic, something that should be capable of curing the worst results in me caused by my mother's death.

Any comment, my two friendly picture guides, resting again today on the top shelf of my desk? Any sadness? Feeling of loss? Regrets? Apologies perhaps? Especially after my previous confession to you about my own struggles with suicidal feelings, my legacy from both of your deaths? Any thoughts on how I can release myself from that inheritance?

CHAPTER 19

Darlings

June 20 -

Dear Jean—

Ind-ya at last. It's 109 degrees in the shade so am "siesta-ing" right now. Drove from Delhi this morning to Agra—about three hours—on a tour, along with three "elderly" gentlemen travelling around the world on a freighter. One turns out to be business manager of the Pittsburg Symphony. Saw some old fort this morning and the Taj Mahal. Have also met here an American couple on motor scooters. They left the States last October & worked their way on the boat. Both very dusty looking. They expect to get back home in about another year.

The hotels are all old-Dominion type. Big terraces & tea in your room before breakfast & again late in the afternoon; houseboys padding in & out carrying trays, water, laundry, polished shoes. I had a scintillating discussion with my "boy" last evening. "Mem," he says, "You ice-skate?"—whereupon he demonstrated a few long glides on the rattan rug. I said yes modestly. Then he quick fired several questions which I guess is pretty standard etiquette here like "You have brother?" "Oh, one brother." "You have sister?" "No sister!" And on & on ad infinitum through every conceivable family connection. Ending up with, "Mem, you married?" Then "No! Well good night, Miss!" And he tip-toed out apparently satisfied with this exchange of "niceties."

Just before I left Saigon I got a letter from Mum telling me about Reid's exam. Darn I'm sorry about that—especially if it delays your plans. "Courage" mon enfant. Do write me c/o American Express Paris & let me know what's up.

Ann

That 1958 letter from India is handwritten on stationery from the Lauries Hotel in Agra, a place that I discover is still in business. Pictures online of a grand establishment complete with lawns exude a fantasy feeling of the British still in occupancy, still in ascendency. Momma's letter again mentions a houseboy; I cringe at her 1950s racist tone; at the same time, I miss her.

The trip she describes is the only time she admits to being on a tour. If I'd been on that trip with her, sharing a hotel room in Delhi or Agra, say, I would've probably felt annoyed with her. Traveling with her is a daydream though; it would be another four years until I was born. Yet I still feel lonely thinking about her and long for her company.

After reading this letter, I return to a fantasy I've had in the past: wishing I could meet my mother somewhere to talk, just for a few hours. Maybe we could meet in the city, the way Momma described meeting her friend, in that letter from the ship at the start of her journey to Vietnam. Back when she thanked Jean, "For coffee for cigarettes for consolation."

I don't smoke, but I enjoy coffee, and I could certainly use some consolation from my mother. What would we talk about though? We'd be like strangers at first, or long-lost friends. There would be awkward pauses while we got reacquainted. Would she appear as the 1950s version of herself from her Jean letters? Chatty, entertaining, in one of her frequent, upbeat, manic moods? Would we talk about what we were both reading? Would she drop a few showy French expressions? Call me "Mon enfant"? Would she ask me anything about my life, my children? I imagine she'd want to know about the grandchildren she never met. I'm sad they never met her; that she never got to know them.

It's not the fact that she wasn't perfect, that she carried an attitude of racial superiority typical of the time and people she came from, that we might not have always gotten along if she were still alive, that keeps me from letting myself miss her even more than I do. She had flaws; I'm not perfect either, which seems too obvious to mention. The problem is that she's dead, that I can't have her again. I'm afraid of facing that bottomless well of missing her. The same fear that sent Dad back to work the morning after she died by suicide. What could Momma say or do to console me anyway? She's not here to say, "Sorry, I never should have left you."

• • •

Next, Momma's tissue paper stationery has a girlish, floral border. She was back home in Sharon. I sense her boredom although she doesn't discuss it directly; and Bill has resurfaced. It's the first of a few rare letters addressed to Jean and Reid together.

Wednesday

You Sweet Things—

I'm sending you this—my only—picture of Bill so you can see what he looks like—in spite of the fact it's so vile of me. This because I have decided currently to marry him. Currently—i.e., as soon as my government check arrives.

So please look & return as soon as possible. How I finally decided—I carded all the available data on a sort of mental IBM. And the answer to "Shall I go to Yakima?" was an emphatic—Hell Yes! A real reasoned response, No?

Will write tomorrow—want to get this in the mail right away.

Your letter was a real boon. Have laughed myself silly over it. I will try to comment intelligibly on Eliot sometime soon. Something to check on you may like:

John Ciardi's collection of poems—"As If."[29]

The Eliot I mentioned I liked (on the porch? The idea "when I am formulated…") is The Love Song of J. Alfred Prufrock.[30] Is that the one you mean?

I will write.

Much love to you
& Cliff of course—

Ann

To the two lovestruck newlyweds, Momma confesses her current infatuation, even entrusting them with her only picture of the object of her crush. No longer with her letter; Jean must have returned Bill's photo as Momma requested.

My mother's plans to marry Bill sound immature, but by this point she does seem smitten. Enthralled enough to have cut her wrists when he backed out? Now that she was home in the States. Asking again, more urgently: "When?" Maybe Bill claimed he was only joking when he proposed, admitted he was never sober.

I let myself picture those events. I can imagine that she, my mother before she was my mother, lost her head, so to speak. Lost her sense of herself, over a man. When she was pressured by her own mother to get married. It feels too painful to picture Momma actually cutting her wrists. At home on Linden Street in Sharon where she grew up, the same house where her father shot himself when she was ten. Alone, in a bathroom upstairs possibly. Or in her childhood bedroom. In 1958, that summer when she returned home from Vietnam, she turned twenty-six. Her birthday was July 22. Maybe she felt too old to still be unmarried. Late 1950s in the United States. If the plan she had to get married suddenly fell through. Only Bill wasn't the married man I thought I was looking for.

Momma mentions a few more books. Poems by Ciardi and Eliot, sounding as if she's referring to a recent conversation with Jean, possibly on the porch on Linden Street. A fragment of one line Momma particularly liked from Prufrock: "...when I am formulated..." It's been a long time since college when I read "The Waste Land." Without doing any background reading, I'm not sure what that line means. And I'll never know what that fragment meant to either Momma or Jean, beyond that they loved discussing what they were reading.

"I'm not liking the Faulkner," I'd confess to Momma, if we met for coffee, if I ever got to fulfill that fantasy. Maybe she'd read some parts aloud to me, explain what she loves about his books, point me to her favorite Faulkner title, make it come to life.

Maybe there would be time to tell her about myself. What makes me happy. Those grandchildren she doesn't know. My husband, kind, patient, quiet, overweight, high blood pressure, hissing CPAP machine at night. How I worry he'll die suddenly because she died suddenly. That's what her death left me with: not a fear of suicide in particular. I must have been too young to truly understand that part of her death. What I inherited was fear of sudden death, sudden disasters. Could I also work in a way to mention that I also don't feel drawn to T. S. Eliot? That my daughter shares Momma's love of stylish clothes?

> Sunday
>
> Dear Jean—
>
> The day after I got your letter asking about T. S. Eliot I was sorting out some old school material & found these notes.
>
> A lazy way out n'est-ce pas? But actually you probably may decipher more from them than I could try to outline in a few succinct phrases.
>
> Let me know if this does any good a-tall! Or what in particular you would like to clarify?
>
> Quartets I know nothing about except from my own reading & rereading. It seems to me though that everything hinges on his TIME concept as in "Burnt Norton" (V).[31]

> Frankly (as a mere literary peasant) I think he's the greatest.
>
> Let me know if this helps. Send back anytime.
>
> And what you think.
>
> Ann
>
> By the way, what are your China and/or silver patterns?
>
> Joyce wanted to know. For wedding gift.

More about Momma's admiration of Eliot. Plus more French. Reid and Jean were about to get married. The woman Momma mentioned who wanted to get them a wedding gift could have been a neighbor. There's no date on that letter; it was likely the tail end of summer. I haven't had time to read or reread any Eliot, am not familiar with his TIME concept. I'd rather read the other poet she mentioned one letter back, Ciardi, whose work I don't know.

• • •

Here at my small desk in Brooklyn, it's a cold spring day. Lately, my two picture guides have been in hiding, in a nearby envelope, not coming out much. Instead, I've been fantasizing about Momma, my ideas of meeting her in different places, such as in a café for coffee. What would that be like? Like anyone, would she say and do annoying things sometimes, like any mother?

The following letter has two parts spaced over two weeks. The farm in Charlestown where Momma camped with Nana was Wheatland, subject of Reid's reminiscing. Dad was Dad Baker, Momma and Reid's paternal grandfather, father of Henry who died by suicide.

In Reid's family history, he mentioned that Dad Baker opened Wheatland for Reid and Jean's honeymoon. At the time of Momma's next letters, Jean and Reid had recently gotten married and moved to Milwaukee, where Reid must have taken a job. I love that Momma calls Milwaukee "the Beer Kingdom." Momma must have mistaken the date of the start of her letter though; in 1958, Sept. 8 was a Monday, not a Tuesday.

Tuesday, Sept 8*

Darlings—

Letters and packages have been pouring in for you both. Mother has organized a local forwarding agency so I trust you get all these things.

I hope you are well-settled in the big city—the Beer Kingdom—by now, and happily so. Needless to say it has been very quiet here. In fact there is tranquillity [sic] all over the place—the peace is downright paralyzing. Except for those few evenings when Trudy plays that thing she plays. I've found myself almost looking forward to these delightfully discordant interludes. Horrors!!

Sept 16

Forgive the week's delay or interim. Mother and I have been to Charlestown. We camped at the Farm. Just loafed around in slacks & sneakers (Mum bought some Keds for the occasion) looking at the cows & cobwebs and ecking [sic] out an existence on canned goods. Thank God for Chef Boy-ar-dee [sic]. Dad disapproved highly of

> this arrangement at first but was won over eventually. However, he stayed at the hotel in town & we drove in to get him every day. This was in every way a superb visit. And of course, Dad talked a lot about the two of you. It's understatement to say he was pleased.
>
> So arrived home to find—huzzah!—your letter.
>
> What a prosaic time we have had in comparison. Certainly nothing has been happening. The status quo is very. I've been playing bridge & golf with Bob. Alas—I like it. Have broken my engagement (if you call it so) with Bill twice since you left. Realize this is a rather shoddy situation to be in but keep feeling that if I create enough pressure I may make a decision—the right one!
>
> Will really appreciate hearing from you just any old time.
>
> Meanwhile—
>
> You are missed.
>
> Love, etc.
>
> Ann

Momma refers to Nana as "Mum" again, as she did in a few previous Jean letters, including the one about being in the crusty Saigon bar with Bill. Interestingly, mum also means mute, as in the mother who didn't talk about her husband's suicide, even to her children. Momma's nickname for her mother. Momma, who was so careful about choosing her own name as a mother.

All of a sudden, my future father is back in the picture. After this, things advanced rapidly on the relationship front for Momma. It's Bill's turn to exit, while Future Dad reclaims the stage, playing bridge and golf with Momma. The Momma I knew never played golf, although that was the one sport my father played for the rest of his life.

Momma writes that she was the one who broke the engagement with Bill—twice. Even calling into question whether it was a real engagement. Again, the pieces don't fit together in the vague story about her first suicide attempt, the time she cut her wrists over some guy, a married man who dumped her. Momma claims she was the one putting pressure on herself, trying to make up her mind. Which decision was she trying to make though? A choice between Bill or Bob? But she acknowledges that Bill didn't seem serious about his marriage proposal. Or was the decision about whether to marry my future father at all? That's the answer that seems to fit better. But even if her "Alas" sounds half-hearted, she also seemed to enjoy herself with Bob who became Dad.

She claims that she found the peace of life at home "paralyzing" though, even gladly welcomed the interruption of a neighbor's discordant instrument playing, alluding again to her horror at suburban life. I'm not certain what precisely horrified her about suburbia. Maybe it reminded her of her unhappy childhood. She was back in the house where her father shot himself in the head, after all. That kind of quiet, small-town life: each family living in a separate house; father at work; mother at home taking care of the children. All that may have presented a familiar picture for Momma, full of unhappy associations. Maybe her feeling of paralysis also arose from the fact that as a young woman at that time and place in history, she had few options outside of marriage and motherhood.

February 12

Dear Reid & Jean—

How this thing came about—Actually Bob and I have been planning to be married since just shortly after you left at Christmas. However he hasn't known until just recently just how when and where he'd be transferred. (Columbus—God!) This is, by the way, a rather nice set-up and I might add—a "promotion." He's to be Asst Manager for a new warehousing operation just being organized for the Middle-Western States. Even if I've never been able to go into ecstasies about "business per se" I am pleased about this—if only I suppose to say Fie on Peggy. So there!

Anyway we picked Easter—about two weeks ago—as a tentative time to coincide with your vacation. And been circling around the idea and all the Details involved ever since. As I mention—La Grande impasse—"Do you really want to do this thing?" Bob kept urging me to at least find out about the church. Next week—manana. So finally (the day I called you) decided can't put it off any longer. Walked downtown. Thought will just stop by church and make an appointment for some time soon. Thought surely nobody will be there. Started to walk past church (on way back up hill perhaps?) turned in instead. Dr. Wells standing at side-door talking to Mrs. Wells, almost just waved & tiptoed on by. However, Dr. Wells just standing there with door open for me. All of which is the real way we happen to be having a wedding.

> Jean—I have no idea as yet about clothes…perhaps I can find something for you at the same time I get my own dress (No—I promise you it won't be a Purina feed bag). It goes without saying that I'll take care of the expense.
>
> I really can't think of anything else at the moment that you should have to do. Certainly appreciate your support—may need it more then—for <u>both</u> Bob and me. Until we really stared this thing in the face he'd been going around like a major general—you know—very convincing: "all you need is a plan of action" type of approach. Organize! Now the past few days he has been decidedly wan—green, in fact. I try not to think of this as being <u>not</u> too flattering to me. He says: "It's not that I don't want to. I really think we should. It's just that it's a big step—you know, like going away to school or joining the army." Great, huh!
>
> Well, I won't weigh you down any longer with these personal matrimonial observances.
>
> Except one more thing. I do want Reid to "give me away." (That's a jarring phrase isn't it?) I don't know what all this entails yet—just that I'd sort of like him to. I mean I don't think I'd walk in with him or anything in an informal ceremony. (Mother says I would). Though I can't exactly picture him just popping out from under a pew and saying "I do." We'll see.

Atypically, Momma didn't sign that last letter. Perhaps she was hyper-distracted with wedding plans. Peggy may have been a smug, well-married former schoolmate. Unmentioned, lingering in the background, necessitating Reid's role of giving away the bride, was their father, Henry, who died by suicide sixteen years earlier. His memory must have hung like a somber cloud over Momma's wedding preparations. In her letter, she sounds like she's throwing herself into the wedding planning though. Trying hard to be happy.

About mid-page in the next letter, there's a sketch, about an inch high, of the dress Momma got for Jean as the matron of honor. The background action of the escalating Vietnam War had receded, replaced for a time by dull Sharon, along with the required domesticity which became inextricably entwined with my mother's denouement.

Momma sounds hesitant about getting married, with her story about barely managing to drag herself in the door of the church for the planning appointment with the pastor. For Jean, she turns this into a funny story as is typical. She also paints Future Dad's pre-wedding jitters in a comic light. I think she and my dad may well have been a good match. Momma sounds in her coming letters as if she's trying to make a go of married life and all that went with it: children, taking care of a home.

Her first choice of what to do after college was an adventure that combined foreign travel and work. I imagine she would have been happier if her life could have continued to include those ingredients. But I don't think the possibility existed yet, of Momma working, full- or part-time. Not in Amherst in 1968, not for a white woman, married to a college professor, with two young children. Also, at that time and place in history, my father might have felt like a failure if his wife worked at a paid job. Momma could have found a volunteer position. To add to the conundrum though, Dad's salary probably wasn't enough to cover childcare, if Momma had worked unpaid outside our home. So, she was stuck at home. I don't know when exactly the small-town life they were living evolved; change was coming for the whole country, with the women's movement, the civil rights movement, and the expansion of the middle class. But Momma didn't hang on long enough to experience those changes.

Wednesday

Jean—

The wedding is marching. Invitations—Dresses—Ordered. Inn reserved for reception.

Have been reading Amy Vanderbilt[32]—long portions aloud—in sheer hysteria. "How do you deal skillfully with an alcoholic wedding guest?" "Double ceremony for twins: Can I have both my husband and ex-husband give them away?" And the terse, anguished: "I am to be a bridesmaid. Do I buy my own flowers? And how do I get to the church?" This last should be signed "Bewildered." I can just see the poor girl standing on a street corner saying—which way to the First Baptist—clutching a bouquet of forget-me-nots.

Bob leaves for Columbus this Sunday, though he plans to come back every weekend until March 28. He's been going around saying things like—Well, if you don't want me now I think I'll just go down & give myself to Christ's Good Will Mission. Really he's very nice. I like him a lot!

Am writing mainly about your dress. Found it the same time I got mine at Bonwits in Cleveland. It's very simple design (sorry, no Empire) in iridescent silk—sort of an antique gold shade. As I said—plain top—and slightly ballooned skirt—size 10. Narrower at the bottom. Not a thin silk.

Gad—I hope you will like it all right. The color I especially like—should be tremendous on you.

Mainly I chose it because I ended up with a more weddingish dress than I'd had in mind originally. (Just didn't see anything in cocktail or semi-dressy variety that "had it.") This is a short, ivory quasi demure type—still o.k. for an informal ceremony according to the experts.

I'll have them make up some kind of hat or small headband for you. What sort of thing would you like? Also any sort of short white gloves and black (or white) shoes will do most nicely—just whatever you have.

Before the announcement appeared in the paper, we decided we might as well stealthily case the jewelry stores for silver & wedding rings. "When are you going to be married?"—"Oh, we're just looking." The epitomy [sic] was in Wenglers. When we were trying to decide on a silver pattern this character asked—"Well, are you planning a colonial home?" Almost a full minute's blank silence before we burst out laughing. Really—what should you say—"We're not exactly planning a home…" You could see this guy peering down his nose, thinking—peasants. Afterwards thought of all the perfect answers—what one might say in this predicament. Like: Early American—very early—a lean-to in fact.

Or

Chinese décor—late Sung Dynasty with smudge pots & oriental hangings.

Alas, too late.

Alas it is late. Let me hear from you soon.

Ann

Momma's attention to the details of the clothes for her wedding reminds me of the envelope of ads for dresses she saved in her Personal file, as well as the box of her clothes Dad rescued from our basement flood in Amherst after she was dead. Momma's love of stylish clothes reminds me of my daughter, of her and Momma's shared love of fashion. I wish she and Momma had known each other; that both my children had known my mother. Both of my children have a close relationship with my husband's mother. Grandma Bess is in her nineties and lives in a retirement community in Florida, where we visit her once or twice a year.

• • •

In my fantasy, I wonder, if I ever got to meet Momma somewhere for coffee, would I yell at her for what she did? The way my daughter sometimes surprises me with her sharp anger. For all the things wrong in the world. My daughter's annoyance comes out as: "Why did you make the dinner I don't like!" When she comes home from college to visit, suddenly like a child again, disoriented by returning to the parental nest.

When do I get to shout something equally strange and ridiculous at Momma, ridiculous because it's too little and too late for what happened: "Why did you have to die the way you did! Why did you ruin my childhood, ruin everything like that!" No, I never got to have that childish tantrum.

May 7

Jean—(et al)

All you did to make the wedding a perfect time—can never thank you enough. Pictures have arrived—"It must have been a good wake!" Bob and John look like solicitous pall bearers in one especially—with candelabra in background adding to the funeral effect.

Enclosing Ustinov story from Atlantic[33] you may enjoy.

Bob and I are going to Sharon tomorrow. Driving on to West Va. with Mother to see Dad. This we just decided to do yesterday—overnight as it were! Since Bob has an extra day off.

Gorgeous chaos getting "settled" (is that le mot?) here. I've planted a row of lettuce and we've acquired a Yugoslavian wicker wastebasket (88 cents each at the local A&P). Also a piece of 5 ft. long "driftwood"—a really agonized looking log found washed ashore along the Olentangy River. Unfortunately we've just begun to suspect it has termites.

Write!

Ann

The wedding came off without a hitch, surprisingly. Though, in the one picture of that day I saved, Momma appears wilted. Her white dress looks slightly homely, with an oversized, ruffly neckline to offset her 1950s tiny waist. Dad grins, looking boyishly exuberant. Next to Momma stands John, Dad's best man and his best friend from college and for a lifetime afterward, looking bashful and wan. Between Momma and Dad is their ringbearer, Kissy, a cute blond boy of six or seven, mentioned in Momma's first letter to Jean from college in 1954, just four years earlier.

On Dad's other side is Jean in the dress Momma put so much effort into selecting: a figure-flattering gold sheath, more perfect than Momma's wedding-day centerpiece. Jean smiles coquettishly, looking more content than my mother on that important day. Barely recognizable as the sharp-edged, salt-and-pepper-haired woman who handed over these letters to me in that Soho loft, forty years later.

Nana might have been the one to snap the photo since she's not in the picture, except her bad eyes make me skeptical that she was the photographer; although she was probably responsible for many of the details evident in the photo record of that day. The elaborate floral table arrangement, along with the selection, if not the actual preparation, of the spread of food on the table in front of the wedding party. Nana, if she had appeared in the photo of Momma's wedding reception, would certainly have borne a satisfied smile, at last witnessing her daughter's marriage.

"It must have been a good wake!" Momma wrote to Jean about the wedding photo. Why the funereal mood? Was it that Momma's heart wasn't in it? Or was it the absence of her father still hanging over her, the wedding, that house, an unhappy ghost refusing to let go?

Many of the other book titles mentioned by Momma, I haven't yet read, certainly not all that Faulkner, not even the Ciardi. I enjoyed the two Salinger stories I found in *The New Yorker* online.

In another online archive, this one for *The Atlantic*, I managed to locate the Ustinov story Momma mentioned. She didn't give the story's title, and there was a series of pieces by that author in that magazine near the date of her letter, May 1959. But when I read the one called, "The Aftertaste," I decide this must be what Momma sent Jean. The story's May publication date matches the letter. The real giveaway is that the story deals, at least in part, with suicide. I find the Ustinov piece annoyingly glib, so it surprises me that Momma liked it enough to mail to her friend. Also surprising is that even at that date, years before her actual death, Momma already had suicide so much on her mind. Why should that surprise me though, given how her father died? He must have been on her mind around the time of her wedding. Wasn't there also that story circling from that time about her suicide attempt, when she cut her wrists?

Glancing back over this last group of six letters written by Momma to Jean between June 1958 and May 1959, it's easy to see that a lot happened to my mother during those years. She returned from being away for two years in Saigon, where she'd worked as a secretary in the US Embassy. Once home, she broke off an engagement with one man, or he broke it off, and then she married someone else. Hiding between those six letters, was there a suicide attempt by Momma when she cut her wrists? I didn't find any shadow of that story in these letters to Jean.

• • •

I return to my picture guides, removing them from their plain white envelope, setting them again on the shelf over my desk. Momma, Grandfather Henry. I know you were a young child in that picture, Momma. I know you never even knew me, Grandfather.

Whatever happened to Bill, Momma? Were you happy being married to Dad, at least at first? Cultivating lettuce, finding Yugoslavian wicker baskets at the A&P, collecting termite- infested driftwood from the banks of the Olentangy River in Columbus where I was later born. Now that you mention it, I do remember those wicker wastebaskets that populated our house in Amherst for years.

Did you really cut your wrists? After your engagement to Bill was broken, whoever broke it? It is you in these letters who sounds hesitant, conflicted. Writing about putting pressure on yourself to make a decision. Saying "manana" and delaying stopping at the church to make the arrangements with the pastor. Even though you told Jean a funny story about Bob looking green with unease, marching around like a major general, barking directions about the need to make a plan of action. Was it you who felt conflicted about getting married?

CHAPTER 20

Wheatland

March 2022. The trip to Wheatland was not what I planned. My daughter was still away at college. I had a trip organized with my husband and son, nothing to do with Wheatland. We were heading to a beach, after two days of driving in a southerly direction. Our son recently got his learner's permit. He loves to drive; the trip included as much driving practice for him as possible. Then an unexpected late blizzard delayed our departure at the start of the school break. Everything was reconsidered in light of the storm and the evolving road conditions. We even considered canceling everything and staying home. Weather bulletins advised: keep off the roads.

At last, midday, a half-day late, feeling alternately brave and foolhardy, we set out. The roads were deserted, and windblown snow and sleet were slung heavily across the windshield. Our plans continued to shift. Our son couldn't get behind the wheel yet; road conditions were terrible. We'd never make it to our first planned overnight stop by dark, a hotel near one of my husband's sisters south of DC; we canceled that reservation. Maybe we'd visit that family on the drive home. On impulse, just north of DC, I said aloud a thought that popped into my head.

"Do you think we could drive to West Virginia tonight instead?"

I had Wheatland on my mind. My husband knew about my current writing project. He knew about my family suicides. I'd been talking to him about my mother, my grandfather, Wheatland too.

Once, years ago, before we had children, my husband and I tried finding my family homestead. That was in a previous lifetime on some summer vacation in that area, not far from where he grew up, the area in which his parents lived at the time before they moved to Florida. We both barely remembered that trip, when we'd only made it as far as the end of a driveway that we thought was the Wheatland property.

"We could stay somewhere near Wheatland tonight," I suggested in the front seat beside my husband. At that late hour, under normal driving conditions, we were within an hour's drive of Wheatland, I realized, looking at the map on my phone. But we had snow, ice, and heavy winds. Low visibility. Could we even make it that far tonight?

At home, in my bin of photographs that I saved the last time we moved, I had one snapshot of Wheatland, a small black-and-white. Even from my single picture, it was clear that Wheatland was a big, old house, painted white, two stories high plus an attic, four tall white columns in front.

One recent afternoon, working at my crowded desk, I searched for Wheatland online, actually found pictures of the place. A Library of Congress Historic American Buildings Survey from 1933 showed four photographs. Four different views of Wheatland. I recognized the house pictured online. It was the same as the single remaining snapshot of Wheatland that I'd saved. The address was listed as Berryville Pike, Jefferson County, West Virginia. Maybe that's what got me thinking about looking for the site of that house again sometime. The old family homestead that Reid had talked and written so much about.

My husband agreed to veer off our route, to add this side adventure. For days before we left, I was rereading Reid's family history. Trying to absorb every bit of information and effort he invested in recording his stories and memories. Wheatland, Reid's beloved summer haunt, refuge after his father's death—my grandfather's suicide almost eighty years earlier, in 1943. I'd even brought a copy of Reid's family history on the trip, for bedtime reading. I'd started imagining a future visit to Wheatland, or at least a visit to the site where it used to exist. But until we turned west on the snowy, icy roads near DC, I didn't realize that I would make that trip now. Even as we changed our plans, headed toward West Virginia, I wondered if I was really ready to go.

Reid's history revolved around Wheatland, West Virginia. My mother, Ann, appears only briefly in Reid's history, darting out from the shadows during the family's annual summer car trip, always asking along with Reid, "How much farther?" Competing with Reid over the single hammock, their favorite, contested place to read in their grandmother Lulu's garden of prickly barberry bushes and locust trees.

Reid related many anecdotes about our relations. J. R., the rich steel company treasurer, and his wife, Maude, of the violet eyes. Dad Baker and Lulu who lived at Wheatland. Sickly Eleanor, her miscarriages, her stillborn baby, David. Even those last two taboo topics were included. But in Reid's history, my mother remains almost invisible. Her suicide, erased. Likewise, the suicide of Reid's father is barely mentioned. The only time in Reid's pages that he refers to the suicide of his father, Henry, is in a bizarrely roundabout manner, as the suicide of Dad Baker's son. Those kinds of extreme avoidances get handed down through generations. No wonder I wasn't certain I was ready to visit Wheatland.

• • •

Dusk, Harpers Ferry. The road grew smaller, darker, winding through the deep, narrow river gorge, the highway hugging the steep mountain sides above the river, darkness descending. Reservations scrambled for with our phone apps while driving. Charlestown, stopping at a hotel up the road from that old family property.

At bedtime in the hotel, I pulled out Reid's family history. Glancing through the pages made me feel sleepy. On my laptop in bed, I peeked again at the Library of Congress listing. Wheatland, the place I hoped we'd find in the morning. Next to me, my husband was already asleep, his CPAP machine humming and whispering familiarly. Our son slept nearby on a pullout couch.

The listing I peered at again by the light of a bedside lamp showed those four pictures. Two of the main house. One of the front, taken at a slight angle, a white brick structure with tall columns, along with a side view. Plus two additional pictures of different outbuildings. The southern property bought by my great-grandmother Lulu's father.

The third picture showed a large rectangular stone building that looked like the two-hundred-year-old German-style barn mentioned by Reid in his history. But what building was in that last picture? It could have been any of the other three outbuildings described by Reid. The library? Henry Camillus's library that used to house his hundreds of books. The workshop? Dad Baker's workshop, originally used as the kitchen at Wheatland. The workshop held Dad Baker's workbench and tools, along with every piece of equipment imaginable. Barrels of chicken feed.

Green glass insulators from old telegraph poles. A balance-beam farm scale able to hold a load of equipment weighing hundreds of pounds. When Dad Baker asked, Reid could fetch any item in that workshop within minutes.

The last outbuilding was the smokehouse where Dad Baker produced the most delicious ham Reid ever tasted. According to my uncle, the smokehouse was the only outbuilding with a dirt floor. In 1993, soon after retiring, Reid revisited Wheatland with his current wife. He found all four original outbuildings, including the barn, still standing, but the main house had already been torn down.

In the dark hotel room, I peered at the grainy pictures from the Library of Congress on my computer screen. It was hard to make out the floor of that fourth photo. Dirt or brick? It didn't look like brick. If it was dirt, then that last picture showed Reid's beloved smokehouse.

Were these three small, square brick outbuildings originally slave cabins? I wondered, peering at the online photos as I lay in the hotel bed beside my sleeping husband. According to Reid, in 1877, my great-grandmother Lulu's father, a prosperous merchant, bought 365 acres of a farm known locally as Wheatland, formerly a plantation. My ancestors lived at Wheatland for not quite one hundred years. I was lucky to know so much about my family history, in addition to knowing about the suicides. With that history circling through my mind along with my sense of connection to this place, I managed to sleep more peacefully and deeply than usual; I had the feeling of a stone sinking deeply into the ground.

Morning broke clear, sunny, warmer, ice still sheeting the parking lot but already melting away from the road edges. More melting ice highlighted tree branches and outlined the sides of tree trunks along the roads, showing the direction of yesterday's fierce winds.

West Virginia. A rural area of farmland with abruptly sloping hills in the panhandle-shaped region of the state carved out from the encroaching edges of Pennsylvania, Virginia, Maryland. As we drove, sappy lines from the song "Take Me Home, Country Roads" flowed through my mind like the waters of the nearby Shenandoah. I rode in the front passenger seat again, glad to let my husband drive. With the icy roads, our son hadn't yet gotten to take the wheel. In the back seat, he burrowed into games on his phone, ignoring our current adventure.

We traveled back and forth along a short span of a country road, searching for where the entrance to Wheatland should be, as near as I could tell from the description in Reid's history. A few miles farther along the route, we passed a small church. The sign outside said "Beulah," a name that tugged at my memory. I grabbed Reid's memoir from the bag at my feet, paging quickly through it until I found the reference to this place. The tiny church where Dad Baker was sometimes invited to preach on Sunday evenings. According to Reid, Dad Baker wasn't an ordained minister, but he was a powerful preacher. Not passionately religious himself, Reid wrote that his grandfather was "not a thunderer of the hell-fire-and-damnation variety." Yet Reid was always moved by the force of Dad Baker's personality and the strength of his faith. Dad Baker who survived the suicide of his son, Henry, and later also the suicide of his granddaughter. Momma.

Turning off the main road, we drove slowly up a dirt drive, turned around. The house at Wheatland was long gone. But it seemed like this really was the land. The property was currently a sheep farm with low wooden buildings and sheep pens to the right of the drive where we stopped the car. Our slow exploration up the driveway and back brought someone walking toward us. A farmer and his dog. Stepping out of the car first, my husband embodied a large, intimidating presence, but gentle and kind. If he were ever magically reincarnated as a dog, he would certainly be a golden Labrador.

The farmer called off his mutt. Untangling myself from the bags at my feet, I stumbled out onto the drive. The farmer whose hand I shook was the minimal amount of friendly, not inviting us up the hill for a look around. A middle-aged man in overalls, almost as big as my husband, listened with a blank face to our explanation of how we thought this must be the past location of my family's farm. I knew the names of the subsequent owners from Reid's history. Henry Heskett, the local farmer to whom the property passed after Dad Baker died. The next owner: Joseph Farland, ambassador to Pakistan at the time. Neither of those names produced a spark of recognition from the reticent current occupant. Even the word that for me held an almost mystical power—Wheatland—slid off the farmer's pale, soft face with no glimmer of recognition. He quickly assured us we must be in the wrong place, urging us to go down the road five or ten miles further.

"People drive up here to dump garbage all the time," the man said. He'd had to chase people off. This could explain his caution with out-of-state strangers.

This farmer guarding his sheep and land, understandably suspicious of unannounced visitors, didn't give us a chance to glimpse any more of the Wheatland property. I continued to feel certain we were in the right place. My husband was even more certain since he used his phone geotag from the Library of Congress listing to guide us to this exact spot.

The more the farmer tried to wave us away, the more certain I felt we were not lost. Gesturing with one arm toward the north, the farmer explained that the road we arrived on was built not many years ago. The original road and direction of approach to this land must have been along the adjoining edge of the property, not the current dirt drive.

I hoped to recognize something from my uncle's descriptions. But I didn't see the tulip poplar that used to stand on the brow of the hill, towering over a hundred feet high, planted in 1897, when Henry's younger brother, Sam, was born. "A gigantic sentinel still guarding the castle that had long since tumbled to the ground," according to Reid.

Instead, here was the current owner, the sentinel guarding his land from intruding northerners. Not allowing us to approach any closer up the drive or spot any markers that would make this place real for me. Those details described by Reid in his memoir. The wisteria tree that stood to the right of Wheatland's front porch. The maple trees that grew near the left front corner of the house. A limestone walkway led from the front porch to a square stone mounting block with two steps, a remnant from horseback riding days. Twenty feet farther out, the circle of prickly barberry hedges. The two large locust trees, great-grandmother Lulu's flower garden. The spot that held the canvas hammock where Reid and Momma both loved to disappear into books.

Maybe some of the original four stone outbuildings were still here as they had been in 1993 when Reid visited soon after he retired. But that was thirty years ago already. Maybe only the foundations of those outbuildings were still visible, impressions in the grass and dirt, on these surrounding grounds so carefully described by Reid.

We thanked the farmer, who had quickly introduced himself when I first shook his hand. I should have written his name down, I realized as we climbed back in the car. If I kept the man's name, at least I could contact him again, maybe invite myself back another time. Instead, with ice still melting from the roads and my husband behind the wheel, we started to drive away, while our son called from the back seat, "When can I drive?"

As we moved slowly up the road, I wondered if I felt Reid's presence here. I remembered that in the nearby hotel the night before, after examining the pictures of Wheatland online and thinking about my ancestors' attachment to this place, I had slept deeply. It wasn't Momma's presence I was searching for here, I realized. I wasn't even sure if she felt at home here the way Reid so clearly did, but she might have. In her letters, she mentioned visiting Dad Baker here with Nana. But the memory of Wheatland hadn't saved her, the way it helped Reid; nothing was enough to do that.

A few miles farther on the road heading away from Charlestown, we again passed the small church marked "Beulah." Like Reid, I wasn't a formally religious person, but I still felt moved as I glimpsed that church. Reid wrote that he never failed to feel inspired by his grandfather's lay sermons. I felt satisfied, seeing a single, solid piece of evidence of my ancestors' existence, the one building described by Reid in his family history that we located.

The white wooden clapboard church looked quiet, even on Sunday morning as we drove past, not one car parked outside. I wasn't surprised to see the church parking lot empty on a Sunday. It was the spring of 2022; the effects of the recent COVID pandemic were still being felt around the country. Congregations weren't meeting in person, even out in the country. Would any of my ancestors have had anything to say about that? Some of them must have survived past flu and other epidemics, like polio in the 1950s.

• • •

Momma, I wonder how you felt about Wheatland. And Grandfather Henry, did you resent being called Junior? Did you detest being a traveling salesman in the company where your father-in-law was the treasurer? Did you hate living in the house that he built for your wife and family? Is that why you died by suicide there? And what did the old family homestead mean to you? The place where you were born. Wasn't there a tree planted for you by your parents, Dad Baker and Lulu? Like the tulip poplar they planted for your younger brother, Sam. If your brother's poplar was still standing, we didn't get a chance to search for it.

CHAPTER 21

The Box

From the Personal file: another newspaper clipping, this one from the *New York Times*, dated Sunday, June 7, 1959. A page of drawings, more ads for dresses, Abraham & Strauss. "Cool, Summer Miracles! They wash, drip-dry, need little or no ironing!"

On the reverse side: a half-page ad featuring furniture from Lord & Taylor. Drawings of wooden cabinets in three versions: buffet, study area, and music corner. "Capturing inner space in a most ingenious way."

Did Momma save this page for the fashion ideas or the furniture? She had recently moved into her first married home. My impression from her letters to Jean and Nana is that she tried to embrace her role as a homemaker, even while turning her homemaking mishaps into funny anecdotes. Termites infesting the driftwood she and Future Dad collected to decorate their newlywed apartment. Repainting Sydney's room multiple times because the first shade they picked—pink—turned out awful.

I'm still betting on fashion over furniture as the reason she saved this sheet of newsprint, based on the other pictures of dresses tucked in her Personal file. That square, brown envelope labeled in pencil: "Dress Designs." Containing six dress ads clipped from various magazines and newspapers, one dated April 1957.

The dress ads Momma saved remind me of the box of her clothes I held onto for years. The clothes Dad rescued when our basement in Amherst flooded. While growing up, I kept returning to the box of her clothes, going over and over what was there and what wasn't; always hopeful, searching for something about my mother I couldn't find. At first, the box wasn't mine, and maybe it never was, but I thought of it as mine, and it became mine because I was the one who cared about it the most. Sydney never seemed interested in those old clothes of Momma's. At first, the cardboard box of Momma's clothes was stored in the basement, the same closet where Dad kept files of old bank statements, a box of tangled ice skates. Above these hung our winter coats, smelling of mothballs.

In the basement at the bottom of the house, the lives of my parents were pressed together like layers of rock; the history of those two separate people with their possessions layered on top of each other, long after Momma was dead. Dad saved those things that had been hers, trying to preserve something of her for us. The hidden layers of their lives pressed down—his life, her life, the life of our family—separate lives and possessions combining, pressing down one upon the other; with one person's life eventually forced out. But some evidence of her existence remained. At the bottom of the house, in the basement. In the box of her clothes.

I went through that box year after year; an irregular ritual I created, practiced alone. Not secret but private. Personal. Like her file of papers labeled with that word. Not something easily explained to anyone. What I was looking for, not spoken of aloud to anyone, barely existing in the realm of words. My habit of looking at her clothes, trying them on, finding an item or two that I'd grown into, could start wearing. I was probably around twelve when I started going through Momma's clothes in the box. Not quite big enough to wear anything of hers. Maybe I said something briefly to Dad about what I was doing, but it never turned into something he asked me about.

Even when I didn't live in that house in Amherst anymore, every time I returned home, during college and after, I would look in the box. At some point, I always went through the contents of the box. But only once during a visit because looking through the box made me feel sad. Whenever I looked at the things in the box—her clothes—I was alone. It felt as if the box contained everything about me, my life, the contents of my thoughts, wishes, dreams; as if it held all the parts of her, who she was at different stages of her life, some even before I existed. Clothes she wore as a young woman; clothes from after Sydney and I were born. Even a few things still in their plastic wrapping, not yet worn.

I went through that box many times, as if each time I would find out something new about her, not knowing exactly what I was looking for. The box of her clothes held no answers to why she died, but maybe the clothes would tell me something about who she had been, what she was like. Some clothes in the box, I looked at repeatedly, started wearing eventually. An irregular ritual prompted by curiosity and loneliness and longing; perhaps the reason I was locked in that repeating pattern. Taking out items one by one. Examining them. Trying them on. Deciding: does this fit? Can I wear this? How do I look in this? How am I like her and not like her?

At some point, the box was moved from the basement to one of the closets in that upstairs bedroom that used to be Momma and Dad's, in the old part of the house. I was in high school when I decided I wanted to make that room into my bedroom.

Dad rarely went in there, but he didn't object to my moving into that room, even suggested we repaint it together, helped me pick a sunny shade of yellow to cover the faded wallpaper. I liked that pretty bedroom, the sloping ceiling, the windows that looked out onto the backyard full of maples and oaks. Around the time I moved into that bedroom, some of Momma's clothes from the box started to fit me, so I started wearing them.

What was in the box? Sadness. But also something else. Her clothes held some of her sense of herself and her abilities that were transferred to me. The plain cardboard box, a mere two feet by two feet, held everything. Everything and nothing, because Momma was still gone.

The first piece of her clothes that I wore: a midnight-blue suede jacket, one shell button at the cinched elastic waist. It was stylish, like nothing else I owned. When I wore it, I felt different: confident, pretty. I wore the jacket from high school through college until I wore it out; it always held the association of having belonged to my mother—a heavy feeling in the background. The jacket was able to transform me from a chubby, shy girl who didn't know how to answer questions about my mother, a girl who liked to read under my bed, liked to eat a box of Nana's cookies, into someone more grown up; outgoing, adventurous even. Someone who had a handsome boyfriend in high school; traveled for a gap year before college. Like Momma, I visited Paris, and other cities and countries in Europe.

The next item in the box: a black patent leather belt, narrow with a silver buckle. Also something I could wear to become someone grown-up, capable. It fit me perfectly. Like the suede jacket, I wore the patent leather belt until it wore out. I went dancing in New York City clubs while working between college and grad school. Later, I discarded the disintegrating belt, something Dad, who always found ways to salvage or repair everything, would never have done.

Two summer blouses. Flowered, cotton, 1950s style, one yellow, one pink. Still in plastic wrappers. Momma must have been saving them, looking forward to wearing them. I wore them from high school until after college, when they became thin and faded and I couldn't wear them anymore. Momma's pants never fit me, too tiny in the waist. There were no socks or shoes in the box; maybe those didn't survive the flood. There were some highly structured underwire bras, like cages, and pairs of floppy underwear like water lilies that I never wore.

A pink polyester cardigan the color of Pepto Bismol. I wore it in graduate school and afterward when I was teaching. Carrying part of my mother with me, the woman she had been. Pretty, young. A thin summer nightgown with a matching robe, pale pink. Momma seemed to love pink. If I had a picture of myself in that nightgown and robe, what would I know about myself? That life could continue even after a terrible death.

A couple of dresses. One, vibrant pink in fitted linen. The other, pale petal-pink cotton, a button-up shirtdress with a matching belt. They each fit the way a glove slides onto a hand. I wore them many times, before, during, and after graduate school, those years when I went dancing at clubs, before I got married, until later when I became a mother. One flame-red silk dress that I could never fit into, gave away to a petite friend.

There actually was a pair of her gloves, also dark blue midnight suede. I only began wearing the gloves in the middle of college when I moved to New York. They became my favorite. Another unspoken part of my mother that I carried with me. I wore them for years until I was a mother and there were holes in all the fingers, and I couldn't wear them anymore.

A heavy, black sweater coat that I wore from graduate school until I became a mother. At some point, I recognized the coat from a picture of Momma in Paris, that college semester abroad. Standing outside a building with "Sorbonne" engraved in large letters over a doorway. Eventually, I realized I looked terrible in the heavy dark coat, that I could get something different that suited me, so I donated Momma's old coat to Goodwill. I don't miss that somber coat, but I wish I still had the picture of Momma when she was a student in Paris. What else was in the box? Loneliness. Longing. Rage. Loss.

I don't have the cardboard box anymore or any of Momma's clothes. I wore many of her things until they fell apart or turned into rags. I don't miss having her clothes. I have all the memories of wearing them. I took everything I could from those clothes and drew those strong parts of her into myself. There's nothing left of her from her clothes that I feel I'm still missing.

• • •

From the plain white business envelope where they rest inside my desk for safekeeping when I'm not working, I take out my picture guides again for help, line them up on the shelf on top of my desk behind my lamp. My mother as a girl, standing on a grassy lawn, trees in the background. Looking slightly to one side, a three-quarter view, gazing into the distance, not directly at me. That short cotton dress, hair in big, white bows. Posed in a thoughtful, almost adult stance as if someone, her father or Nana, said: stand here for your picture.

Beside her is her father, my other photo guide. He looks directly at the camera, at me. Maybe it was Nana taking his picture. Although with her famously bad eyesight, I wonder if she was ever the photographer. Henry is half-smiling, half-somber.

Today, it's him I miss. He wasn't especially young when he died. But still, there's always the story of the life that could have been when someone dies early. Especially when the person dies by suicide, there's always the question of the life they didn't get to live. If Henry had lived, he would have been sixty-seven when I was born. I probably would have gotten to know him. I wonder what kinds of things we would have done together when I was a child if he hadn't died.

My paternal grandfather, Grandad Willy, was a grim man who drove a truck delivering gasoline to gas stations before he retired. Those Missouri grandparents rarely visited because that grandmother was afraid to fly. Once when they did visit, Grandad Willy secretly colored in the eyes of my favorite white plastic pony with blue pen, then wouldn't answer my enraged child's questions about who wrecked my toy. I never understood why he did that. He seemed to enjoy teasing me, like a child himself, although he was in his late sixties at least. Maybe that's partly why I never imagined the fun I was missing out on with Grandfather Henry, since my one living grandfather was someone I disliked.

So, Momma, Grandfather, what was your relationship like? Were you your father's favorite, Momma? I think that's what Dad told me. Is that why you died by suicide, like your father, Momma? While Reid, Nana's favorite, managed to stay alive. And what would you have thought about me wearing those clothes of yours, Momma? After you left.

CHAPTER 22

Jeanne

Monday

Jeanne—

I will sit down and write this long-neglected letter. Right now. As for the long silence—I'm the one to have been beating my brow on that score—And I have, naturally with the best intentions…

Alphabets and Birthdays[34] was perfect. Especially since had never seen this sample or particular style of Gertrude Stein's. You know how I—I think the word is "admire"—her. Sending an article from Atlantic on her you may be interested in—by none other than that "friendly old critic" J. Malcolm Brinnin running to true iconoclastic form.[35]

As for the lamp—the amber glass base sounds ideal. I can hardly wait to see it. Also Bob answered with a sort of fanatic zeal when he read this portion of the letter. You know he has developed a real passion for bottles—which I now and then hint must have Freudian implications but which he distinctly ignores. So far we have only 2 rather un-unique whisky bottles and another really fascinating chunk of uneven blown glass, green and very heavy. This latter gem B. brought back like a war trophy from a solitary antique expedition of his own.

Wild Strawberries[36]—we saw just last week. Also the Seventh Seal.[37] My own reaction to these films best summed up by the fact that—I have nothing to compare their impact to. No nice summing up of values or technique. An utterly new experience.

For us this fall has been fairly uneventful. Mainly taken up by considerations of and about babies, not to mention the baby. Gradually getting used to the idea that this thing is going to happen. Have been decidedly fine except for an occasional fit of lethargy—your "hit by a 2 x 4" struck a familiar note. Encouraging in a way to know it's just not me. Also, I sometimes get the impression I'm being used as a football dummy. Definitely not a quiet child.

Have been working one afternoon a week at the Children's Hospital here. So far just in one of the nurses' stations on one of the regular wards—in very routine capacity, copying schedules and that sort of thing. This—with one of the neighbors whose husband is in law school and who also has much unused time. ("Freelance" volunteers). I have much less of a "crowded china shop" feeling about tiny enfants. From this close quarters observation they seem somewhat more indestructible than before.

Bob has been spending most evenings building his hi-fi set. Also we have been house-hunting not too seriously but with an eye to next Spring or Summer. Mostly old farmhouses. The ads we've checked out have been misleading to say the least. One in particular really sounded like the one—perfect bucholic [sic] setting, woods, lake, not to mention greenhouse on the property. We pictured some quaint little celarium [sic], shady and secluded. This in fact turned out to be a shed-like house 50' from the main highway with the damnedest, biggest greenhouse I've ever seen. A huge deserted hulk—more like a bombed-out factory junk yard than anything else. Bob kept saying the property did have possibilities though. $5000 worth of canvas drapes and we could have moved in. What I mean is, you can eventually get discouraged from this kind of thing.

By the way, I'm taking a watercolor class. (To borrow an old phrase of Reid's—"this will jar you"—at the YMCA.) Bob decided to take one of their hobby courses in Real Estate and talked me into going along with him at the same time. Which actually is a pretty good compromise—since the Art Museum is just too inconvenient right now—(distance, time, and pregnancy-wise).

So far I have only tried one still life—the apples look like peaches and the water jug is drowned in its own pigment. The teacher was very encouraging though: he said—"Well, I've seen worse first attempts." He had suggested I try tempera—for beginners—but what madness! I'd insisted on transparents. "At least" he said "you're not afraid to use the paints—that's good!"—this as the whole thing was sort of oozing together and I was frantically fighting water shots!

> I'm still not reconciled to Thanksgiving. It would have been such a superb holiday. We of course are still going home—tho not sure about Christmas, at this point. Will be thinking of you all and planning on bigger and better reunions.
>
> Love, Ann

For some reason, my mother started sometimes addressing her friend with that Frenchified version of her name: Jeanne. Following this letter, there are only four more letters to her friend, the last two also addressed to "Jeanne." The somewhat arch and distant tone of the new pet name doesn't bode well for their friendship. Momma's letters to her friend became less frequent during this last period, but probably they were both simply busy with their families.

I cut some details about the couple of TV shows Momma describes, which date the letter to late fall 1959. *I, Don Quixote*, aired on November 9, 1959, and *The Moon and Sixpence* aired on October 30, 1959. Those TV movies highlight Momma's boredom during her pregnancy though. Even more than bored, Momma sounds unhappy about being pregnant. Her "occasional fit of lethargy" makes me think of the low mood and energy swings of her possible bipolar symptoms. Or maybe she was just tired from being pregnant.

When I was trying to become a mother, I had multiple first-trimester miscarriages. Every time I was pregnant, I felt extremely nauseous, not just in the mornings, and each pregnancy I lost was emotionally wrenching. I saw numerous specialists, but the causes of my miscarriages were never understood or solved. After almost a decade, my husband and I gladly abandoned the world of experimental drugs and fertility doctors and decided to form our family through adoption.

Our decision wasn't related to a fear of a genetic link I might have to the history of suicide in my mother's family. I never struggled to become pregnant, but my body couldn't stay pregnant, which isn't the typical problem treated by the fertility industry. The most advanced medical solutions available at the time didn't work for me.

Nana once told me Momma was born by cesarean section, such a strange tongue twister to me as a child that I always struggled to remember those words. I remembered Nana's other stories: the stillborn first baby she and Henry buried on Christmas Day; her multiple miscarriages before Reid and Momma. There were also her stories about her blood ailment that made her tired for years and required her to take the tiny white pills she always carried in her silver pocket watch. I never worried about inheriting a genetic trait for suicide, but I wonder if my fertility problems were caused by a different inherited genetic link, if the underlying cause of my undiagnosed miscarriages was possibly a blood-related disorder not understood at the time by fertility specialists, since my physical difficulties were so similar to Nana's.

• • •

The next letter, in January 1960, confirmed that the prize for first baby went to Jean and Reid. Their daughter, Robin, was born in late January or early February, barely ahead of my sister, Sydney, who arrived just after Valentine's Day.

> Dear Jean—
>
> It seems as if I've been planning to write forever—since Christmas, the baby, the long letter which Bob and I both enjoyed hugely, and on and on.

Can't tell you how pleased and excited we were when the News finally arrived. How are you by this time? We talked to mother briefly just after she had gotten back from Milwaukee. Very anxious to see the pictures. Assured her that I was "organized"—hardly the word. Appears that Bob has been completely won over by your description of a daughter. Not that he has utterly deflected [sic] to the other side! But he has been reverting often to the subject (once pronounced closed) of what-to-name-a-girl. Think Robin is unique.

The package has really been welcome, the change of "costume" downright delightful. Everything is very chic and very appreciated! The green and white is especially intriguing and unfortunately I have now passed the stage of wearing "with aplomb" that type of one-piece. Have been reading, rather ironically at this particular time, Edna and Ilka Chase's Always in Vogue[38]—recommend it—an Algonquinian type review of "la mode." So meanwhile here I am rapidly taking on the appearance of a healthy dirigible and feeling as if, at any moment, I might just disappear with a loud POP.

The information on natural childbirth has really been enlightening. Not that I'll probably be able to do much with the exercises at this late date and sans guidance—though I have been lying around on the floor breathing like mad. However, it's the only thing that's given me any idea of what actually to expect during labor. Even with a tour of the hospital here and an ob. willing to answer all questions, the whole project up to now has had a formidable aura about it of "the clinical," "The assembly line." So thanks for sending this along. From all reports, it sounds as if you hardly had time to put the NCBA's recommendations into practice!

Saw the out-of-town opening of A Thurber Carnival[39] with Tom Ewell, the choice being Columbus apparently since Thurber is a native son. Surprised to see that it is opening on Broadway next month—can honestly say this without even trying to be condescending. Sketches of some of the fables the best. Also Basil Rathbone as Satan in J.B.[40]—a real coup seeing this. Rathbone quote fell ill immediately following the performance unquote and was in the hospital here for almost a week—ptomaine poisoning. A superlative after-touch. Last, as a real blow, just notified that Hal Holbrook is to be here in the Mark Twain thing.[41] March 2! This as an alternate to another program, some organ recital, later on in April for which we held tickets. March 1 is standby date but damned if I'll miss this. So what do you think of the Veterans' Memorial as a fair substitute for Yankee Stadium in the olde "where was you born" cliché?

I have seen so little of Bob lately that we're developing a passing-in-the-corridor complex. The warehouse, after a year, is finally just getting into operation and he has been working practically a double schedule, Saturdays and late most evenings for the past month. He is definitely considering a change of scene—completely off the record comment on my part, please. But the operation here has apparently developed into something rather different than expected. In any case, we have given up any idea of a house or even a temporarily cozy little niche ici, and meanwhile typing tentative inquiries round and about. Which situation I suppose may go on an indefinite time without the right thing or anything turning up. I mention this only as a commentary on the status quo.

Really must close and get this off in the very next post, as scanty a record of events as it is.

Love to you all—

And do write,

Ann

Momma still doesn't sound happy about being pregnant. As I've come to expect from her letters to Jean, she turns her discomfort into a funny story. Actually, she sounds anxious, underprepared, and plain unenthusiastic, about both childbirth and motherhood.

Dad's story of Momma's first experience of giving birth: she hated it. She was given more drugs than she wanted. She hoped to use as little medication as possible, he said, but instead was completely numbed by the doctor from the waist down, so she couldn't feel anything. That must have been frustrating for someone born by cesarean who wanted to experience giving birth.

Dad said Momma vowed to take as little anesthesia as possible for my birth. He said he thought she had a spinal block for Sydney's birth, while for mine she was given an epidural. Not exactly natural childbirth either time, despite Jean's loan of a book on that subject. By 1962, when I was born, there still wasn't much support for that approach. Dad said he wished he was allowed to be present when both Sydney and I were born, instead of being stuck in a waiting room and handed the stereotypical cigar, the only option for fathers during those decades.

I don't know if my parents made it to see the Mark Twain thing with Hal Holbrook in Columbus. Years later when I was in junior high, around the time I moved into that upstairs bedroom and he handed over Momma's letters, Dad, a fan of Twain's, also gave me a paperback by that author, possibly as a birthday present, and encouraged me to watch an evening TV special featuring Holbrook as Twain.

> Wednesday
>
> Dear Jean—
>
> My Hat—being tossed through la porte. Since all news seems so much old news at this point, I will just begin…
>
> Happily mother sent these pictures on to us. Bob's comment about the one with the big smile—I don't know what it is exactly but that's Jean all right. Frankly I'm not sure you just didn't stick your head through the hole in the canvas like in one of those old carnival tintypes. Admit it.
>
> We do have by the way a very nice baby—still cranky aux fais but thoroughly delightful. Yes, she is smiling—even giving forth now and then with what I consider a small, tentative chuckle—that and "talking" at everything and everyone including the Teevee. Until just the past few weeks Bob has referred to her as "the angry young baby"—or could she be! Right now she is sleeping happily—(that is should say happily she is sleeping) in playpen. Our apartment is more and more taking on

the air of a comfortable kindergarten. In any case, agree that a baby is a fine thing to have around—in fact she has so completely intruded herself upon the scene that cannot imagine having been without one.

The child is starting to Be heard. Must go—but at least will get this in the mail to break the long silence.

The Fugitive Kind[42] is in town. We are seeing it tonight. Enjoying much Wake Up, Stupid.[43] Have not read much else of late except the grocery circulars and the free Gerber Foods offers that arrive daily.

Love to you, Reid, Cliff—Robin—all—
Gad—I am glad about next year for you all—sounds wonderful.

Ann

Back to addressing her friend as "Jean," Momma decorated the top of that letter with a line drawing: a jaunty hat, topped by a daisy. Illustrating the saying, "To throw your hat in the door." An outdated expression meaning, "To see if you're welcome." There's no date on her letter, but *The Fugitive Kind* opened in mid-April 1960, so the gap since her previous letter was maybe only several months, despite her apology for the delay, not much longer than usual.

Now that Sydney was born and Momma's physical struggle with pregnancy was over, she sounded more upbeat. When I initially read these letters before I was a mother, I felt uncomfortable learning that my mother felt less than pleased with pregnancy and motherhood.

While I didn't actually give birth, I did become a mother—twice—and the experience gave me a new perspective. Any idealized notions of perfect motherhood I once harbored evaporated. Months of waking to feed a baby multiple times a night, along with a crying baby keeping my husband and me up for hours, drove out those idealized ideas. I experienced, either first- or secondhand, most common childhood ailments, plus a few lesser-known ones. One time I even caught scarlet fever. After that, I read the parts of Momma's letters about motherhood with new eyes. Picking up on any whiffs of Momma's less-than-perfect contentment with being a mother didn't bother me. I even felt reassured by her confessions to her best friend. The problem wasn't her complaints to Jean about motherhood. The problem was that soon she wouldn't have that Jean friendship to lean on.

After my sister's birth, Momma's Jean letters tapered off; both women were married, with at least one child apiece. Reid's job made him move his family to Vermont, perhaps related to Jean's later love of that place. And wow, all those books Momma was reading. I'm still back at *Dubliners*, *Rock Wagram*, and *The Idiot*.

• • •

Dear Momma and Grandfather Henry, I'm leaving your pictures inside the envelope today. I feel unsure about how to talk to you, or what to call you even, Grandfather. Grandfather Henry? I have that picture of you, but I can't quite imagine you. You died over eighty years ago. Henry Baker Jr. And Momma, yes, it might have been nice to have you around to help me during my years of miscarriages and my family's struggle to fit together the pieces on our path to adoption. But I wonder how much help you would have been. Were you already starting on your downward trend?

CHAPTER 23

Parachute

April 1961. One of the last items from Momma's Personal file. An article from *McCall's* magazine:

400 FAMOUS PEOPLE, AND HOW THEIR CHILDHOOD AFFECTED THEM

What their parents, schools, and difficulties were like. A survey of special interest to parents of gifted children.

Why did Momma save this magazine article? Was she trying to figure out something about how to be a good parent for Sydney, her first child who recently turned one? Did she tear the article out of that magazine herself or did someone send it to her (Jean or Nana maybe)? The glossy pages smell of dust and ink and are brittle with age as I gently unfold them. I've read this article from Momma's Personal file before, but don't recall what's here; only remember a familiar feeling of resistance to digesting this information.

In the ongoing debate about nature versus nurture in child development, I don't give precedence to either side, instead landing somewhere in the middle. This article, from a study of "the intellectual and emotional climate in families producing eminence," sides with nurture, not a scrap of nature or genetics, predictable for 1961.

While probably not concerned with how to raise a genius, maybe Momma worried that her family history of suicide would negatively affect her own child. The article optimistically predicts the outcome of a troubled childhood will be a creative type: novelist, playwright, actor, even a comedian. Thumbnail sketches of various "eminent" men and women provide evidence: Charlie Chaplin, for example. Reading the article, though like swallowing medicine, isn't as bad as I feared.

• • •

In a memory from Amherst, Sydney reclines on the low branch of an apple tree. A family outing to an orchard to pick apples, a quaint New England activity. Possibly 1967, a year after we moved there, not long before Momma died. Sydney would have been six or seven; I was about five. Sydney climbed a tree, and Momma or Dad snapped her picture, posing in a red sweater, a hand-knitted gift from Nana. A minor miracle that Nana could knit with her bad eyesight. The sweater had a pointy hood and zipped up the front. Syd looked like a sulking elf perched on a low tree branch. After getting her photo taken, she refused to climb down. For ages, my parents attempted to coax her off the branch.

We used to have a snapshot of Sydney in the tree, wearing that red sweater, legs outstretched along the tree branch, arms crossed stubbornly at her chest, looking cute. Making herself into a roadblock to our parents' plans. I don't remember how the scene ended, how they got her down. Probably not gracefully. Probably with Sydney crying, maybe with promises of rewards or threats of punishment. I remember that Kodak snapshot, but it's not one I wish I kept.

• • •

My daughter, who's often annoyed with me for reasons I rarely see coming, will soon graduate from college, will probably be living at home again, the way it was for over a year of her college career during the pandemic. I'm trying to head off a return to that tense time, the four of us crowded together into our small apartment, the new home everyone in our family helped select with the plan in mind that our daughter was almost out of the nest. Now apartments in the city are increasingly expensive and hard to find; it looks like she'll soon return home for at least a while, looking for a job, deciding she is sick of school, putting her grad school plans on hold.

In desperation, I started a weekly study group with her, completing the exercises from *What Color Is Your Parachute?* the career and job exploration book from the 1970s that's still updated yearly. My twenty-one-year-old daughter and I started meeting weekly on Zoom this spring, joined by my husband. Soon also joined by our daughter's boyfriend, who's interested in what we're doing. The two of them Zoom from one of their rooms at college, with my husband and me on the couch in our Brooklyn living room. I wish all colleges offered free career planning groups for students based on this *Parachute* method. I lost my mother; now I get to be the mother. I find this challenging, satisfying, healing.

• • •

Grandfather, I can't imagine you were ever much fun to be with, working all the time, drinking too much. Traveling salesman for Sharon Steel. Shooting yourself in the head with a rifle near midnight on a Sunday and dying, while your wife and children were probably sleeping, not far away. An act of both bravery and cowardice. I don't imagine it's easy to shoot yourself. Or maybe you were just drunk. But not too drunk to get the job done. Who did you think was going to find you, did you even consider that? It must have been Nana. No wonder she was sick for years afterward.

Momma, did you ever think of writing to your father after he was gone? Even though you were such a letter writer, I can't imagine you considered addressing him in writing. Then you might not have felt compelled to repeat his act. You must not have tried talking to him either. Reid said you never even talked to each other about your father's suicide.

CHAPTER 24

Nana

For decades, Momma's letters to Nana sat on a shelf in my office of the house in Brooklyn, in the box from Reid. My typed transcript of the letters—that abridged version—I saved in a file cabinet. The next time I moved, to this smaller apartment in Brooklyn, I must have thrown the box out. I don't remember deciding to throw out those letters. I must have been in an overly eager cleaning mood.

When I unpacked in the new apartment, I didn't think about things I hadn't kept. At first, I didn't miss Momma's letters. When I started my project of writing about her, I looked everywhere for that box of letters from Reid. That's when I realized I'd actually thrown that out. Finally, I found the typed transcript, that shorter version. Not the originals, not Momma's handwriting. With relief, I opened the transcript and started to read. The first letter was from February 1961, mentioning one-year-old Sydney dragging around her doll, the gift from Nana.

Momma's next letter was addressed to Nana at Jean and Reid's in Vermont, I knew from the transcript, even though I no longer had the original envelope. Momma, along with Dad and Sydney, were staying at Nana's on Linden Street in Sharon, the house where my grandfather shot himself.

June 21, 1961

Dear Mother,

...Hilda said you knew him and would be interested and concerned—though frankly I can't see any advantage over your hearing it now, to when you get home. Mrs. Dann also called to comment on and add to the latter item. (She saw the door open the other night and thought you were here.) I'm afraid I've been away from Sharon too long to appreciate the town's most resourceful, though well-intentioned, prying. Really formidable.

Nothing definite about a job. The best possibility is still the Electronics Co. Meanwhile Bob is becoming more than acclimated to not working. All sorts of time for golf and more complicated stock market charts.

Now holding Sydney in my lap with one hand and madly trying to finish this up with the other.

At the start of the letter, Momma complains about a neighbor who insisted Momma clip and mail a local news item to Nana in Vermont, about the Sharon businessman who recently shot himself in the head. The man's suicide must have resonated with both Momma and Nana, although Momma wrote nothing about that.

• • •

When I was young, Nana always smelled sweetly of face powder and Joy perfume, with a cloud of short, white hair, styled weekly at the beauty salon. She wore thick glasses and low pumps that matched her outfits. She had an ongoing love affair with food, an ongoing battle with her waistline. She used the services of Mrs.

H., a seamstress who regularly took in or let out the waists of her dresses and skirts, so everything fit perfectly.

After Momma died, Nana visited Amherst several times a year, staying for weeks at a time. We visited her in Sharon every summer too. Nana tried to be a doting grandmother, even if she couldn't fill all the gaps left by Momma's absence. When she couldn't be with us, Nana mailed presents to me and Sydney. At Christmas, our birthdays. Along with frequent boxes of homemade cookies. Her specialties: peanut butter, banana walnut, oatmeal raisin. When a box of Nana's cookies arrived, I ate them without stopping while I did my homework. After Momma died, I grew chubby on Nana's attempts at mothering us through homemade sweets.

> August 2, 1961
>
> Dear Mother,
>
> ...planning on some neglected maternity shopping this afternoon. Can already forsee [sic] the day when I am caught with nothing. In fact it's about here. Actually I do have a few things to get along with, just want to pick up some blouses so I won't have to be ironing every day. This in-between period is certainly the most disgruntling of all!
>
> Still nothing definite jobwise. Opportunities and leads <u>have</u> kept cropping up—so in any case we've been subsisting on a number of possibilities.

Momma's comment about maternity shopping is the first time she mentions to Nana being pregnant a second time, even indirectly. The first time in her letters to her mother that my presence was noted. Nana and Momma also kept in touch via telephone though, so it seems Nana already knew. Again, as with Sydney, Momma sounded annoyed about being pregnant. Before I was a mother, I felt sad and surprised when I read how unenthusiastic Momma sounded about being pregnant with me. But in this later reading, I remember my own physical misery during the times I was pregnant.

> August 18, 1961
>
> Dear Mother,
>
> Will thank you in advance for sending the maternity things out...did want to get them before the trip even though I knew you'd be sending them soon. And as I mentioned I can really use them. A week ago I was patting myself on the back for being so 'skinny' still—when all of a sudden—well I can't avoid the fact any longer that I do seem to be having a baby.

The trip Momma mentions: the long drive at the end of the summer to visit Dad's parents in Missouri. My other grandparents, the grandfather I never liked. Again, Momma jokes about her lack of enthusiasm for being pregnant with me.

> October 21, 1961
>
> Dear Mother,
>
> I've been trying to have dinner ready right when Bob gets home—and it's worked wonderfully. I have so much more <u>time</u>. A whole evening to catch up on cleaning, mending, ironing, reading—while he disappears into the lower depths, his den. Also I've had to type a few papers for him. He spends the whole day—from 8:00 to 5:30 or 6:00 at the University. Although he has

> only one morning class three days a week, there's so much outside research that it's the only way he can manage to stay 'caught up.' He has really been enjoying the work and the classes though.
>
> Tonite [sic] we're finally going to see 'La Dolce Vita.'[44] So sorry that you and I missed it. There are so many things on right now—concerts, folk-singers, plays, lectures all at once—that we can't possibly get to, that I just have to close my eyes on the entertainment page and refuse to think about it.

Nana must have visited recently; that letter was one of the infrequent times Momma wrote to her mother about films, concerts, plays, lectures. She sounds like she was working hard at being the ideal housewife, even laboring as Dad's typist, which I can't imagine was fun for her. Pregnant, cooking and cleaning, with a toddler, working as Dad's unpaid secretary too.

> October 30, 1961
>
> Dear Mother,
>
> Bob has really had a fantastic amount of work. He's been studying a good deal on the weekends too, as well as the 6–8 routine during the day, with 4 or 5 hours of 'homework' on top of that at night. Rather rigorous schedule—but we've all been enjoying it tremendously.
>
> I keep thinking how much fun it will be with you here this Christmas when the baby 'arrives.' Getting very excited about the prospect.

When I was in elementary school, and later junior high, I sometimes visited my grandmother on my own. Nana could talk forever about her physical ailments. Her arthritis. Hammertoes. Bunions. Bad eyes. Cataracts. Reid wrote in his family history that his mother was sickly as a child and had a lazy eye, but there was more to her health problems and her dwelling on them that I heard about as a child than he recorded in his family history. Nana's skin was thin like tissue paper. The veins on her hands bulged like purple worms, and she always had at least one giant bruise on one of her arms or legs, oddly shaped like the outlines of distant countries. Whenever she bumped into anything, even lightly, she got a dramatic bruise—from the medicine she took, she told me. In her pocketbook, she carried a silver pocket watch case that held the tiny white pills she added to her tea, two at a time, along with milk and sugar. Her doctor prescribed the daily pills. A blood thinner, maybe she said. Or maybe she told me some of them were saccharine.

When my mother was a girl, she took care of Nana. My mother, Ann, who was such a good girl, my grandmother told me. Always helping Nana in and out of the bath, in and out of bed. Nana, who was sick for years after her husband died. Momma, who was ten when her father died by suicide. Nana never said the word "suicide," not about her husband, or later about Momma.

In that last letter, Momma finally sounds excited that I was about to be born, but it's Nana's visit she's equally anticipating.

> November 25, 1961
>
> Dear Mother,
>
> The doctor said last week that the baby has already dropped down—sometime before Thanksgiving. Said that this is not unusual so early—and that even though it <u>can</u> mean a

> somewhat-before-expected-delivery, he is still definitely counting on January 12. The only drawback is that I can really <u>feel</u> the difference—as if I've suddenly gained additional ballast.

That was me, dropping like a bowling ball with six weeks to go before my birth. I arrived a day early, not on the twelfth as predicted. The anniversary of Momma's father's suicide. Probably not a welcome coincidence. Wherever I go, I still prefer arriving early.

• • •

OK, my two picture guides, I'm taking you out of your envelope today, even though it feels uncomfortable to be always making these sad comments to you both who are actually dead.

Momma, what did you used to call your father? Did you call him "Dad" or "Daddy"? Or did you call him "Father"? I'm not sure what Reid called him either. It's that thing about suicide making a person vanish, how no one talked about you, Grandfather.

CHAPTER 25

Reading List

Judging by the movie Momma mentioned, this undated letter must have been written around December 1961. Although she says it was a year since her last letter, it was actually longer, more like a year and a half. This is Momma's second-to-last letter to Jean, again using the new Frenchified version of her name.

> Dear Jeanne,
>
> I have been downright thrilled and pleased with the bracelets. They are lovely, Jeanne—really a welcome surprise when they arrived—and have certainly been very much appreciated. I initiated them first off with a navy maternity-type shroud and felt (yes, actually) CHIC. Which is quite an accomplishment at this advanced stage of "with child." So you can see, you really saved the day and my morale!
>
> How to catch up on a year's correspondence; it can't be that long. Just been thinking how pleasant it would be to have a private wire through to Vermont, to simply pick up the phone and chat about ideas (what have you been thinking?) or just plain events (your job? new faces?). Questions questions. Really, we will have to arrange for one sometime. Without the intermediary of the US Post, or the trials and tribulations

of child waking early, neighbors dropping in for coffee, door-to-door salesmen, market surveys, etc. etc. plus all the rest of the daily barrage of trivia, from diapers to dental check-ups. For NOW I'll simply start pecking away at random, come h--- or high water if it takes all winter! Allons.

Bob is at a project meeting this afternoon (Sunday). He has really been busy the last few months, getting back into the routine of school and hoping to get his MBA in three quarters—by Spring. How all this came about is something we're still absorbing since he didn't actually decide to go ahead with his master's until a few weeks before the term started this fall. As you probably know from mother, he did leave Westinghouse last spring. Though any number of developments which could be labeled as "promising" "interesting" or "possible" kept turning up, things were still in a rather indefinite state by the end of the summer. So-o-o, here we are and enjoying it much. Bob, after being rather skeptical about the whole thing (a kind of practical snob) has been very much stimulated by the program, professors, and prospects. In fact, he's somewhat more than enthusiastic. Meanwhile, the cellar has been turned into a "study" (I use the term loosely) with cardboard packing cases made into partitions, 50 cents worth of lime for whitewash, various other odds and ends, including a rug (too glamorous a word for it) from good-will, a lampshade for ten cents, a door which now serves as a huge desk. We're thinking of sending photographs and drawings to American Home or a like-magazine for the ultimate in do-it-yourself articles. You know something like "how I made my basement into a den for $7.93..." The neighbors were sure we were constructing a fall-out shelter.

We enjoyed all the news and bits of information about all of you gleaned from mother. She loved her visit with you. A passing remark of hers has turned into one of those beautiful pieces of incidental intelligence that keeps popping to mind whenever I try to imagine what it's like up there (combination rugged individualism, Utopian god's country, isolated frontier and what have you). "VERMONT: they don't have very good television reception!" Perfect.

Books. I'm finally sending Cliff's T. H. White[45] back after a really unforgiveable delay. Also the Styron pocket edition:[46] I know how you like him too and just taking a risk on your not having been able to get this one yet. Have you by any chance seen the new San Francisco lit magazine Contact (William Carlos Williams among the editors). Got a few of these through Marlboro—and will be glad to send them on to you. As the result of an article in one of them by I. Hayakawa,[47] (a Japanese American English teacher writing on of all things the negro question) have been delving into semantics. His books in particular plus some others.[48] Fascinating. Had thought this field restricted merely to a dry study of words and symbols without any broader implications. Anyway, you might be interested in some of this. Kerouac—enjoyed a lot of On the Road[49] but certainly not all of it. Laughton read from this when he was here last year and it was downright lyric. For weeks afterwards I kept thinking in terms of "like sure man…" also took your advice on E. M. Forster[50] and found myself arguing with him all the way though it—just couldn't take wholeheartedly to the concept of the noble savage. Have wanted to try more, however. Breakfast at Tiffany's[51] we just SAW (had read it, also you mentionned [sic] the Christmas story[52] which Bob and I had read out loud [sic] together before and loved). The movie is bastardized some, but a MUST. What else? Portrait of Max, Bernard Berenson's biog[53] (adore the name Sylvia Sprigg or is it Sprig?) Years with Ross[54]—all of which I can't recommend because I know you must have seen them first. Finally got around to sampling Swados—False Coin.[55] "Durl's" Black Book.[56] Have you read Nabokov's Invitation to a Beheading[57] (this one I can send you too)? Sean O'Faolain's short stories,[58] Brendan Behan,[59] Gore Vidal's City and the Pillar.[60]

Forgot to mention the clothes in Breakfast at … one big-brim black hat in particular, with great stiff satin streamers (cream) down the side, I'm sure will drive you wild. Fabulous things.

Mother also mentioned that you were still getting lots of records from the library, something we've been doing too on a kind of skimpy pot-luck basis, though. Have you ever heard Faulkner reading from his own books? This is one of the weirdest experiences I've ever had. For some reason I've always approached his prose on a Ronald Coleman frequency as if Y. County for all practical purposes, and even if it was about the South, lay somewhere in a clean uncluttered realm north of Westchester. Really jarring: what does this drawling character think he's doing reading the Sound and the Fury! Needless to say, after getting used to the idea it was just right. Something else both you and Reid would enjoy—Shaw's Don Juan in Hell,[61] an old recording with Charles-es Boyer & Laughton and Sir Cedric Hardwick. Do try to get this. We were also apparently re-playing John Brown's Body[62] about the same time as you.

It is now and actually has been for several paragraphs, Thursday. I told you I was just going to forge on. Now I'm simply going to close up and send this on as a first installment, to let you know we are still alive. Even with all the big gaps in information.

Would love to hear when you have the chance. We do miss you-Reid-Cliff-Robin. The picture of S.—she is wearing the blue and white dress you sent, really my favorite. For this pose she was surrounded by so many toys, papers, keys, etc. in a harassed attempt to pacify her long enough for the shot, that we had to settle for head only. Thought you might like to see it. She is really a time-consuming and demanding little item—or what to do with yet another. I am really put to shame by reports of how good Robin is, especially about playing by herself. These reports usually come on simply awful days when I've reverted to Spock in despair to find out my lord what to do. Not to say she isn't pleasant to have around a good part of the time. Have been able to take her to nursery school a few mornings a week which really helps. (Usually on Sundays at the Community Church near here, and again in the middle of the week for a terrific seminar on the psychology of religion.) A dual boon, and one that several friends "Here in the Court" have been taking advantage of too. So now she talks often about "kind-garten and boys." I always amend this to "boys and girls" which she completely ignores. Much more impressed with the first.

Don't do what I do—do what I say—> which is Write.

Ann

P.S. Thanks so much, too, for letting me use your M-clothes again. Shall I send them back to you or burn them?

The Court was our apartment complex in Columbus, Ohio. Momma refers more than once to being pregnant, but only indirectly. It seems Jean already knew, probably from Nana, who just returned from a visit to Vermont. In her joking way, Momma sounds enthusiastic about domestic life and her thrifty home decorating. But her gloomy attitude about pregnancy and the accompanying maternity clothes resurfaces when she refers to Jean's loaned navy "shroud."

The letter mentions a treasure trove of book titles, along with a supplemental list of listening and viewing materials. Momma's diet of mental stimulation while she was pregnant with me. Maybe she was also showing off for Jean, rattling off her impressive list. Or maybe this was another of Momma's high-energy manic phases, brought on by her heightened anxiety over my approaching birth. Or was this simply how she coped with the reduced physical activity of late pregnancy: reading, watching movies, listening?

I also wonder about those bracelets from Jean just before I was born, possibly a Christmas gift. Jean must have known Momma liked bracelets. Did she know about the scars on my mother's wrists? Did she know anything about Momma cutting her wrists? I can imagine that Momma kept her suicide attempt a secret from her friend. The mention of the bracelets reminded me of that story, the jilted marriage proposal that Momma managed to hide even from Dad, until after he married her. The bracelets could have simply been a gift from Jean, who knew only that Momma liked wearing them.

• • •

I get out my envelope with my two picture guides: my grandfather and Momma as a girl; placing them as usual on the shelf above my desk. It's summer here in Brooklyn, close to your July birthday, Momma. I think of asking: did you first try to kill yourself by cutting your wrists, after you came home from Vietnam, when Bill told you he wasn't serious about getting married? How did you find out he wasn't planning to marry you after all? Another telegram? Then you decided you could be happy with Bob, Future Dad, instead, when he started coming around the house on Linden Street? But you hid those scars on your wrists with bracelets, until after you were married. It sounds like you were happy being married, at least for a while, until maybe motherhood overwhelmed you, added to your other struggles. Dad loved you a lot. Once, he told me his pet name for you: Pigeon.

Dad told me many times your suicide wasn't my fault. Did anyone tell you that your father's suicide wasn't your fault? Dad said you felt like your father's suicide was your fault. How did he know that? Did you talk to him about how you felt?

I can't keep up with your prodigious appetite for reading, that list of books from this second-to-last letter to Jean, the bracelet letter, when you were pregnant with me. Multiple books from your reading list deal in some way with suicide. *Rock Wagram*, for example, is one of the things you read back when you were still in Saigon, four years before this almost-last letter to Jean. In that Saroyan novel, the main character also has a father who died by suicide. Were you always thinking about suicide, about your father?

CHAPTER 26

Mum

Next, a note scrawled on the back of a Valentine's card, a month after I was born. Momma sounds happy; Nana recently visited to help.

> February 13, 1962
>
> Dear Mother,
>
> Have been slightly busy! Can't tell you how much you helped and how missed you've been. Hard to keep ahead of Hilary—she is thriving—8 ½ pounds now. Must say she has us all a little awe-struck.
>
> Sydney is 'adjusting' gradually.

A year after Momma died, when I was seven, I asked to be taken to see Momma's grave. We were visiting Nana, our annual summer pilgrimage to Sharon, the first summer Momma wasn't with us. After a week or more at Nana's, we always continued to our other grandparents in Missouri. I hated that part of the trip, days of driving in the broiling car, visiting a bunch of Dad's relatives along the way. But I loved staying with Nana. In return, she doted on me.

In Nana's eyes, the ranch house where she lived at the end of her life was a few steps down from the comfort and luxury of

Linden Street. But to me, visiting Nana in her clean, new house, having her cook and care for me, was a luxury. In Amherst, I had no mother to take care of me. We had different student renters, "the girls," moving out before the end of every year. I had to do housework every week, a constant source of tension with Sydney who dragged her feet about helping, and left piles of her unfinished homework in the kitchen. We had Dad's poster on the kitchen wall, the friendly gopher professing to eat problems for breakfast.

The summer afternoon at Nana's, when I asked to visit Momma's grave, Dad and Nana refused. Dad hated cemeteries. The idea of visiting not just anyone's grave, but Momma's, was too painful, like holding a fresh burn next to a hot surface. I heard his annoyance and pain in the way he abruptly said, "No." The same way he took the phone from me in the kitchen that day and barked in the receiver, "There is no Mrs. Plattner."

Nana probably would have taken me to Momma's grave; she still drove to familiar places like the beauty parlor, supermarket, and church. But she wouldn't go against Dad's wishes, not in front of him.

I threw myself on the floor in the doorway between Nana's tidy kitchen and her formal dining room, what she called her sunken dining room because of the single step that led down to her gleaming mahogany table. The room, which smelled of lemon furniture polish, was a favorite place to play for me and Sydney. It reminded me of a swimming pool with its emerald-green wall-to-wall carpet, always perfectly clean and smooth. That afternoon, instead of playing, I lay on the green carpet, sobbing. Sydney had already occupied herself somewhere else.

"She must be tired," Nana declared, letting me know I was too old for what she usually called "that kind of childish nonsense."

My tantrum wasn't something I planned. I cried without being able to stop myself, wanting something I couldn't name. The only wish I could manage to say: "I want to see Momma's grave."

Dad and Nana left me crying on the floor at the edge of Nana's dining room. One of the few times I remember when Nana didn't do everything she could to make me happy.

> February 20, 1962
>
> Dear Mother,
>
> ...this is one of those few benign moments when I feel terribly 'organized' and self-righteous about it all. The apartment is fairly neat, clothes in the washer, table set, everything ready to pop in the oven for dinner. I've been managing everything this way ever since you left, but no matter what the preliminary preparation all hell seems to break loose at 6:00, with a wild scramble to get all of us fed. The baby's eating cereal and vegetables now—and while I'm feeding her, Sydney invariably joins in the chaos—either littering the floor with tons of food or else picking that moment to throw a temper tantrum or undress herself. So Bob usually arrives home to a screaming, half-naked, pablum splattered household. I've taken to barricading myself in the kitchen with the gate and just ignoring it all.

Nana's ranch house stood on a street of similar houses across from a sprawling park. On random weekend mornings, a few Shetland ponies appeared somewhere in the park, brought by a man offering rides, but we always had to hunt for the ponies.

When we were at Nana's, Momma and Dad always took us to find the cute miniature horses.

> March 1, 1962
>
> Dear Mother,
>
> The baby has been just an angel the past week, like a well-timed clock-piece, sleeping from 9:00 or 10:00 at night (tho' sometimes later) until 5:00 a.m.
>
> Did so enjoy talking to you on the phone. Wish we could do it more often.

That first year we visited Nana without Momma, that same summer when Dad refused to take me to see where Momma was buried, he took us to find the ponies. When we found them, he paid the man for our turn to be led in a circle, seated in a saddle on the back of one of the sweet ponies with the long tails and wispy bangs. Sydney was nine already, maybe slightly too big to ride a Shetland. Still, she went first. Not even halfway around the path in the grass, the pony turned its adorable head and chomped down on Sydney's bare knee. Her mouth opened wide to let out a scream.

Dad rushed to help Sydney, yelling at the man. "How could you let children ride these dangerous animals!"

Sydney, quiet after her single scream, continued sitting on the shaggy Shetland while Dad shouted at the pony's handler. I felt stunned that the pony had bitten her but also relieved it happened to her, not me. That was the last time we looked for the Shetlands when we visited Nana's. Was it always like that after Momma died? Dad, easily irritated, angry. Crybaby big sister. And me: resentful, silent.

• • •

Oakwood Cemetery in Sharon is still there. The name chimes a familiar tone in my mind when I google the name. The wooded grounds in the pictures online look familiar, but maybe most cemeteries look similar. I'm pretty sure Nana did sneak me there once to stand by Momma's granite gravestone. That could have been during one of the solo visits I made to her home outside Pittsburg when I was in junior high; one of the times she bought my plane ticket to come see her, before she died. By then her eyesight was so bad, she hired a driver to take her to and from the airport.

Momma wrote two letters in May 1962, thanking Nana for her recent visits to care for me and my sister while Momma and Dad went apartment hunting in Ann Arbor; they planned to move that summer so Dad could start a PhD program at the University of Michigan in the fall.

> [Late June, exact date illegible], 1962
>
> Dear Mother,
>
> Bob arrived home Thursday night. The news: we have a house! The one I described to you. Bob called me Wednesday to tell me his offer had finally been accepted—with stove and refrigerator thrown in. This is the one with the apartment to rent on the second floor...We still don't have an exact moving day. Probably early next week.

On a visit to Sharon when I was eight or nine, a year or so after the pony bit my sister, Nana drove me in her pale blue Plymouth across town to show me the two houses on Linden Street. My grandmother complained the whole drive about how terrible it was that the current owners painted the bricks of the houses with white paint. The current owners were ruining the bricks with the paint, or they were ruining the bricks by not keeping them well-painted. Something about moisture seeping into the bricks near the ground at the back of the house. She went on for so long about the bricks, the paint, the moisture that it sounded like she was talking about one of her own illnesses, not houses.

I lay in the back seat, so bored I barely lifted my head to glance out the car window as we inched past the houses on Linden Street. I didn't think about the fact that Nana was almost blind and rarely drove anywhere anymore. I didn't know I should be anxious, riding in the car with her behind the steering wheel. Only years later did I wish I had sat up and stared at those houses as Nana drove slowly by. The place she once lived with her parents, where she grew up. Where Momma grew up too. Where Grandfather Henry lived until he shot himself.

• • •

On the computer at my desk in Brooklyn, I look up the Linden Street address in Sharon. There's a picture of a brick house set far back from the road. A long, grassy front yard. A modest house, far from the grand mansion Nana conjured up in my childhood imagination.

Next door stands the house where Nana's parents lived. White front columns, but not huge. Online, I can even view pictures of a few interior rooms, which gives me a creepy feeling. These people who lived there: Eleanor, the young girl with thick glasses, her lazy eye. Her mother, Maude, with the pale hair and violet eyes. J. R., the scholarly-looking businessman with a neat goatee who died after a car trip to Tucson. The same J. R. who didn't want Eleanor, his sickly only child, to move away, so he built a house for her next door when she married. The house where Eleanor's husband shot himself in the head on a Sunday night after eighteen years of marriage. Leaving Eleanor with two children, Ann and Bake. I feel as if I might glimpse these people in those matching brick houses. But no, the rooms are empty; those people, gone.

• • •

If you wrote to your father, Momma, what would you tell him? Dear Dad… if that's what you called him, when you were ten and he shot himself in the head, and Nana-Mum had the fake "accident while cleaning his rifle" obituary printed in the town paper.

Dear Daddy, it was so stupid and selfish what you did, you wrecked my life. I never stopped missing you. Never stopped blaming myself.

I can't get her voice right, even though I've had her voice with me now through all her letters, to Dad, to Jean. Now, these Dear Mother letters that go on and on. What that writing teacher wanted me to cut, cut, cut. Just as Momma had cut her wrists. Then cut herself right out of her own picture, out of my life.

I know there must have been a rage in her that she turned against herself. If she directed that rage at her father instead, what would she say? What would you say, Momma? There he is in that picture next to you on the shelf over my desk, both of you tucked beside each other behind the base of my lamp.

Tell him, Momma, what a stupid selfish shit he was, but that you still love him. How do you go from rage to forgiveness? What bridge takes anyone from here to there?

CHAPTER 27

Playpen

Sunday

Dear Jeanne,

When the telegram arrived I was absolutely limp with delight, and with an almost-tinge of amazement as if it hadn't been after all something we'd been "expecting all along." And what a coup to surprise everyone, and with a mad dash in the middle of the night. And a boy at that! Bob and I both so terribly pleased for you and will enjoy hearing more-and-all-about-him.

Your letters kept us entertained for days: Reid's—such a pleasure to read (and "see" Washington again.) I was still chuckling this morning over perky alias Cosmo McMoon, The YWCA, et al. Oh yes, and I'll send the Maud Harris book back. It has been a favorite.

I must tell you about the real estate agent when we were up here for the first time "looking." He kept showing us places, very patiently, yet all the while nudging into the subdivision type areas. In spite of our trying-to-be-polite oh, no's. At one point he described one section of "downtown" with a grand flourish and mentionned [sic] "all sorts of queer people." Really from the way he said it I imagined everything from ax murder to general mayhem. Until he added (I was frankly beginning to panic) "You know" as if that explained it all, "People from all over the world..."

Talk about comic relief.

I had a rare excursion this morning to bookstore by the campus while Bob stayed home and watched les enfants. Usually I take Sydney & Hilary Everywhere so that it was a real treat just to browse. Wonderful dark damp bookstore with rows and rows of pocketbooks, books half uncrated, here on shelves or in jumbled piles on the floor, aisles so negligible it was hard to squeeze past someone coming the other way. Everything from Mickey Spillane to dietary aids to Eugenie Grandet and back again, to a stack of Faulkner anthologies hastily propped up by the cash register. Children's books, too, and toys. Scores of model airplanes, balloons, Dr. Seuss but no "Jack and the Beanstalk." After reading all the titles, thumbing here and there, checking the critics, I came away reluctantly with a mere "Three" by Gore Vidal,[63] "Pale Horse, Pale Rider,"[64] and Jean Stafford's "The Mountain Lion."[65] Next the market where shades of the old cracker barrel there were a half a dozen big brown paper bags on the floor filled with bagels and various other hand rolls. A girl standing in line with a poppyseed-covered one clutched in one hand, changed her mind, put it back and took another. The milieu after Columbus is—to be slightly canny—"exhilarating." Like being suddenly catapulted from Isaly's to Istanbul. A rather exotic reference I'll admit for moderately attractive, conservative little Ann Arbor. Nevertheless, I find myself constantly cataloging detail as if it were an end in itself. Sights, sounds, sensations bigger than life-size. Amazed even by, and perhaps especially by, the trivial. So I'm delighted with the beady sandles [sic] all those "queer people," Indians, Chinese, many accents mixed in with the smooth shaven, the Village Store or just simply the overworked housewife pack. A Ben Casey type in a white medic coat buying a pound of butter and a box of thumbtacks. The big triumph though was on the way home passing two ladies peering under the hood of a stalled car—both wearing white gloves and identical pillbox hats, one blue, one yellow, absolutely spilling over with huge floppy roses. The original gold-dust twins?

Have just hung up from Mother's call. "Todd." I vastly approve. I do like it.

I mentioned we had lost our quote interesting unquote roomers. After cleaning up the apartment this past week I am not sorry—or how to feel you know someone intimately without even trying. After scotch tape on the walls, cobwebs hanging on the bathtub, and a grease splattered kitchen, I'm convinced that Bohemians age better in art or at least at a respectable distance. They casually dropped the information that they were leaving in less than a week over Martinis one evening after which could barely manage to be civil. Not that the fact was so world shaking in itself, but it couldn't have come at a worse time with just getting settled and Bob so utterly tied up with school and how in heaven's name do you go about being a "landlord." Anyway, we've been frantically painting, patching and (this time) compiling a lease with help of New Covenants and the "Handy Legal Advisor." Our new tenants—please don't snicker—football coach at the University high school and his wife a dental hygenist [sic]. The only way I can describe them is that they're so terribly young and dewy that it's almost painful. She is trim, petite and he's hardly taller than I am but awfully healthy looking. He's also enrolled at the University and just <u>how</u> one goes about getting a "doctorate in physical education" we've spent many hours musing about. Without having yet met him, Bob is certain he's a frustrated intellectual.

I really had better close up this rambling account for the evening and PREPARE 1) for a visit from Bob's parents and brother this next week and 2) the following week expected measles for <u>both</u> Sydney and Hilary. At this point I don't know which prospect is the most enticing.

Tell us all about the house—it sounds fabulous—when you can.

Ann

That was Momma's last letter to Jean, although there's nothing in it that signals the coming breakup of their long friendship; no evidence that the loss of that friendship was another step in Momma's decline. It was 1962, probably early fall. I was almost a year old. My parents were settling in Ann Arbor, soon after Jean and her family relocated to DC.

Reid's Cosmé McMoon alias refers to the Mexican American pianist, composer, and accompanist for Florence Foster Jenkins.

I wonder if Momma would have enjoyed the mediocre 2016 movie version of that story, starring Meryl Streep as the infamous tone-deaf soprano.

Momma's description of her visit to a local bookstore near the university portrays herself as a kid in a candy store, although she only bought three volumes. I can still picture one of those books, *Pale Horse, Pale Rider*, on the bookshelf in our Amherst living room, several moves later and several years after she was dead. A paperback with a thin, white spine, evidence she had existed.

Among the authors and titles she mentions not getting that day: Mickey Spillane, American crime novelist; plus *Eugenie Grandet*, Balzac's first novel from his Comédie humaine cycle. The Maude Harris Momma returned to Jean must have been a children's book she read to Sydney, maybe also to me.

A single short word scribbled in that last letter, I puzzled over for ages, unable to make out Momma's writing. Did it say "Italy"? That didn't quite fit. One more brisk google: eureka! I got it. Like *Pale Horse, Pale Rider*, not on its own anything important about my mother's life. But learning that Isaly's was a chain of family restaurants in the Midwest from the early 1900s until the '70s feels as sustaining as finding the right food to satisfy a ravenous craving. That image doesn't quite capture the feeling I want to express though. Momma would've been better at finding the right words. If she was still here, I would ask her.

The Gold Dust Twins, I learn from looking it up: a popular radio program from the 1920s, named after the equally popular Gold Dust soap powder, an early advertising-world product tie-in. Both product and program were phased out in the 1950s with a dawning awareness of the racist logo: a demeaning caricature of two black children, the original Gold Dust twins.

Of the tenants Momma describes—a pair of bohemians that came with the Ann Arbor house, and the doctoral candidate in physical education and his trim wife—none fit my memory of the time I was woken in the night and carried upstairs by Dad. The renters I remember were two young women who lived upstairs and sometimes babysat for us.

One story Dad sometimes recounted about Ann Arbor, one of the few that included Momma, had nothing to do with her hospital stay. His story could have been called "The Playpen," and featured a classic piece of baby equipment. Momma didn't use ours to contain me and my sister though. Instead, Sydney and I were allowed to explore our apartment while Momma climbed inside the pen, turning the enclosure into a protected reading spot. She must have needed that reading sanctuary. I remember my own homemade reading spot beneath my bed, in my new bedroom in the addition, built by Dad after Momma died. I imagine reading satisfied her craving: for meaning; for calm, when Syd and I were small. I picture Momma sitting cross-legged inside our playpen, behind the net walls, her head of short, dark hair bent over the pages of a book.

• • •

Our college-graduate daughter is living at home with us in Brooklyn again, in our compact, crowded apartment, while working full-time in the city, the job she successfully got after dropping her grad school plans, completing our *Parachute* career-exploration activities; saving up so at some point in the future, she can afford to rent her own apartment, a place she hopes to share with friends. A hard-to-attain dream in our current city.

I meet her in the city for lunch in the middle of a workday. We sit face-to-face in a dimly lit, nearly empty Mediterranean place near Grand Central, and I try to listen to what's going on in her life. Once before, a couple of months ago, we met in this same lunch spot. I'm proposing we make these dates more regular, maybe monthly. Something I didn't get to do with Momma. Soon after the start of lunch, her gnocchi, my salad, a leaky teapot, a waiter hovering forever, I'm mopping up wasted tea, and she's already annoyed with me. A suggestion I made of someone she could ask about her resume that she wants to update. I try asking her other things, but I can tell she's still irritated that I tried to advise her when she didn't ask for help. Even talking about clothes, a favorite topic of hers, doesn't help.

After lunch, we walk together along chilly fall city streets. I feel like weeping when I hold the arm of her jacket for a minute in the doorway of her office building. Sometimes when my heart is open, like after one of these mother-daughter lunches, a minor goodbye still feels like a major farewell. I remind myself I'm going to see her at home in a few hours. It's her turn to cook. On her night, she makes margherita pizza for the family; takes her dinner into her room, talks to her boyfriend on the phone while watching shows on her laptop. These times of seeing her alone are brief, like sighting a wild animal, a stylish, fashion-loving one.

• • •

Well, Momma, I have no more new thoughts to share with you right now. I'll leave you to read in the playpen, or let you sit there beside your father on the shelf over my desk.

No, OK, I do have one question, if you can listen to one more angry rant, hopefully my last: what were you thinking when you decided to have children? Was it a sort of knee-jerk, automatic, nothing-else-to-do-but-this kind of decision? Or did you genuinely think about it, consider if you actually wanted to be a mother, and then give the decision the go-ahead in your mind? After weighing all the options and choosing this one: motherhood. Deciding you were ready to give it your all.

Because that's what I tried to do, when I made my motherhood-or-not decision; and then had to decide over and over to keep trying, through many miscarriages; and through the stop-start, repeatedly deciding to try again, in the jumping-over-hurdles, complicated process of adoption.

No, I get it, it was the tail end of the 1950s when you conceived Sydney. Then the early '60s when you must've decided to keep going and have the typical two kids, evenly spaced two years apart, to get the project accomplished as soon as possible as many parents did back then and still do. After all, you were almost thirty by the time I was born. Probably you also thought: let's give them both a playmate; one can always entertain the other. Maybe also, after turning your ticker to the question of kids or no kids, you might have entertained the notion of a "what the hell else am I supposed to do with my life in a 1960s pre-feminism, lack of many other options for women" world? Well, you certainly made a mess of everything, you know, leaving the way you did.

Also, it's interesting to note your rating of a visit from Bob-Dad's parents and brother as equal to contracting a case of measles, since I also never felt much fondness for that side of the family. Another thing we have, or had, in common.

CHAPTER 28

The Big Storm

> Sept. 14, 1962
>
> Dear Mother,
>
> Bob starts school Monday; today got his courses scheduled. Tomorrow registration. This place is such a huge factory that it's a real ordeal. Sydney also starts to kindergarten the 17th. Had to take her for a 'teacher-child conference,' and she could hardly be dragged away. When we got home she burst into Hilary's room to tell her all about it: 'go to a big building, Hilly…' She was so absorbed that when I walked into the room at this point she shouted—'No, Mommy, go away. I talking to Hilly.'

The return address on that letter to Nana: West Huron Street in Ann Arbor, Michigan. In my typed, abridged draft of these letters that I saved, I recorded the street name but no house number. Our new house had a yard with a cherry tree. I have a memory of seeing a stream of water rushing out of the high, leafy branches, down the trunk. I have no explanation for this image. Maybe Dad snaked a hose up into the branches of the tree, but I don't know why he would have watered it like that.

October 22, 1962

Dear Mother,

I'm so sorry I missed you. I had been thinking of how nice it would be to talk to you that day—but surpressed [sic] the urge to call. Money. Money. Believe it or not, I just figured up that we have spent $75 in doctor bills this past month. Mostly office calls as I keep trotting Sydney and Hilary alternately across the street.

In spite of which have really been gadding about (for me—that is, relatively) this past week, with the book sale the night you called, a visit to the University art gallery one afternoon, … Also went to the first of the APA productions (the professional theater group here)—'We, Comrades Three,' given a mention in today's NY Times in the theater section under Prognosis: Hopeful. This is an original drama by Richard Baldridge, playwright-in-residence, and is possibly destined for a Broadway run next year. Bob and I both have tickets for Ibsen's 'Ghosts,' next week with Eva Le Gallienne.

When I google those plays, I find *We, Comrades Three* made it to the Lyceum Theatre on Broadway but not until December 1966 and only for eleven performances. Eva Le Gallienne starred in Ibsen's *Ghosts*, at the Lydia Mendelssohn Theatre at Ann Arbor's University of Michigan, October 24 to October 28, 1962. I think the plays Momma had Dad see with her were part of her personal life support system.

Our house was small and white and sat on a corner. Soon, Dad built a fence, a tall redwood enclosure around our yard. Maybe our house on the corner inspired him to protect us and keep us out of the street. He wasn't usually such a protective parent, apparently not objecting to Momma barricading herself in our playpen, while Sydney and I roamed freely through the apartment.

> January 7, 1963
>
> Dear Mother,
>
> After we had waited and watched your plane leave, waved good-bye, etc.—explaining how you were going back to Sharon, Penna—Sydney asked in a very forlorn voice, 'Where's Nana?' as if she hadn't realized at all that you were really leaving. We all rather felt the same way yesterday.

When we were old enough to explore the yard on our own, Sydney discovered a knothole in the fence. Small enough to fit into one child-sized palm, the circle of wood slipped out when my sister pushed on it, opening up an eye-level peephole. She showed me how to put my eye to the miniature window, an opening to the world beyond our yard. A world made more alluring and important because of our separation from it. There was not much to see out there though: the street was dead quiet, hardly anyone walking past on the sidewalk. Maybe it was summer at the time, the nearby university not in session.

> January 17, 1963
>
> Dear Mother,
>
> In spare time have been absolutely immersed in 'Ship of Fools'[66]—interesting but falling somewhat short of expectations.

Sydney and I took turns carrying around the borrowed knothole when we played in the yard, careful to always return the missing piece to the fence afterward. Dad eventually found out about the removable circle and ended that game, nailing the knothole permanently in place. Sydney and I protested, but Dad didn't get it. What was so special about being able to remove a piece of wood, peer out a tiny window, then replace the disc like a perfectly fitted puzzle piece? He worried about the knothole getting lost. The discovery of a secret window and the fascinating world beyond our yard were nothing new to him.

Another paperback made it through the move to a different state; *Ship of Fools* sat on the living room bookshelf in Amherst near *Pale Horse, Pale Rider*, surviving longer than Momma. *Fools*, another book on my must-read list, even though Momma commented it failed to live up to expectations. I tried reading that book by Porter once before but was put off by the long list of characters. Of interest: one of *Pale Rider's* three novellas contains another suicide story. Momma was truly obsessed.

> February 6, 1963
>
> Dear Mother,
>
> Guess what! Bob is taking French this semester. I've just been reviewing pronunciation with him. He can take two courses to fulfill his language requirement—this is a five-hour beginning class—(8:00 in the morning of all things.) What a thing to have to plunge into at this point.

My mother, the French major who lived in Paris her junior year of college. Her knowledge of that second language helped land her a Foreign Service job in Saigon. Back in the US, living in a college town, housewife with two young kids, no paid employment, tutoring her husband in elementary French, hiding in a playpen to steal a few minutes to read. I can imagine she felt unhappy, even trapped, during those Ann Arbor years.

> [Date illegible, February or March] 1963
>
> Dear Mother,
>
> We painted Sydney's room—ivory. This time in an enamel which should be easier to wash. It had taken on a really 'used' look to say the least. Actually, we put on a pink first which turned out on the walls to be a shade too awful to describe. (We kept saying it couldn't dry that way but it did!) So the next day we did the whole job completely over again. Sydney was carried away with the whole project—when we ran out of paint the 2nd time and had to go out to get some more she wanted to know, 'What color are we going to paint it now?'
>
> I know how overwhelming it must be for you about Jean and Reid. I just can't accept it I guess. (Bob's typical inflexible reaction somehow says it best: why that's the goddamnedest thing I've ever heard of!).

That sounds like something Dad would say. This is the first reference to Jean and Reid's breakup. This also sounds like the Momma I've come to know from her letters: covering up the heartbreak she probably felt at the dissolution of Jean and Reid's marriage with a comic story about another home decorating mishap.

> [Date illegible again, probably late June] 1963
>
> Dear Mother,
>
> Finally heard from Mrs. Rose at the Family Planning Services just after you had left. I do have a doctor, enfin, and will be seeing him initially July 15th. However, I won't actually be starting in with him until the end of the month. As yet I have no idea of what he charges—will have to find out at the first appointment. Anyway he comes recommended by both Dr. Hall and head of the University Hospital Psychiatric staff. At least something will be started—and please don't worry, I know I will be able to manage all right this summer—truly I feel much rested and much less tense after your very pampering visit. I can't tell you how marvelous it was just to get out some and not have the children <u>all</u> the time. Will never be able to thank you enough for coming to help out.

This is the first mention by Momma of starting to see a psychiatrist. As far as I know, she never sought help from any type of therapist before this point. All I know about her history of psychiatric problems was what Dad told me when I was older about the scars on her wrists, that she cut her wrists around the time she returned from Vietnam, the "married man who dumped her" story, before she married Dad.

Once again, Nana's recent visit to our family in Ann Arbor made all the difference to Momma. My sister and I were both home with her almost full-time. The parent-run coop preschool Sydney attended, where I also soon went, didn't provide Momma with much of a break. I know from what Dad told me at some point that she had additional volunteer responsibilities, including regular weekly or monthly hours helping in the classroom, taking care of more preschoolers.

> July 29, 1963
>
> Dear Mother,
>
> … Saturday night we went out with Bob's friends from New Zealand. A really marvelous evening. A German festival type thing out in the woods with a real oom-pa oom-pa band, Tyrolian costumes, and all. With simply mobs of people (we met several other couples in the business school there, too), picnic tables, huge pitchers of beer, and much Student Prince atmosphere, it turned out to be a real gala affair.
>
> I'll let you know more about the money thing later. My first actual appointment is this evening. I'm sure we'll probably be billed by the month and unless or until I let you know differently, anytime that is most convenient for you to send a check during the month will be all right here. Lord, that will run $80–100 per month depending on the number of 'Mondays.'

Nana was apparently paying for Momma's psychiatrist. Up to this point, it never occurred to me to request information about my mother's psychiatric record from that period in Ann Arbor. Finding out more about Momma's life following her suicide attempt when I was three felt overwhelming. But with Momma's picture in front of me over my desk, along with my grandfather, "my two suicides" as I've started calling them, the idea begins to gel. I start poking around online.

My mother was hospitalized sometime between the spring of 1964, when the Nana letters ended, and the summer of 1966 when we moved to Amherst. Fortunately for me in this case, HIPAA protection lasts only fifty years, I learn from reading online; if any health records for my mother still exist, I should be able to access them.

Momma never names her doctor in her letters, only the hospital. A place in Ann Arbor that still exists, but the blurb on their website says the current building only opened in 1986. When I call the number listed online, not surprisingly, the first thing I'm told by a friendly, youthful-sounding female receptionist: University Hospital has no records older than 1986. When the young woman on the phone transfers me to the hospital PR department, they promptly disconnect my call.

> Sept. 13, 1963
>
> Dear Mother,
>
> Bob has a very tight schedule this semester. You know, he has, theoretically, a 20-hour a week research job to augment the fellowship. This will apparently entail doing various projects for Dr. W., one of the professors, but so far he hasn't been pressed into doing much of anything. It is unlikely, however, that this euphoria will last. In any case, it has given him extra time to prepare for his French reading exam next week.
>
> About the money for the psychiatrist—here's a run-down: 2 appointments in July and 4 in August came to $120. Exempting Labor Day Monday, there'll be 4 appt's or $80 for September. So with the initial $100 check you sent, it will take another $100 to cover expenses up to the end of this month. If you wish, and to avoid any unnecessary dickering back and forth

> about this, you can merely count up the Mondays in any month and send the appropriate amount after this. We are of course keeping track of all this as a loan. I wish there were more I could tell you about it except 'the cost' but it's simply not the sort of thing I can discuss—so far just a lot of loose ends and a lot of 'talk.' I hope you won't be offended by any lack of communication on this score.

Momma's decline: increasingly more focus on payments for her psychiatrist; fewer details about things she enjoyed, like books, plays, movies, music. No more Jean letters.

> November 24, 1963
>
> Dear Mother,
>
> ...You asked about suggestions for us—I thought I mentioned Folk music recording while you were here—Joan Baez in particular. There is really nothing else that we need or would enjoy so much. Of course if you can't find this particular 'artiste,' anything else in the same line would be just fine. This is something you can just send to both of us and we truly <u>don't</u> expect anything else.
>
> Before I forget, I will only have 3 doctor's appointments to pay for this month. How much good will come of this, if any, I have no idea as yet. I am taking a new drug, Tofranil, along with the Librium. From the little I understand about it the two have somewhat opposing effects, so that between them I feel quite 'chemically stabilized,' more than enough to carry on. Joking aside, I do feel fine.

> I have been busy this last week collecting information from various University departments and museums—rewriting a section of the guidebook that the nursery publishes and sells throughout Ann Arbor, updating and revising. In fact I was in the middle of telephoning yesterday and trying to wind the project up, when word came of the assassination. At which point all lines were immediately tied up, and everything ground to a halt here at the school and in the town as I suppose they did everywhere else.
>
> I have spent as much time last night and today as children and routine have allowed tuned in to the events on radio and TV. A rather awesome experience, not just the tragedy itself, but seeing this sort of thing for the first time given the full mass media treatment.

On my computer, I look up the names of the drugs Momma listed. Librium: a sedative. Tofranil: an antidepressant. The accompanying basic info includes warnings about the need to report any new or worsening symptoms, especially any suicidal thoughts, to your doctor. A downer and an upper; no wonder Momma felt "chemically stabilized." I guess her psychiatrist missed the signs of her worsening symptoms, which soon arrived.

As I grew up, I frequently asked Dad, "What was Momma like?" One line I remember him saying: "She was always really up or really down." He sounded sad when he gave me that description of Momma, as if he carried a heavy load of apologies about her, adding, "When I came home at the end of the day, I never knew what to expect. I had to leave you and your sister with her though. I had to go to work." He was talking about Ann Arbor when he was in graduate school.

I didn't remember Momma always being really up or really down. Reading that last Nana letter, I remembered Dad's words. I wondered if it was the medications Momma took that shifted her mood up and down. But how much was she already like that, before the mood-altering drugs? I remembered the word "mania" from Grandfather Henry's death certificate. If he was bipolar, was Momma bipolar too?

Momma mentions rewriting a section of the nursery guidebook, part of those volunteer duties for Sydney's cooperative preschool. Maybe Momma, who previously worked as a secretary, enjoyed having responsibilities beyond home and childcare.

The assassination of President Kennedy took place on November 22, 1963, two days before that letter. By "awesome," I think Momma meant not wonderful, but inspiring apprehension and fear, a more outdated use of the word. She was also commenting on the relatively new, mesmerizing, and magnifying power of the news media, particularly television.

Nana must have gotten Momma and Dad the requested Joan Baez album. By Christmas that year, Baez had two albums out, Volumes 1 and 2, released in 1960 and 1961. It was the first of these that I think Nana gave Momma and Dad. When I look up the albums online, the cover of Volume 1 leaps out at me, a familiar image engraved in my mind. A head-to-waist shot of young Joan Baez, strumming her guitar, her name printed in red caps across a stark black-and-white photo. One of several dozen vinyl records in that wooden cabinet built by handyman Dad, where years later in Amherst, when I was about eight, I found Momma's file marked Personal, preserved like a fossil, pressed between those music records on the far-right side, weighed down by the geological eons of our family history.

That album is listed on someone's online catalog of 1001 albums you must hear before you die. When I search on Spotify and listen to the folk songs from that record, each one makes me feel like crying and throwing up, each mournful, haunting song evoking the lonely atmosphere of motherless years from my childhood.

January 27, 1964

Dear Mother,

Bob's exam Saturday was practically an all-day affair.

As I mentioned, last week was busy. Got your cookie dough finally all rolled out and cut so that we have all been enjoying this post-Christmas treat. Took some of them to the Dame's meeting on Tuesday—the program was a talk by 'Mrs. Michigan' (or how to make almost anyone feel like an incompetent housekeeper by comparison). Actually she gave a most informal and amusing chat on all the trials of becoming a title-winner. She was, by the way, one of the top-ten in the country. Frankly, though, Bob was more amused than anyone by the occasion, since I spent about two hours beforehand 'getting groomed-to-the-teeth,' for this event: at least makeup, seams straight and all that.

Then Saturday night Bob and I saw the Stratford Players in the Hollow Crown—a kind of pastiche on the kings and queens of England (from many sources). Wonderful satire. Afterwards went to Winnie's for a late party with a few other couples from the business school.

Poking around online, I find The Royal Shakespeare Company performed *The Hollow Crown* in Ann Arbor on Saturday, January 25, 1964, part of a tour of the US and Canada, more of Momma's lifeline.

I remember from around then, Momma invited a friend over for drinks after dinner, the only time I recall that happening. I begged to be allowed to stay up with the adults. Instead, I was sent to bed early so Momma could see her friend. My sister must have been in bed already; Dad could have been out at school. My bedroom door didn't lock. I could have run into the living room, interrupting Momma and her friend. Instead, I got out of bed, threw myself on the floor and cried until I fell asleep. An earlier version of the tantrum I had when I didn't get to visit Momma's grave.

The time in Ann Arbor, when I woke up, I found myself on the carpet by the door. It must have been almost morning. My body felt stiff from sleeping on the floor. I realized no one came in to check on me during the night.

February 5, 1964

Dear Mother,

Have been at a Nursery meeting this evening. Tomorrow night a Fine arts lecture on Architecture. Last week was quite busy, too, with Interior Decorating and Nursery meetings, the Russian film 'My Name is Ivan'[67] (winner of all kinds of prizes this last year), a sherry party Sunday afternoon at Morgans', friends of Bob's in the Business school. Friday night Winnie and Frank came here for cocktails, etc. and then we all went out to dinner, and back here afterwards for coffee, brandy and dessert. This was a kind of post-celebration of the pre-lim though Bob still hasn't heard the results.

I received an incredible letter from Jean. Quote…I realize you are suffering from illness, and have been for a prolonged time, and are not exactly in schoolgirl bloom, etc. etc. Unquote. No mention of Christmas gifts. Rather demoralizing to say the least—the kind of thing that leaves one with a 'what the hell does she mean by that' impression, since everything couched in innuendo—no straightforward statements. I know I shouldn't even mention it since I know you have had Jean and repercussions up-to-here. But I am curious to know if all this is based on mere speculations on her part—after you said you had never mentioned anything to her about 'my problems'? Enough of that. Though I would be interested in your opinion.

Jean and Reid's marriage had fallen apart. It was over a year since Momma's last letter to Jean. It sounds like Jean wrote something about Momma's psychiatric problems that my mother found insulting. Momma carefully phrases her question to Nana about how Jean knew about her problems. The offending letter must have marked a break in the friendship between Momma and Jean. My mother no longer wrote letters to her old friend, at least none that Jean gave me.

March 14, 1964

Dear Mother,

This week's 'news' can mostly be condensed into 'the Big Storm.' Tuesday we woke up to a real blizzard, after days of clear weather. Sydney came

> dashing in early in the morning to ask what all the cars were doing out front. Well, I took a quick look, and West Huron was one big traffic jam—with four solid lines of cars moving at a snail's pace. That was just the beginning. Bob did manage to get over to school, but the snow continued all day without let-up. All plans for the day were cancelled and we just stayed home and hibernated.
>
> Our biggest news: Odetta is going to be here tomorrow night. Bob got tickets, so at last we'll be able to see her in person.

That's the last letter I have from Momma to Nana. News about a snowstorm and plans to attend an Odetta concert. Seated at my desk in my cozy Brooklyn bedroom, a lifetime later, fall 2022, I search the weather history for March 10, 1964. It did snow that Tuesday, but I can't find a record of how many inches fell that day. Instead, I locate a *Michigan Daily* ad for that Odetta concert, March 14 at the university's Hill Auditorium. Tickets were incredibly cheap by today's standards: one dollar, $1.25, and $1.50. The charge for each of Momma's psychiatrist appointments, also unbelievably inexpensive by today's prices: twenty dollars a pop.

The March 14 date of the Odetta performance in that letter is confusing though. Momma wrote that the concert was the *next* day, but the ad lists the concert on the *same* date as Momma's letter. Probably she put the wrong date in her letter. I assume my parents got to hear Odetta's concert. By the next day, the big storm was over.

• • •

After reaching a dead end trying to access Momma's hospital records, I don't want to give up. Maybe I can at least learn something about the history of the hospital. Poking around online, I find not just one but two historical associations in Ann Arbor. With a sort of hopeless, what-the-heck feeling, I email a few questions to both. According to both websites, resident historians can take up to two weeks to answer. Surprisingly, within days, someone from one of the places responds: due to HIPAA, there's no way to acccss the medical records of another person, unless I'm the patient's designated proxy.

How could I be my mother's designated healthcare proxy? I silently fume. HIPAA didn't exist when Momma was alive. The woman who emailed me might be a historian, but she doesn't know that HIPAA only extends fifty years into the past. Even I know that from a little online research.

When I email the woman again, she sends back a link to the 150-year history of that Ann Arbor institution. The hospital, described in its online history as a rugged fortress on a hill, humbly claims credit for bringing the shade known as hospital green—chosen over basic white for its quality of restfulness on the eyes—to the walls of surgeries and hospitals worldwide. Also included is a link to the hospital's Release of Information Unit, where I can finally fill out forms requesting records for deceased individuals.

• • •

Note to my two suicides: Momma, Grandfather. I continue to drink a lot of tea when I look at your papers. The tea reminds me of Nana, her pocket watch filled with the pills she always added to her tea, whether it was saccharine or medicine for her mysterious blood ailment or both.

Momma, Grandfather, I don't think either of you meant to pass on your problems the way you did, dropping that sense of sadness down to the next generation like Nana dropping her pills into her tea. I take my tea with milk. No sugar, no saccharine, no medicine. The sadness is still there, hard to escape.

Momma, I finished reading *Dubliners* and loved it; I read it before in graduate school but didn't remember much. What did you think of that book of stories? Did you like it as much as you loved almost everything by Faulkner, your favorite?

CHAPTER 29

Bake

June 2002. Reid visited me in Brooklyn. He came to New York for a conference, a meeting related to his hobby: genealogy. He stayed at a hotel in the city, braving the subway to Brooklyn for lunch one Saturday. A short visit carved out of his packed weekend.

I hadn't seen Reid in years. Hadn't met him in person many times in my life. Momma's older brother. Her painful story always kept us apart. There were those phone calls I made to him when I was in my twenties, grad school, when I was first trying to learn who my mother had been, to understand why she died, and write about her.

I was forty already that June when Reid visited. A pale, balding gentleman in his early seventies, tan raincoat, brown leather briefcase. In person, he reminded me even more of Nana than he had on the phone years earlier. He had the same jelly-filled donut body that I remembered from Nana. A similar gentle, refined way of speaking.

Over the years, Reid wrote me an infrequent card or note from Ohio. He still lived in the remote southeastern part of the state with his current wife, the post-Jean one, in the retirement cabin that was Reid's self-proclaimed attempt to recreate his idyllic childhood memories of Wheatland, his paternal grandparents' West Virginia home.

The day Reid visited, we drove to the nearby Brooklyn Botanic Garden for lunch, a warm day, a pleasant place for an outdoor meal. Reid sat in front, my husband driving, while I rode in the back with our two-year-old daughter. We didn't yet have our son. That family car trip to Wheatland with my husband and teenage son was still two decades away, after Reid was already dead.

During the drive to the BBG for lunch, Reid mentioned something he already told me years before, during one of those phone calls when I was in grad school. "My father was drinking a lot during those years."

I couldn't see my uncle's face from where I sat, just the pale, soft back of his neck. I didn't know why he was telling me that again. I didn't say: You already told me that before. Isn't there something new you can tell me? This wasn't a typical conversation for my family. Despite my occasional hard conversations with Dad about Momma's suicide, in my family we rarely talked in an open, spontaneous way about these relatives who died by suicide. Maybe seeing me made Reid want to talk about his father.

My husband, quiet by habit, chauffeured us smoothly through the thick, Saturday afternoon Brooklyn traffic, while our daughter entertained herself with a Sesame Street picture book in her car seat beside me. At the outdoor eating area of the garden, we took turns carrying our food on trays from the counter to the free table we managed to grab.

During lunch, Reid and I didn't talk about Momma—Ann, as Reid called her. It felt like a relief not to talk about her. Not to be trying to learn or understand anything about her right then. We ate cold salads. Warm chili. A hot dog cut up for my hungry daughter. Carrot cake for dessert. The adults drank iced tea. My daughter sucked watered-down juice from her bottle. We talked about Reid's genealogy conference, what he thought of New York City (he hated it). What his grown children were doing (living all over the map). I probably mentioned Jean's visit, a few years earlier, the letters from Momma she gave me. We sat under a sun umbrella, midafternoon between crowded tables.

In the car on the way home, I rode in the back again, my daughter strapped into her car seat beside me, in this brief, contained time and space. My daughter's eyes drifted closed, her head lolling to the side. My husband attempted to speed through traffic so we wouldn't waste the precious reprieve of naptime in the car. I tried asking Reid: did he know anything about Momma's earlier suicide attempt? Dad's story about the scars on her wrists, how she wore bracelets to hide the marks. With Reid in person, this was my chance to ask.

In front of me, my uncle sat up straighter, appearing surprised even from the back. He attempted to swivel his plump middle toward me, to pierce me with his soft blue eyes, so much like Nana's. "Yes," he said. "Ann did often wear bracelets."

But no to the rest of it. Reid assured me he never knew anything about an earlier suicide attempt. He never saw scars on her wrists. As far as he knew, she first tried to kill herself when we lived in Ann Arbor.

"Nana went there to take care of you," he said, "when your mother was in the hospital." Again telling me something I already knew.

Back at our house, my husband volunteered to carry our sleeping daughter inside, to transport her without waking her, like a piece of delicate china, so we could all lie down for a welcome siesta. Miraculously, the princess remained asleep when placed in her spot on our family bed. I showed Reid the couch in our living room where he could make himself comfortable. But he declined, glancing at his wristwatch.

"I should brave the subway again, I'm afraid." He apologized for the shortness of his visit.

From his briefcase, Reid slipped a thin, white paper tube into my hand. "Your family tree." The fruit of his genealogical research, he explained. He made one for each of his children, grandchildren, nieces. I noticed my tube, the width of a sheet of typing paper, was marked in pen in one corner with a tiny blue H.

I felt only a slight interest in my family tree from Reid, beyond struggling to unroll the tightly coiled paper, taking a cursory peek at the interlocking web of names that unspooled from right to left across the page, ending on the far edge with my name. A piece of paper that I had no extra energy for then, I placed the tube on a high shelf in my office, along with the papers and letters related to Momma.

Several months later, a package arrived in the mail from Ohio. Another gift from Reid: that family history, the remaining fruits of his genealogical labors. His memoir containing those stories about my relatives. Eleanor, J. R., Maude, Dad Baker, Lulu, and more names, tracing back through a dozen generations to my ancestors who crossed the Atlantic from Germany and other parts of northern Europe. Some of whom ended up at Wheatland. Little mention of those two main characters though. Momma. Grandfather Henry.

• • •

Over a decade has passed since Reid died, age eighty-one, following several strokes at the end of his life, years when we were not in close touch. If Reid was still alive, and he and I had one more chance to talk, I would ask him to try again to tell me about Momma. I don't feel hopeful, even if he never had those strokes and could still speak, that he would remember anything more about my mother. Anything that would explain her to me or bring her clearly to mind so I could let her go.

• • •

So far, I've faxed two requests for Momma's medical records to the U. of M. Hospital's Release of Information Unit in Ann Arbor. First, I called the information number listed on their website, waited on hold for fifteen minutes, spoke to one woman. Asked my questions about how to complete their two-page form. Was told about a second required form, another two pages. Spent half a day filling everything out; walking to UPS; getting the second form notarized; faxing the hospital all four pages of completed forms, plus a copy of my driver's license. Yes, just the front, the woman on the phone at the Release of Information Unit assured me.

Two weeks later, back comes an anonymous email response. I am now informed that I must also supply a copy of the deceased patient's death certificate, along with my "corrected" application.

Really? You didn't tell me that when I was on the phone asking in detail how to submit my request for medical records *of a dead person*. That the patient in question was dead was no secret. That was the whole point of the second required hospital form: Affidavit of Heir. You can't be an heir unless the patient is dead. That is the second, and real reason, that HIPAA is a moot point. I am entitled to access the medical records of my deceased parent.

Within days, I ordered and received a copy of my mother's death certificate from a town clerk in Massachusetts. I now own another piece of paper about Momma. A sad document detailing facts I already know. The day she died: Sunday, February 25,

1968. Circa 4 p.m., according to her death certificate. Suicide. Long ago, I learned to look these cold details in the face: the exact way she died. Even as a child, I had to digest that information. Now I need to fax this personal information to an anonymous hospital bureaucracy. At this point, my request includes six pages of documents. Will the malfunctioning hospital bureaucracy respond with another method to delay or deny my request? At least their bureaucracy is somewhat creative. Each "no" from the hospital has been different.

• • •

Ah well, Momma, Grandfather, I'm not taking your pictures out of the plain white envelope today. I can speak these thoughts to you silently in my head without peering into your faces. Were you both always either really up or really down? Were you alike in many ways? I managed not to follow in your footsteps. I promised my father. I promise myself, my husband, my children. I have not, will not, don't dare do what you did. I have to tell your story. Maybe I don't really need your help, don't need you to guide me. You would each tell a different story anyway.

CHAPTER 30

Ann Arbor

The second-to-last paper from Momma's Personal file: a full page from the *Ann Arbor News*. Saturday, June 20, 1964. I was two and a half. What prompted her to save this? Numerous items cover the front and back of this sheet of newspaper. Advertisements, listings for church services, small-town news. I've examined both sides of this musty yellow page many times. If my mother knew someone mentioned in one of the local news stories, I don't recognize any names. If the item important to her was one of the shorter items, wouldn't she have clipped out just that part?

On the reverse side, the main article covers most of the page:

Here Are Provisions of Senate-Passed Rights Bill

The center article, plus two related pieces, details this civil rights legislation. The Senate bill, soon signed by President Johnson, prohibited discrimination in public places, provided for the integration of schools and other public facilities, and made employment discrimination illegal. Were these the issues my mother cared about enough to save this page? A sheet of newspaper dating from the time we lived in Ann Arbor. At the start of those years when she stopped writing to Jean and Nana. Near the time when she almost died by suicide and was consequently hospitalized. In my child's memory, she was gone for two weeks. I never knew her diagnosis, only that she was in a mental hospital following a suicide attempt, and Dad only told me that many years afterward.

Despite her suicide attempt, somewhere around the time of that saved newspaper page, did Momma feel connected to something hopeful happening in the country, the civil rights movement? Is that why she saved this piece of newspaper? In a few years, by the winter of 1968, she was dead.

• • •

As I grew up, I was always asking Dad: "What was she like? What do you remember about her?"

She was always really up or really down. She was the most alive person he ever met. They met by chance at a picnic at a lake, two weeks before she left for a job on the other side of the world, in Vietnam. It was 1956. He was thirty already. He never fell in love before; never had any previous serious girlfriends. They saw each other every night until she left. He didn't ask her not to go. They got married soon after she came home. I collected these fragments and stories and facts he told me, along with her letters to him that he gave me.

One more thing Dad later mentioned about the time in Ann Arbor when Momma started seeing a psychiatrist. The doctor told Dad that Momma wasn't opening up, wouldn't talk about her problems. Dad also told me this story at some point when I was older, about her suicide attempt in Ann Arbor when I was three.

"She was taking an evening class," he said. She came home around nine. He was studying at the kitchen table. When she went into the bedroom, instead of saying "good night" as usual, she said, "Goodbye."

Later, when he found her, he remembered her words, realized how strange that was. At the time, he was distracted, focused on his work. Sydney and I were already asleep in our rooms. When he went into the bedroom to go to sleep, Momma lay on her side of the bed, on top of the covers, still dressed in slacks and a blouse. When he touched her, she was as cold as winter.

"I never felt anyone that cold before," Dad told me. On the bedside table, he found an empty bottle of pills. He ran into the kitchen and called her doctor, who called an ambulance, told Dad to meet him at the hospital.

I vaguely remember being woken up in the middle of the night, brought upstairs with Sydney by Dad to the women who rented the top-floor apartment. My eyes felt tired, the lights too bright. Later, Dad said Momma was away in a hospital. She would come home soon. I was too young to visit her, I was told. Nana came to take care of us.

Another day around that time, Nana was in our kitchen, cooking. Momma was still away. I knelt between Dad and Sydney in front of our living room window, trying to see something out in the yard.

"Don't you see the rabbit?" Sydney kept asking, pointing at the yard.

I only saw a brown ball of fur. Dad said it was a mother rabbit, sitting on a nest of babies. I wanted to see the babies under the mother rabbit. Dad and Syd both said they could see that. As hard as I squinted, I could only see the brown mother rabbit. My eyes felt blurry, like when I was woken in the middle of the night and taken upstairs. Nana was the one who had bad eyes. Why couldn't I see the baby rabbits that my sister and Dad were looking at?

When Momma returned from the hospital, she brought presents, memorable for their strangeness. I felt obligated to thank her for these unwanted gifts after I was told by Dad and Nana that Momma made them herself in the hospital.

Sydney and I each got one identical present. Rectangular wooden jewelry boxes, the tops inlaid with tiny sky-blue tiles. Inside, the boxes were empty, the bottoms covered with dark purple felt. I was too young to own any jewelry to put inside my box. The second present Syd and I got was different. Mine was a small, boring rug, woven from yellow and brown rags. Dad said I could keep it on my bedroom floor. Sydney got a circular plate covered with the same sky-blue tiles as our jewelry box lids. The plate was for hot things, Nana explained. I didn't understand how or why Momma made these things. I didn't like her weirdly grown-up gifts, but I couldn't tell her that. The gifts that partly matched but didn't match opened a space between me and Momma, between her and our family, a space that seemed like it didn't exist before, that had no words to explain it.

Another afternoon, I stood in our yard beside Dad. "There," he said, kicking at the dry dirt with the toe of his shiny leather work shoe. "This is where the mother rabbit kept her babies."

I expected to see a hole, something that could hold some baby rabbits. Instead, I saw a shallow indent in the dirt. I felt no sense of discovery or wonder. How could a rabbit keep her babies there? I tried to picture what a baby rabbit looked like. I wasn't even sure.

"Where's the mother rabbit now?" I glanced up at Dad, so much taller than me. "Where are the babies?"

He looked distracted. "I don't know, she must have moved her nest."

• • •

Brooklyn, 2022. Passing from fall into winter. A year now that I've been working on these papers. In our small, new apartment, there's one more thing of Momma's I still have, besides all the papers: a red leather billfold. How I came to have this old wallet of hers, I'm not sure. Probably it was in the box of her clothes Dad saved from the basement flood in Amherst.

I found the billfold in my file of family papers, even though it didn't fit and kept sliding out. It must have been me who stuffed Momma's old wallet in there with my papers. The red leather is slightly faded but still a cheery, cardinal red. The slim billfold snaps open, releasing a dusty smell.

Inside are some pictures. Dad, looking unbelievably young. A tiny, pleased smile hovered at the corners of his mouth. He's dressed in a work suit, with horn-rimmed professor's glasses; glossy, short, dark hair, not yet gray. I don't know how old he is in the photo. Probably taken in Ann Arbor when he was a PhD student, occasionally lingering in the background when Momma wrote her Dear Mother letters.

More pictures: me and Sydney. Both of us babies, toddlers, children. Solo portraits and together. In yards, bedrooms, living rooms. Columbus, Ann Arbor, Amherst. The history of our family wedged into one slim billfold. Along with that, there's one more important item. Not just a driver's license with our Amherst address, after Ann Arbor. Another ancient ID: a rectangular slip of paper containing our street address in Ann Arbor. Written in pen in Momma's hand. 1111 West Huron. A detail that was almost lost when I carelessly discarded those original copies of the Nana letters along with their envelopes.

From the computer at my corner desk in my cozy bedroom, I look up that address on West Huron in Ann Arbor. The house at that number doesn't look familiar. It's more like peering through layers of water into a half-remembered dream. A two-story, white clapboard house with a steeply peaked roof, green shutters. A tiny place. Not on a corner at all. The high wooden fence that Dad put up, enclosing the place like a fortress, is gone. Is there still a cherry tree in the backyard? I can't tell from the single online picture. Remembered places always look so much smaller later on. My childhood family, the mother I lost, are not there anymore. Looking at the picture of that childhood home doesn't tell me much, only makes me feel empty, like the inside of that jewelry box from Momma, and my memory of that yard where I couldn't see the babies under the brown mother rabbit.

Decades later, having raised two children myself, I can understand needing to have my own time to see a friend. Being too tired to check on a child at night. Even finding one of the children asleep on their bedroom floor. Deciding to leave my child to sleep on the floor instead of risking waking them by moving them into bed. But I would at least bring over a blanket, a pillow.

I have no lingering wish to revisit that house in Ann Arbor in person, the same way I no longer have any desire to visit Momma's grave. Nana must have taken me to Oakwood Cemetery at some point, without telling Dad, to see those granite stones embedded in a row in the grass. The family burial plot. J. R. Maude. Henry. Ann. Now Reid and Nana too.

• • •

This morning while I'm working at my desk, I listen to Pete Seeger on Spotify. "John Brown's Body" is amazingly available, along with Seeger's entire catalogue. I don't remember any of his records in that cabinet in Amherst, but we had other albums. Peter, Paul, and Mary. Barbra Streisand. I would make up dances to different songs, fling myself around unselfconsciously on the oriental carpet. "John Brown's Body" makes me want to lie on the floor and sob.

Instead, I get myself to call the Release of Information Unit to check on my application. I'm overdue for a response. No waiting on hold today. Almost immediately, I get through to someone, a different person this time. I remember to ask her name: Aaliyah. She requests the name and birth date of the patient in question, tells me they're running behind on their customary seven to ten business days to respond.

"The records are there? There is a record for this patient?" I practically stammer. I was expecting more delays, a flat denial. My mother was never a patient there; no records exist.

"Yes, yes," Aaliyah assures me. "Your request is here. But it can take up to thirty days," she apologizes. Explaining I'll get an invoice. As soon as I pay, I'll be able to view the record.

There's no mailing or photocopying involved, so what is the payment for exactly? I don't ask. A record exists. Of what happened to Momma, years ago when she was in the hospital. A time I barely remember and know little about.

Delay I can deal with better than denial. I can wait the remaining days. What am I expecting to discover though? The exact dates she was in the mental hospital? A diagnosis maybe? How bad can what I find out be? Knowing something is better than knowing nothing, I tell myself. Bracing myself, not sure what to protect myself from. Do I even need protecting anymore? That all happened so long ago.

• • •

The day Nana died was a Wednesday, the day before Thanksgiving. She lived until 1975, the year I was in eighth grade. I came home from school as usual, except I arrived home lightheartedly, knowing it was a long weekend.

Dad, Sydney and I were looking forward to going to Nana's at Christmas. Usually, Nana came to our house for that holiday. I forget why we were planning to go to her house that year instead. She wasn't sick. At seventy-eight, she had all her usual health problems: arthritis, bad eyes, bad feet. Maybe hosting Christmas that year was something special she wanted. Nana loved to celebrate, loved to cook. She already had the holiday menu planned out, a month in advance.

A favorite expression she frequently recited: "Let's eat, drink, and be merry, for tomorrow we diet." She always lingered over the last word, pronouncing it as "die." Then as a surprise, drew out the final syllable: "die-et." Her private commentary on diets as a kind of death.

When I got home from school, I saw Dad sitting in the roller chair at the desk in his room off the kitchen, which surprised me. Usually, he arrived home around five, right before dinner. He called me to come in. Sydney was already there, curled into the petite upholstered chair by the door. I braced myself for bad news, I just didn't know what kind. It seemed Dad told Sydney already; her eyes and nose were red from crying.

"Nana died today," Dad said as soon as I perched on the edge of his narrow bed. He delivered the rest of the news immediately in one dose. Nana was alone in her house when she died.

"Reid called and told me," Dad said. When the man from next door who often helped Nana with chores found her, she was already dead. She lay on the floor in her TV room. She must have tripped on the rug. By the couch where I often sat next to her to watch her afternoon soap operas. *Days of Our Lives. As the World Turns. Dark Shadows.* And her favorite, *General Hospital.* Her short yellow shag carpet. Her cushiony, flowered couch. She must have hit her head on the side table, then bled to death on the carpet.

Dad said, "We'll go next weekend, after Thanksgiving. To clean out her house." He said we couldn't go to the funeral; he had to teach. I knew he hated funerals. None of us said: this is too much like when Momma died. I cried, but not a lot. Dad's nose glowed red like Sydney's.

The doorbell rang, startling us. I remembered I had plans with friends. I left Dad and Sydney at home together. One of my school friends waited outside our side door to the kitchen. I grabbed my winter coat and ran out, not able to fully escape, a cloud of sadness hovering around my head like Nana's perfectly styled white hair.

My friend and I joined another friend at the bus stop up the street across from the telephone company. We liked to ride the free college buses. We caught a bus to the bookstore at UMass, each picking out a white paper bag full of assorted candy, sharing the candy when we got on another nearly empty bus. Most of the college students had already cleared out for Thanksgiving. We rode over to Smith College, across the river and back as dusk settled down, laughing at our own jokes. I'm not sure which two friends I was with that day. I'm pretty sure it was snowing. My candy: miniature, chewy mint Christmas trees.

At some point, I told my friends, "My grandmother died today." I felt sick from eating too much candy. Sometimes I ate a lot of Nana's cookies when a box arrived in the mail. That wasn't going to happen again. We weren't going to her house for Christmas.

One of the friends said, "Oh, I'm sorry," looking surprised, probably that I was riding buses around with them when my grandmother just died. We kept eating candy. I didn't even like candy. Nana loved food, loved eating.

A week later, we drove to Nana's in Sharon. At age thirteen, when I made that drive with Dad and Sydney, I didn't think: this is the last time I'll drive to this place with my family. When I was in Nana's house, I realized: this is the last time. We went through her things. Reid had already been there, taking what he wanted. He left a note, called Dad while we were there, apologizing that he couldn't stay to see us, saying, "Take anything you want to keep."

We took some of Nana's furniture, what we could fit in our car. Old Blue had been replaced by a new VW van, but we still couldn't fit Nana's flowery, soft couch or her mahogany dining room set. There was a flat cardboard box in her basement: Nana's ancient, floor-length wedding dress. Something she saved that she always wanted Sydney and me to have, to wear when we each got married. Sydney and I looked at the dress, took turns holding it up from the box. No way: too much lace, too scratchy. We shook our heads, laid the dress back in the box, and left it there.

There wasn't much left to eat at Nana's. We were there one day, sandwiched between two nights. We ate food from the pantry. Canned peas. Cold hearts of palm. Strange foods that didn't go together. Her fridge, her freezer, already empty. Usually, her freezer was packed with at least three kinds of dessert. A carton of ice cream. A store-bought icebox cake. A kind of frozen dessert with whipped cream like a cloud that Nana made and kept in a giant bowl in her freezer, and I wish I remembered the name.

From a dresser drawer in her guest bedroom where I slept when I visited, I chose one thing for myself to keep. A pristine bar of oval soap, still in its box, pale blue like Nana's eyes.

• • •

From the desk in my Brooklyn bedroom, I look up the weather in Amherst on the day Nana died. Thirty-seven degrees Fahrenheit. Windy, snowing. Just as I remembered, riding the buses, eating those sickening mint Christmas trees.

CHAPTER 31

Release of Information

I found her. I feel like I could disappear into a deep well, a solid weight tied to my ankles, pulling me straight down feet first, cold water closing over my head and cutting off my air supply, strangling me, mercifully forever.

No, that wasn't me—that was Momma—she was the one who died. Not by drowning though. Somehow, I cut the weight of her off my feet, separated myself from her. Long ago when I was a child. Maybe I decided to do that after she left me to cry myself to sleep on the floor in my room in Ann Arbor. Maybe there were other times, too, that I don't remember that added up. But cutting myself loose from her in my mind to save myself, to not go down with her, that wasn't what killed her.

The information that arrives in the email from the hospital helps confirm what I already knew. She was already dropping to the bottom of a well.

• • •

The email that arrives contains two separate attachments. Online, I pay the unexplained fee: $6.89. Then open the first attached document, the smaller one. What I find: a copy of my own application to access her records, ten pages long, now part of her hospital record. Years afterward, someone came searching for her, a daughter: myself.

Next, her file, 118 pages. The documents inside are difficult to understand. Out of chronological order in places. Pages and pages of detailed technical information, numbers, medical jargon. Charting her weight, analyzing her blood chemistry, measuring her urine output. What is peritoneal dialysis? What is an endotracheal tube? What is a Bird respirator?

I print out the entire file. Read and reread. Make notes, highlight important words and events. Mark significant entries with colored Post-its. The file contains different kinds of spidery, scribbled handwriting, impossible to read in places. Every term I don't understand, I look up. I'm building a picture of what happened. What, when, where. All the W's.

Who: "White woman. 33-years-old."

Who and what and when: "In-Patient Notes. 1 Dec 1965. 33 y/o white female enters in a coma after ingesting 2500 mg Tofranil and 1000 mg Librium at 10 PM on November 30, 1965."

Where: "Patient was brought to the ER at 2 AM in a comatose state and was unresponsive to gross pain." All the W's mixed together. And why? Why did she ingest those drugs, why did she try to kill herself?

"She has been followed by Dr. A. from NPI who states he had seen her one day PTA and she gave no indication to him of suicidal tendencies although she is markedly depressed." PTA? Prior To Admission. Not parent-teacher association.

"1 Dec. 65." On page two. "In-Patient Notes. Scar on L wrist." A small, neat circle drawn around a single, handwritten capital L.

In my memory, I've searched for evidence of those scars Dad once told me about, proof that she tried to cut her wrists before they were married. I even asked Reid, but he claimed he didn't know about any scars. Now here is evidence. There was a scar on her left wrist. Not her right one that I remembered examining when I sat next to her in the front seat of the car; the time I didn't remember seeing any scar, only her watch and her pale wrist. Now I learn there was a scar, but only on her left wrist. Noted in only one "In-Patient" note taken by one of the doctors who first treated Momma in that ER. Maybe it was a faint scar, not obvious.

Several pages mention two previous suicide attempts before this "2 AM ER" trip following her drug overdose: "Patient has attempted suicide 2 times previously...Patient has at least twice attempted previously to suicide...Has attempted 2x before... Who apparently twice in the past has had suicide attempts." The scar was possibly evidence of her first suicide attempt. This drug overdose was attempt three then. What about attempt number two? I have to search through to the end of these convoluted pages before I untangle that question.

On a later form. Pages and pages farther in. "1 Dec 65. 33-year-old white female. Just admitted after ingestion of Librium and Tofranil in massive amounts. Brought to ER at 2 AM. Admitted comatose, unresponsive to pain or any other stimulus and periods of apnea. Patient lying in bed—slow pulse—slow respiration—tongue is flabby and falls back—pupils equal and round—small reaction to light—no coronal (no blink reflex). No reflexes—no reaction to pain."

There she was. My mother, almost dead. She tried to die, but she didn't. Apnea: she stopped breathing temporarily.

"Patient was not lavaged due to 4-hour lag between ingestion and time seen in ER." "Lavaged"? Is that a French word? Washing out of an organ such as the stomach, to remove drugs.

“Endotracheal tube was passed when patient became apneic.” “Endotracheal tube”: a breathing tube inserted through the mouth or nose.

“Patient is married and mother of 2.” That was her, Momma. “Mother of 2”: those words don’t appear until five pages into the repetitive, disturbing details. Hours, days, weeks, even months passed while she was in the hospital. Succeeding pages restate, add on, abruptly change topics. Why: hardest of all to understand.

“Mother of 2.” I was the second of those two, a small person hidden behind that number. I was in the background of this report, years ago. This happened to me also. At the time, I didn’t understand what was happening. Later, the ages of the children appear: “3 ½ & 5 ½.” At another point: “4 & 6.” Momma was still in the hospital for my fourth birthday: January 1966. For Sydney’s sixth birthday in February too. I have no memory of my birthday that year. I dig farther into the record to comprehend. Short doses so I don’t make myself sick from looking at this.

• • •

I remember the perfect birthday party Momma created for Sydney, the undersea-theme basement birthday, the handmade decorations. That must have been the following year, Sydney’s seventh birthday, after we arrived in Amherst, when Momma must have been trying to have a life again. All those sequined fish cut from colored construction paper, fishing-themed children’s games. The pink frosted cake. That was Amherst. After this suicide attempt and hospital stay was over. Momma survived.

But by the next February, 1968, two years after getting out of the hospital, she died by suicide. Sydney’s eighth birthday came a week before Momma’s death. That couldn’t have been the year Momma planned and executed the elaborate children’s party.

> In-Patient Notes. 1 Dec. 65. 4:30 AM. No response to pain. Dr. P. called and suggested dialysis in view of massive doses, no lavage, and recent onset. He states Librium not able to be dialyzed but suggests peritoneal dialysis on basis of Tofranil. —Dr. S.

"Peritoneal dialysis": using the inside lining of a person's abdomen to act as a natural filter to remove toxins; requiring insertion of a soft tube or catheter into the belly.

> 6:45 AM. Endotracheal tube pulled because patient gagging and fighting tube. Moving air well. —Dr. S.
>
> 6:30 PM. Vital signs stable. Dialysis running well. Responding to pain. —Dr. S.
>
> 2 Dec. 8:30 AM. Patient somewhat more responsive. Opens eyes and attempts to move in a very confused manner. Turns head and tries to move extremities. Has <u>very</u> brisk reflexes. Did not recognize me although this was the only question she answered definitively. —Dr. A.
>
> 2 Dec. 65. Vital signs stable. Patient lethargic but answers questions. Will discontinue IV and start on clear liquid diet. Will discontinue dialysis after next exchange. —Dr. S.
>
> 2 Dec. 65. Peritoneal dialysis discontinued and catheter tip sent for culture. —Dr. G.
>
> 3 Dec. 65. Vital signs stable. Alert. Eating well. Will transfer out of ICU when bed available. —Dr. S.

> 3 Dec. 10:30 AM. Patient recognizes me and is aware of her suicidal attempt. No contraindication psychiatrically for transfer to regular ward although because of her obvious history of suicidal attempts some precaution would be advisable. She no doubt will require psychiatric hospitalization when her physical situation is stabilized. —Dr. A.
>
> 4 Dec. 65. Alert. Vital signs remain stable. Will try to determine disposition with Dr. A. Believe patient responding and no longer will require medical treatment soon. —Dr. S.
>
> 5 Dec. 65. Doing well. Very hostile today. —Dr. S.
>
> 5 Dec. 65. Patient apparently depressed and agitated. If she is physically in shape I would recommend transfer to NPI which I will look into. —Dr. A.
>
> 6 Dec 65. Medical work up negative. Will transfer today. —Dr. S.

She was in the hospital for three and a half months. December 1, 1965 to March 18, 1966. First in the ER, followed by several days in a bed in the general ward, after which she was transferred to the fourth level of the NPI, the Neuropsychiatric Institute. For the first week in the NPI, she was seen by Dr. D. The author of a two-page hand-scribbled note.

> Admission Note: 12-6-65. This is a 33-year-old noticeably depressed white married woman who was transferred today from Medicine where she had recovered from a very nearly successful suicidal attempt. She had taken 100 Tofranil

and 120 Librium tablets, and was barely pulled through on the Intensive Care Unit with artificial respiration and peritoneal dialysis. She has been a private patient referred from Family Service to Dr. A. for 2 ½ years and during that time has tried suicide three times.

She has a history of stormy behavior in the home with lots of impulsive hostility toward her husband and children (ages 4 & 5) but usually taken out on herself, e.g. by her breaking some valuable possession of her own. Beside this characterological picture of symptoms, she is obviously paranoid.

Upon admission to the 4th Level NPI she was very subdued, and on the point of tears. Her husband informed the social worker that he was sure she is still suicidal. Her first remark to the doctor was that in spite of Dr. A.'s fine recommendation, she hates women, and she proceeded to fix a stony stare on the doctor while puffing a cigarette. Later she relaxed a bit, said she had mixed feelings about being revived from her suicide attempt because this time she thought she had really "fixed it." She had no outstanding complaint either, she said, but had simply found the children fussy. It had been both her and her husband's observation that they had not been making any progress with Dr. A. lately. Patient states she likes to paint—does not like sports.

Impression: depressive reaction—probably paranoid schizophrenia.

Disposition: admit and watch. OT & RT as tolerated. Supportive psychotherapy. —Dr. D.

I don't completely trust the report by Dr. D. I understand from her comment that she must be the female doctor upon whom Momma fixed a stony stare while puffing on a cigarette, saying she half-wished her suicide attempt had worked. Dr. D.'s line about Momma's three previous suicide attempts is confusing. In multiple places, the reports say there were two previous attempts. Maybe Dr. D. makes mistakes with numbers. She got the number of pills wrong, inserting the number "120" for Librium, while everyone else wrote "100." Dr. D. also gets the ages of me and Syd slightly wrong. Minor mistakes, yet multiple ones, multiplied my distrust of this doctor's report, adding to my dislike of what comes across in her "Admission Note" as her ice-cold clinical style.

Also confusing is Dr. D.'s sentence about Momma: "It had been both her and her husband's observation that they had not been making any progress with Dr. A. lately." A typical freshman college writing mistake of unclear referent? Not surprising given Dr. D.'s disorienting third-person reference to herself as "the doctor," the recipient of Momma's stony stare and ill-tempered comment about hating women. Does "they" in Dr. D.'s line refer to Momma and Dad? Or to Momma and her psychiatrist, Dr. A.? If the former, this is surprising since that would mean Momma and Dad were both seeing Dr. A. for a type of couples counseling, which might have been warranted, but I don't think that's what was happening, even given the stormy relations in our home reported by Dr. D. So the line could refer to Momma and Dr. A.: *they* were not making any progress lately, which makes more sense given Momma's suicide attempt while under Dr. A.'s care.

That Momma reported she "found the children fussy," I don't find surprising. Given the dates, Syd and I were five and a half and three and a half when Momma entered the hospital. Children that young are always a lot of work. I feel sad that it sounds like Momma was too depressed to enjoy being with us much then, which confirms what I remember from those Ann Arbor years. Dr. A. had Momma on a lot of psychiatric meds, which apparently didn't help. All that Librium and Tofranil, the uppers and downers used to keep her "chemically stabilized." Instead, Momma used them to try to end her life.

Scouring further into the report, I see that after one week in the NPI, Momma came under the care of a different clinician: Dr. C. Possibly male this time, possibly a better match for Momma as a doctor.

Dr. D.'s initial paranoid schizophrenic diagnostic label for Momma didn't stick. By the time my mother left that institution, she had other words attached to her. "Emotional disorder": this label sounds broad and bland. For insurance purposes? Bestowed by Dr. C. at Momma's mid-March hospital discharge. Plopped into the report midway through, not at the end of her stay there where I would expect to find it. Followed by a dozen more pages of lab reports: blood work, charts of Momma's detoxing dialysis. Plus a progress report: three days on the Bird respirator. Not a respirator for birds. A modern, efficient machine was invented in 1958 by an American engineer and aviator, Dr. Forrest Bird.

Finally, another diagnosis, also placed midway through instead of at the end. Since I didn't find another diagnosis by the end of these documents, this label must have been what followed Momma when she left the NPI. Delivered by Dr. C., who I know only by his/her scribbled last name. His/her almost illegible writing. This final diagnosis was delivered upon Momma's discharge in a form letter to Dr. A., to whose outpatient care Momma was returned. The diagnostic label is a mouthful. Unlike the earlier generic, covering-all-bases "emotional disorder," this second label covers all bases in a different way. By using as many terms as possible: "Personality disturbance passive-aggressive type with hysterical features—borderline." Like cooking when you want to use up all your leftover ingredients but can't quite decide what you're making. This diagnosis for Momma's mental illness was one of the things I thought I was looking for when I decided to seek out her medical records. Now that I have the diagnosis, I find it as cold and empty as an old refrigerator.

• • •

Hey Momma, I had to search for where I tucked away your old childhood photo again today. You, that little girl with the big white bows on both sides of her head, hands clasped behind her back, standing in the grass, gazing into the future, legs firmly planted, slightly knock-kneed. It's you I came looking for today, not your father with his own misery that seems to have gotten you started on your unhappy path.

I feel overwhelmed and stuck, reading through this medical report of yours, trying to make sense of what happened to you.

CHAPTER 32

Amherst

The last Personal file item. A sheet of yellowed notebook paper with a drawing of a horse saddle, each part of the saddle meticulously labeled. Momma's handwriting, her drawing. No date. Why a drawing of a saddle? This time I know the answer, at least in part. I was there for the horseback riding afternoons. Was this a recommendation from her new psychiatrist in Amherst? Try something new, a healthy, outdoor activity.

1967, our second fall in Massachusetts. Most weekends, Momma took me and Sydney riding at a farm in the country, a short drive away. I was in kindergarten but wasn't big enough to ride. At that Western ranch, to be allowed on a horse, the top of your head had to reach the top rail of the corral. Those Saturday afternoons, I was left behind in the barnyard to entertain myself with imaginary horseback riding games, while Momma and Sydney rode real horses in the ring and even on long trail rides. From Momma's drawing, it seems she was trying to memorize the name of every part on a Western saddle, studying with an ambitious thirst for perfection, more driven than the average weekend horseback rider.

• • •

Fall 1967. In the backyard in Amherst, there was a shed. A small brown toolshed under the trees at the far end of the yard, surrounded by ferns. Sydney and I were allowed to turn the shed into a playhouse, where we spent hours and days inventing imaginary games. A rusty metal fence enclosed the yard. Soon after we moved in, Dad ripped out the old fence, an unexplained reversal of his fence-building activity in Ann Arbor. Here, with a much bigger yard, we were released into the woods.

The first surprising plant I found in the woods beyond the shed had a threadlike stalk with a drooping, cup-shaped head, each one ghostly white, the stalks growing in a single clump. I didn't know what they were called. When I ran inside to show Momma, she looked it up in a book.

"Don't pick this again," she told me, along with the name: Indian pipes, also known as ghost plant.

With the fence gone, my world stretched beyond the backyard into the woods behind our house that reached all the way to the edge of town. In the other direction, the range of my known world extended across our street to the backyards of the houses along the other streets in our small neighborhood, crouched beside the university, the place Dad worked.

When we were outside, my sister and I played with the neighborhood kids. Nick, one of the only boys in our gang. He lived across the street and was in Sydney's class at school. Peggy, the unspoken head of our gang, not because she was the oldest but because she was the biggest bully. Peggy's two brothers didn't usually hang around with us because they were teenagers, and they were boys. Deb, a girl my age with long orange hair and a scalp crusted black with dirt. She became my best friend. Frances, my age but short and tough, with two younger brothers. We didn't let them play with us because they were too little. Angela, with ten brothers and sisters, all much older. Angela was almost blind, and her head swiveled and bobbed constantly, so we all knew we had to let her play with us. My sister, one of the oldest, but not the boss of our gang. At home, she bullied me, but in the world of our neighborhood, she was sometimes a chicken and a crybaby.

• • •

Spring 1967. The next plant I found also grew in the shade on the side of the shed. A warm day. I was alone for a moment when I spotted the single, delicate flower. I didn't know what it was, so I picked it. Again, I ran into the kitchen to show Momma. She didn't need to look it up.

"Lady slipper," she told me. A bright yellow globe-shaped sack. Like a baby bootee.

I got another reprimand: "Don't pick this again." Along with a new word: endangered. This flower, even rarer and more special than the Indian pipes.

• • •

Summer. In the woods behind our house, there was a stream. After Dad tore out the fence, the stream still divided our yard from the neighbors' yards. The stream flowed away from town, through the woods, a stone's throw from our house, then passed in a tunnel under the street and continued through the backyards on the side street called Nutting. Nutting originated across from our driveway, then ran downhill a few blocks before ending at the parking lot on the edge of the university. Our street was called Fearing. Nutting and Fearing. The strangeness of those names was softened by the presence of the stream, which never had a special name except "the stream."

In the woods, there was a path called the shortcut. When we took the shortcut into town, it followed the stream in the opposite direction from the flowing water. Near the path, not far from the stream, stood a small, empty house built of stone with a slate roof, the windows always dark. The kids in our gang always ran past it. We said a witch must live there.

Soon the path veered away from the stream and cut through the woods, coming out between two buildings at the top of our street, close to the edge of town. One building on the corner was the telephone company, a solid brick block that never seemed to be open, with a parking lot that never held more than one or two cars. Next door was a gray, rambling fraternity with a wraparound porch. On the weekends, the porch was usually full of college students holding giant tumblers of beer while music blared from open windows, and an abandoned couch sat somewhere in the yard.

In the other direction from the shortcut into town, where the stream ran under the street, we sometimes played a game of dare. We tried to crawl through the cement tunnel to the other side of the street, on our hands and knees in the trickle of water. Once I made it almost through the tunnel to the point where the light seeped in from the other end, led by Peggy in front. Behind her crawled Nick, then my sister, then me, on our hands and knees in the narrow dark, with my friends Frances and Deb following behind. But Sydney got scared and started to back out, so I had to inch backward, too, on the cold, wet cement, Frances and Deb crawling backward behind me, both of them pissed off, especially Frances.

Ahead of Sydney, Peggy and Nick made it through to the yard of the house on the other side. By the time they crossed back over the street, my sister had run off to our house crying. Later, she returned with a message from Momma. Syd and I were not allowed to play in the tunnel under the street anymore.

One backyard belonged to an old man who lived with his dog. He limped with a cane and grew raspberries under a white net. We loved to sneak down the staircase along the side of his garage into his enclosed yard and steal his berries from under the net, enjoying the thrill of escaping each time before he and his dog could catch us, coming down the stairs, cutting off our only escape route. The advance sound of the dog's yapping alerted us with enough warning so we could get to the stairs before the man started down, limping with his cane, the dog following behind to protect him, before leaping out to bite one of us. The thrill of the narrow escape equaled the satisfaction of devouring stolen berries.

The man's garage held a closed door with a window. Once, I stopped to peer through the window into the dark interior of the garage, filled with ancient lawnmowers and rusty appliances. On the floor, behind the closed door, stood several inches of water. I knew I risked being caught on the stairs by the man and his dog, so I tore myself away and ran after my retreating friends. Angela of the bad eyes and bobbing head was never with us when we snuck down the stairs into the man's yard because she couldn't run.

There was a grape arbor, a place we sometimes ran and hid. Dark and enclosed, behind one of the houses on Nutting. Overhead were wooden beams where vines and leaves hung down. Hiding in the enclosed cave below the vines were Concord grapes, thick-skinned, sour and green or soft and purple, the insides slimy.

• • •

Summer. Inside a closet one day at Angela's house, I first saw a litter of baby kittens. We were never allowed in Angela's house near the corner at the far end of our block, opposite from the direction into town. Her solid stone house was off limits, full of her ten older siblings, packed with junk, people, and animals. That day, Angela snuck us inside to show us a surprise. One or two at a time, we were led up some steps, into the back of a dark closet. There in the dimness, inside the low drawer of a dresser, crammed full of towels, beside the hairy belly of a mother cat pushed aside by Angela's pale hand: a balled-up mass of squirming, mewing kittens. Eyes closed, barely recognizable as cats. The mother cat looked up accusingly. Angela's house smelled bad, better not to breathe. I ran outside with everyone else as fast as possible.

• • •

Fall. Standing beside Sydney in our warm, yellow kitchen, both of us in flannel nightgowns after our baths. My sister smelled of clean laundry, wet hair. Sydney held the tin cake pan level while Momma slopped steaming gray pablum into it, telling us, "This is the same cereal I fed you both as babies," entrusting us with the task of feeding our kittens.

The day before, Dad drove our family to a farm near our horseback riding place. Sydney and I were allowed to pick one kitten each from a straw-filled box on the barn floor. Sydney pointed to a black one, so I picked the cream-colored one. On the drive home in Old Blue, with the kittens in a cardboard box on the back seat between us and the car's sour milk smell surrounding us, Momma told Sydney and me, "You can each name your kitten." By the end of the ride, Sydney was calling her cat Blackie, so I named mine something equally plain: Whitey.

After Momma filled the cake pan in Sydney's hands with pablum, I followed my sister through the dark rooms to the porch door. Through the glass pane on the top half of the door, I could see the dark porch outside. Through the door, I could hear the desperate, high mewing of our kittens on the porch floor, although I couldn't see them.

"Open the door," Sydney directed, flicking on the light switch for the porch.

The instant we stepped onto the newspaper-covered cement floor, the smell of cat pee stung my nose. We were surrounded by the baby kittens, clinging to our ankles below our nightgowns. They wanted what Sydney was holding.

She lowered the pan to the newspaper, and instantly our kittens shoved their furry, whiskered faces into the steaming pablum, licking and panting as if they wanted to bury themselves in the sticky paste. Sydney and I stood together shivering, wrapping our arms around ourselves, trying not to breathe in the cat pee smell. From overhead, the single light bulb rained down a harsh light.

We didn't know what was going to happen. At the tail end of winter, Momma was going to die. But not just die, she was going to die by suicide. A year later, in the spring, Sydney's cat Blackie was going to get sick with leukemia and die too. Whitey would live for decades though, longer than most cats, keeping Dad company after Syd and I left for college. First Syd departed to a distant university. Then I left, too, for a nearby college; later to the Big Apple, half a day's drive away, where I've continued to live for decades.

Standing on the glass-enclosed porch on that chilly night, my sister and I paused to watch our kittens lapping up the dish of steaming pablum with such energy and desire to live.

"Here," Syd said after a minute. Leaning down to show me how to plunge my index finger into the warm pablum, drawing up a thick fingerful. The mush tasted slimy, an illicit treat. As soon as we returned the empty cake pan to the kitchen, Momma asked, "Did you eat the pablum?" She must have been watching us through the window in the porch door.

"No," we lied in unison.

"Don't do that again," she scolded, followed by a lecture about germs and how kittens need their food.

Outside the glass walls of the porch: darkness. Our friendly daytime yard, the swing set, the shed, the stream, the woods in the distance, the shortcut into town, all unseen, hidden in the black night.

• • •

Spring, a washed-out, lukewarm day. I found myself crouching next to my sister on the curb of a parking lot in the center of town, staring at my sneakers, clutching the edge of a white bedsheet with bright, multicolored words painted on it like one of our childhood paintings. While Momma stood talking interminably to some moms nearby, Sydney read the words from our bedsheet aloud: "Make Peace Not War." At the time, I didn't understand what we were doing, that this was a protest against the war we were brought to by Momma.

• • •

Winter. One day, the TV stayed on all day. Our small, black-and-white television sat in the corner behind the door to the living room, on an oval table with a white marble top. Words scrolled down the screen, white letters like snow rolling down the gray glass. Maybe it was snowing outside and that was why I was inside. Sydney was at school, and I couldn't read yet, at least not anything as complicated as tiny, moving words.

Somewhere nearby, Momma was vacuuming. When she came through the living room dragging the vacuum cleaner, I pointed at the screen. "What's that?"

"Names of people who died in the war." She barely paused, pulling the vacuum after her toward the stairs to the bedrooms on the second floor, her sadness like the droning of the vacuum. The names continued rolling down the screen.

• • •

Fall or winter, close to Momma's death. I heard voices yelling and something breaking. Momma's voice shouted words I couldn't understand. A heavy object slammed against something. Noise of china shattering. My sister's hushed voice, trying to reassure me, "They're fighting. It's only Momma and Dad."

We stood in the upstairs hall, outside the door to our bedroom. At the opposite end of the hall, behind their closed bedroom door, it sounded like giants crashing into each other.

Later, I saw the statue that Dad glued back together and returned to the top of the bureau in their bedroom. Something Momma kept from Vietnam. A slender woman carved from black wood with arms stretched overhead, pulling long, black hair upwards. The statue was as narrow and as long as my mother's forearm. White lines showed where Dad glued the woman together.

• • •

Fall. Puffballs. The third strange plant. Found in the same area, the shady side of the shed, out of view of our house. This time, I was with Sydney and the neighborhood kids playing chase when I spotted something on the ground: round, white-and-gray clumps like shriveled golf balls or the heads of unknown creatures poking through the leaves. I stomped on each one before someone else stepped on them first. Each mushroom was perfect, not overripe. Each one released a puff of smoke when I crushed it with the toe of my sneaker. Three satisfying puffs. Sydney called after me as I ran away, leaving behind the flattened plants: "Puffballs!" Naming them, like it was the answer to a secret spell.

• • •

Rain, so probably fall or spring. The basement flooded. It happened more than once before Dad figured out how to stop it. The stream passed so close to the side of our house that when it rained a lot, our basement flooded. It flooded that way until Dad put a sump pump in the basement.

• • •

Each of those memories is like a snapshot, all of them tumbled together, like a pile of photos on a counter or inside a box. This is a collection of memories, not in the right order, from the year when we moved to Amherst, after Ann Arbor, the last months before Momma died. The disorder is part of the story.

One more thing I remember Dad told me once after I grew up. When we moved to Amherst, Momma didn't like it as much as Ann Arbor. At the time, Amherst was a small, quiet town. One restaurant. One traffic light. No shoe store. A college town, but a restrained New England one. Momma liked Ann Arbor better, but even there she tried to end her life.

• • •

Summer 1967. A snapshot. My sister, me, and Momma. In the backyard of the house in Amherst. By the combination climbing-gym swing set. A year before she died. Dad built the swing set from junk he found at the dump: metal pipes, pieces of wood for the swing seats. He probably bought the chains for the swings, assembled and painted everything. He's not in the shot. That must have been him taking the picture.

Momma stood between me and Sydney, in front of the low bar. We perched on the bar like two birds, one at each of her shoulders. To keep her balance, Sydney gripped the vertical bar up to the high bar. We knew how to hang from that high bar, how to drop to the ground. Outside the frame of the picture stood the rest of the swing set, three swings total. One each for Sydney and me, plus an extra for a friend.

The bar where I perched at Momma's shoulder was four feet from the ground. One of my hands rested on top of her head for balance. I remember what it felt like to rest my hand on her head. I don't remember the exact color of her hair, but maybe it was black since this came after the hospital. Her face looked soft and young in that picture.

When I look for the photo in my box of pictures, I can't find it. Then I remember: before I moved, I had a fat photo album. The kind you stick the photos in. When I tried to pull out that picture of Momma, me, and Sydney on the climbing gym, it started to rip. I couldn't save the photo. It was stuck, tearing, disintegrating. I thought I used to have multiple copies of that picture, but that was the only one I had left. Now I just have the version I remember, full of uncertainty, like the way I balanced with one hand resting on Momma's head.

• • •

No message for Momma or Grandfather today.

CHAPTER 33

Ann P. Records

OCCUPATIONAL-RECREATIONAL THERAPY PROGRESS REPORT. 1-10-66. 4th Level NPI.

Mrs. P. is a short woman of medium build who looks her stated age. She was referred for ward O.T. on 12-6-65 and attended twice, after which she was rescheduled for regular O.T.

She is a very soft-spoken, aloof woman, who does respond, however quite superficially, when approached by staff. She usually exhibits a constant smile and her manner is coolly polite. Mrs. Plattner's only approaches to staff have been project-oriented, that is, either asking for supplies, or more infrequently, for assistance. Interaction with patients is infrequent and appears less reserved although this is limited to patient N. and ex-patient Y.

From observation, she appears very engrossed in her work and remains involved for the entire period. She has been quite independent, either working in a familiar area (ceramics) or on very simple, uncomplicated projects. —Jenny G., OTR

Another chilly clinical report signed by a female clinician, this time from occupational and recreation therapy. Again, describing Momma's voice as soft, just as Reid told me in one of those phone calls when I was in grad school in my twenties, and I hadn't wanted to accept that as one of her defining traits.

"Medication Records." Every medicine Momma was given is recorded in detail by amount and time of day for pages and pages. So many different drugs, treating coughs, colds, insomnia, itching. Basically, no Librium or Tofranil for two weeks after she overdosed on them. Soon, Momma was transferred to the NPI, and Dr. D. started her on the Librium again, but in a stronger dose than when she overdosed. No more Tofranil though. When Dr. C. took over, she/he continued Momma on that anti-anxiety medication. In other words, Momma was being calmed down.

Immediately after putting Momma back on Librium, Dr. D. also tried giving her Mellaril. I look it up: used to treat schizophrenia. After one day, Dr. D.'s note states: "Discontinue Mellaril!" Whatever happened, the exclamation point says it all. The Mellaril must have backfired. Probably why the medication, along with the paranoid schizophrenia label, didn't stick.

After one month in the NPI, in addition to the sedating Librium, Momma started taking a sleeping medication several nights a week. Chloral hydrate, aka knockout drops, no longer available in the US due to health risks to the heart, not to mention overdose fatalities.

Two weeks before her discharge from the hospital, Momma's Librium dose was reduced to the same amount she was taking prior to the suicide attempt that sent her into that hospital. Just no more of that other drug, the upper with the name like "topper": Tofranil.

• • •

After several days of study, even I, layperson nobody, my mother's daughter, can tell that a few important items in her medical file are missing. After two weeks in the hospital, on December 14, 1965, three psychological tests were administered by a psychologist; a trainee supervised by someone else, the scribbled note says. The WAIS (partial). Rorschach. And TAT. Names of tests I could look up but decide not to because what will I really learn? They sound like characters from T. S. Eliot's *Old Possum's Book of Practical Cats*, like Momma's cat, Macavity, in Saigon: Bombalurina, Jellylorum. But those tests sound more like the names of sickly cats, experimented on for too long in medical labs.

Results of those psychiatric tests? Not here. A noticeable omission, especially since so much else is here. Results of Momma's routine chest X-ray. Results of the gynecological exam she underwent due to vaginal itching, a few weeks after her transfer to the NPI. My mother's vaginal itching. More than any daughter would want to know about. Where are the results of her psychological testing? They should be part of her medical record at the hospital where the tests were administered. Tests that must have been used to diagnose and treat her mental illness, as well as to justify her stay in that Neuropsychiatric Institute for insurance billing.

Also missing: any notes on therapeutic treatment, beyond medication. The supportive psychotherapy recommended in the "Admission Note" by Dr. D., the chilly female psychiatrist Momma fixed with an equally cold stare.

They did *try* to help. A dozen pages of "Clinical Records" diligently taken by different nurses. Pages of columns recording my mother's attendance at OT and RT; along with walks, any other special activities, passes given, visitors. If Momma made a phone call, that was noted. Doctors' visits, meaning her psychiatrists. Twice a week, she saw Dr. D., then Dr. C. One time, a week before discharge, she again saw Dr. A.

Every daily recreational and occupational therapy session Momma declined or agreed to attend was ticked off, columns of Y's and R's. Y for yes, R for refuse. At first, she refused more than agreed. More OT and RT were offered. More Y's began to be ticked; she was becoming more agreeable. They were giving her Librium. "Movie" is ticked with a Y almost every time. She loved movies. Does "Caf" mean cafeteria? She usually said yes to "Caf." Refused bowling; refused bingo every time. Said yes to GT several times though. GT for group therapy? Was this the supportive psychotherapy recommended by Dr. D.? However, this group therapy was provided by occupational and physical therapists, not psychotherapists.

• • •

On December 25, Christmas Day 1965, after living in the NPI for three weeks, she got a day pass, her first. That Christmas in Ann Arbor when Momma must have reappeared for a single day following weeks of absence: I have no memory of that. A blank. Not of her leaving again either.

Sunday, January 9, another day pass. Again, on Tuesday, January 11. Significantly, that Tuesday was my birthday when I turned four. Just like the Christmas that would have come only a few weeks before, when Momma similarly reappeared for one day, I have no memory of my birthday that year. Another blank. Most people probably don't remember their fourth birthday. Now I know why I don't remember mine; why I saved a blank spot instead of a memory. Probably that birthday was especially bleak. January 11 was also the anniversary of Momma's father's suicide. Did any of Momma's psychiatrists, Doctors A., D., or C., have a clue about that? Would they have permitted her to return home for one of her first exits from her protected hospital sanctuary if they had the remotest understanding of anything that made her tick? To go back to the place where she recently lost it enough to overdose on all her psychiatric meds. On the anniversary of the day her father died by suicide. "Sure, let's try that out as one of the first days to send her home to be with her husband and children." Did Dr. C. think that? Or did he just think: blank?

The dozen pages labeled "Physician's Orders" are filled with scribbly handwriting, first by her doctors in the ICU: Dr. G., then S., followed by A., who checked on her several times. Followed by Dr. D., then C. in the NPI. The pass for the January 11 visit home was granted by Dr. C.

On January 13, immediately following her visit home for my birthday, Dr. C. scribbled the following note: "Suicidal Precautions." Followed one day later by: "Out of suicide precautions. 6:30 PM." Nothing further. What were the suicide precautions? I wonder. Watching her? Keeping her in her room?

Dr. C.'s January 13 note is the only one for suicide precautions during Momma's months in the NPI. Except for the first days when she entered that department of the hospital, under a suicide watch. After a day in the NPI, her new temporary home, Dr. D.'s note records: "Discontinue official suicide precautions. Permit walks, special activities with ward groups."

In the "Clinical Record" section for those corresponding mid-January days near my birthday, the anniversary of Momma's father's death, the nurse's meticulous notes record no suicide watch. Also, why did only doctors earn the privilege of illegibility, while nurses had to maintain strict neatness in handwriting?

• • •

On January 23, Momma was transferred from the fourth to the sixth level of the hospital. Presumably, a different floor or different area in the hospital. More privileges perhaps, less security possibly.

On February 24, Momma was allowed to visit the beauty parlor before returning home for the weekend. "On pass," the notes say every time she was allowed out. During the three and a half months she was gone, she came home on pass eleven times. For a day, an overnight, building up to multiple times when she returned home for an entire weekend before she was eventually released for good. I don't remember anything about those back-and-forth times when she came home briefly, followed by more days and weeks when she was absent.

During those months, Dad visited Momma in the hospital twenty-nine times, the medical report shows. He never mentioned anything about that: going to see her over and over. Not when I was a child. Not later when I was grown up either. Except for those few times when stray bits of this story came out. Telling me I was too young to visit her in the hospital. Later, maybe during that time in high school when I moved into my parents' old room and asked more questions about her, telling me that it wasn't just a hospital, it was a mental hospital. Later still, when I was grown up, blurting out that her hospital stay in Ann Arbor didn't follow her first suicide attempt. There was an earlier time when she cut her wrists. He said she came home from the hospital a changed person, started dyeing her hair black.

• • •

"Physician's Orders." December 12. "Permit daughters (aged 3½, 5½) to visit today (dining room)." —Dr. D. I think: she got our ages right that time.

"Physician's Orders." December 16: "One visit per week. Sunday only, to include husband and children. No other visits." —Dr. D. Emphatically underlined. The way Momma used to underline things in her letters, but with more enjoyment than Dr. D. exhibits in her work.

December 17. "Visiting and phone as follows: Husband may visit only on weekends (Sat. and Sun.) and bring children Sun. Pt. may phone home daily one time between 1 and 2 P.M." —Dr. D. "Pt." for patient. Then Dr. C. took over. Visits with children were prescribed two more times, once in January and once in February, for our birthdays. Momma was permitted to come home on a pass more regularly. Presumably, children's visits no longer needed to be prescribed.

On the corresponding dates in the "Clinical Record" section, when I compare what the doctors recommended with what the nurses recorded as actually happening, I see that children's visits are mentioned on two dates only. December 19: "HUSB–DAUG" is written twice, one above the other, as if this happened two separate times on one day. And on January 30, this note: "1:45 p.m. Family."

Yes, I use counting as a way to manage my sadness, reading this bleak record. Well, at least Momma was given daily starch baths, as attested to by the nurse's notes in the "Medication Record" section.

I was there in the background. My mother was in a mental hospital, for months, not weeks. Momma whom I missed and needed when I was that child. They tried to help her, but they failed. They would probably say it was her fault: she was beyond help. *They*: her collection of psychiatrists and nurses might say that.

What if I compare what was recorded by those doctors and nurses with what I remember about the children's visits? I know my memory has not always been reliable regarding this story of my mother, and I realize I'm biased in her favor. The medical record indicates that I visited Momma in that mental hospital, possibly in an institutional-style dining room as prescribed by Dr. D., on December 19, 1965, when I was three and a half. Perhaps again as recommended by Dr. C., on January 30, 1966, when I was four. Despite those records, I have zero memory of being in a hospital or visiting Momma there.

What I remember: standing with Sydney in the living room of that Ann Arbor house, and being told that Momma was in the hospital, but I was too young to visit. Maybe that was the same day the cryptic note twice said: "HUSB–DAUG." But why twice? As if I *was* there, a cutoff half daughter, and the half that was subtracted was my memory.

I think Sydney did go. She is the first "DAUG." Maybe the second note was a simple mistake. The later January note about a family visit could mean Dad took Sydney again, although I think it's more likely he brought Nana that time, and left Syd and me at home with a babysitter, maybe the renters on the top floor again. Dad, maybe together with Nana, probably did decide I was too young to visit Momma in that hospital.

What about all the times the record says Momma came home on a pass? I also don't remember that. I only remember being given those odd craft projects as presents. I thought the day we got those presents from Momma was when she arrived home for good. But maybe we got the gifts on one of the days she reappeared briefly and then went away again.

I've been wrong before, but I trust my memory over this report. I don't think I was ever in that hospital. But I could have forgotten, blocked out everything as too much to understand at the time.

I don't wish I got to visit Momma there. At age three, I felt annoyed about being told I was too young to do something my older sister got to do. Now I'm grateful I never had a disturbing image of Momma in that institution saved in my mind. I was too young to have any perspective or context, and the person I might have seen would have been a sedated, distorted, half-lost version of my mother.

Instead, I stood in the Ann Arbor living room with that low window that looked out at our flat, grassy yard with the wooden fence built by Dad, and the cherry tree, and I couldn't see the babies under the mother rabbit even though Dad and Sydney kept pointing at the yard beyond the glass, asking me repeatedly, "Don't you see the baby rabbits?"

• • •

On the last day of February, the strength of Momma's Librium doses was cut from 25 milligrams to 10 milligrams, still four times a day. On March 9, the "Clinical Report" by a nurse notes Momma said yes to roller skating. Significant, since reportedly she didn't like sports. On March 16, she attended a party, then was allowed out on a pass for three hours. Not into the care of her husband for the first time. Alone.

Where did she go, I wonder, during those hours, by herself for the first time in months? What did she do, wandering around outside the walls of that fortress on a hill? Did she go back to the bookstore near the university she described to Jean, in a letter from the fall of 1962, soon after she moved to Ann Arbor with her husband and two young children? That wonderful dark, damp store with rows and rows of books. Her doctors must have been testing to see if she could leave the hospital alone without harming herself. Before they sent her home.

On March 18, 1966, a note in the "Clinical Report" section says she last saw Dr. C. at 4 p.m. Then under the column labeled "Remarks": "Disch to husb w meds 5:10 p.m." On the same date, under "Physician's Orders": "Discharged to care of her husband. —Dr. C."

She came home. Presumably, she continued her weekly visits with Dr. A., continued taking her daily doses of Librium, the same 10 milligram capsules she was taking when she overdosed on them. Just no more Tofranil, the topper-upper.

• • •

There's one more significant piece of information I learn from this long medical report. Just before the end, another out-of-sequence report repeating details about the 2 a.m. trip Momma made to the ER when she overdosed on her psychiatric meds (one hundred Tofranil and one hundred Librium), the near-fatal overdose that led to this long stay in the NPI.

Then the final two pages. At first, I don't understand what I'm reading. It looks like another restatement of the 2 a.m. December 1 ER visit in 1965. But the details don't match. At last, I locate a difficult-to-read stamp, blurred because the numbers overlap a printed word: "DATE." This is the only identifying date on these final two pages. I decipher the faint numbers: "10.13.63." Put that together with these other words on this page: "EMERGENCY SERVICE. REASON FOR VISIT: took 50 Librium. Arrival time: 12:40 A.M."

Not the same ER visit. Not December 1, 1965. Finally, this explains the repeated references in the earlier ER reports to Momma's *two* previous suicide attempts. Momma's *first* suicide attempt is likely accounted for by the scar on her left wrist. Here in this hard-to-decipher report on the final pages is the missing information about her *other* previous suicide attempt. "10.13.63."

I feel overwhelmed and my head swims when I try to unscramble the story of these multiple suicide attempts. I grew up only knowing about the time Momma died by suicide. In Amherst when I was six. Plus *one* suicide attempt in Ann Arbor when I was three, which I'd barely known about. Dad's story of Momma's other attempt when she cut her wrists didn't even come out until I was an adult.

Emerging from these last confusing pages of this medical record is evidence of a third suicide attempt. The writing on the last page of this ER report from October 13, 1963 is scribbly, a few words nearly impossible to make out. The signature at the end: "Dr. A."

> HISTORY PHYSICAL EXAMINATION AND TREATMENT: 31-year-old white female likely took 50 (10mg) Librium caps at approx. 11–11:30 P.M. on 10/12. Husband discovered she had taken them and called private physician who called police and recommended being seen in ER. Patient has had known psychiatric illness in past and is under care of private psychiatrist. Pt. has attempted suicide in past with one general hospitalization. Pt. has not vomited nor has there been sign of respiratory distress. No unconsciousness.
>
> Mental Status: Pt. is somewhat drowsy but not unconscious; lying on operating room table but recognizing individuals and objects. Speech slightly retarded but not slurred. Thinking clear.

> Affect somewhat depressed. Orientation and memory is good at this point and infrequently.
>
> Impression: Acute depression with suicidal gesture.
>
> STATE WHAT DISPOSITION OF CASE WAS MADE: Home to continue in care of private psychiatrist. Gastric lavage! —Dr. A.

So many strange things about that last page of these medical records. That line that trails off ungrammatically with the word "infrequently." Infrequently what? Or am I reading the scrawled word incorrectly? Even more importantly, that single word: "gesture." How to interpret that word with its emphatic underlining? How did Dr. A. conclude this drug overdose of Momma's was a gesture? Not a serious suicide attempt requiring hospitalization. Because the number of pills wasn't enough to kill her? Because she wasn't unconscious? But still serious enough to warrant his urgent directive to pump out her stomach, with an exclamation point.

Strange that the form is signed by Dr. A., yet his top paragraph mentions the patient was "under care of private psychiatrist." Dr. A. doesn't clarify that the psychiatrist was himself. Odd, the shared habit of these multiple psychiatrists of referring to themselves in this detached-from-self, third-person manner.

Also, what about the reference in that same paragraph to another past suicide attempt of Momma's, followed by a hospitalization, but not in a mental hospital? I assume that was the time Momma cut her left wrist, as evidenced by the scar noted in one of the 1965 ER reports.

She tried how many times to die by suicide? No wonder my head swims when I sort through her several suicide attempts.

First, the time she cut her wrist, if the 1963 ER report reference to a previous attempt meant the wrist-cutting time. Second, the time Dr. A. called a gesture, when Momma took fifty Librium in October 1963. Those two times, plus her bigger drug overdose in 1965, add up to three. Maybe Dr. D. was right when she counted Momma's suicide attempts and arrived at the number three.

Sitting at my small corner desk in my bedroom in Brooklyn, the same workplace where I've been examining this long medical report, I look once more at Momma's Nana letters. According to those letters, my mother started seeing a psychiatrist at the end of July 1963, when I was not quite two. No sooner did Momma get her hands on the Librium than she OD'd on it, in mid-October that year, according to that last page of hospital records.

Momma's next letter to Nana, November 24, 1963, barely a month after that "suicide gesture":

> I am taking a new drug, Tofranil, along with the Librium. From the little I understand about it the two have somewhat opposing effects, so that between them I feel quite 'chemically stabilized,' more than enough to carry on. Joking aside, I do feel fine.

After Momma's October suicide "gesture," Dr. A added an antidepressant drug, Tofranil, to the Librium in his prescription.

Three more letters from Momma to Nana. January, February, then March 1964. Then the letters stop. Momma stopped writing. Or maybe Reid decided not to send me the rest of those letters, if there were more. I don't know what scenario is most likely, maybe that the drugs left Momma unmotivated or in no condition to write more letters to her mother. That last letter of Momma's from March 1964 is the one that talks about the big blizzard and the upcoming Odetta concert.

It took less than two years from her October 1963 suicide gesture to the end of November 1965, when she tried again, again took all her meds at bedtime, arrived back in the ER of the same Ann Arbor hospital in the middle of the night. But this time when she swallowed her entire supply of meds, she had a bigger supply. She ingested all of both drugs, the Librium and Tofranil together. It nearly worked.

One question: which time was the one Dad told me about? Why didn't he ever tell me there were actually two times when Momma overdosed on her psychiatric medications at bedtime and ended up at the ER in the middle of the night? Did he forget? Mix up the two times so they blended into one in his memory, both so similar, both leading to an ER visit. Once when Momma was sent home after having her stomach pumped out. The second when she arrived in a coma, needed a respirator and dialysis, ended up in the mental hospital. For months, not weeks. Did he feel it was too much to tell me about? Or maybe he tried to forget it all ever happened.

Also, why did Dr. A. keep Momma supplied with so many drugs? Her psychiatrist had no clue she was suicidal? By 1965, she had already tried two times. But he thought one was just a gesture. Momma wrote to Nana, "I do feel fine." She was lying to her mother, or to herself. Also, to her doctor. Or to everyone, maybe hoping the drugs, the visits to Dr. A., were helping.

• • •

After studying Momma's hospital record for days, weeks even, I searched online for Doctors D., C., and A. The psychiatrists who treated Momma in Ann Arbor. Those first two doctors, I can't figure out who they were or are from their scribbled names. But Dr. A. has an unusual-enough name, something that sounds like a type of medication. I find him on the first try. He's still alive unless the online record is outdated; highly likely because he'd probably be in his nineties by now. Around the age of Dad, if he were still alive. Dr. A. is listed as still practicing, not in Ann Arbor but a different Midwestern city. Do I want to contact him? Ask for information about my deceased mother? His former patient who tried to kill herself at least twice under his care.

After she was discharged, it took Momma another two years, but she did eventually die by suicide. Did Dr. A. know that? Would he tell me his impressions of her? Would he still have any medical records, any written notes about their therapy sessions? Do I even want to know what diagnosis he gave her, after she exited that Michigan institution with that word-salad diagnosis from Dr. C.? Do I even want to hear Dr. A.'s description of my mother, after those images of her delivered in the language of various hospital personnel? Would Dr. A. know the name of the psychiatrist Momma started seeing in Massachusetts? At some point, Dad told me she started seeing a different doctor after we moved to Amherst. Dr. A. must have forwarded Momma's records to the new psychiatrist. Would I next attempt to track down that psychiatrist as well? The doctor who was treating Momma when she died? Where does the search for her end? How do I find an ending to this story of her that I want? An ending for Momma that I get to decide this time.

Why: never solved, not really. In the ER that time in 1965 when she nearly died, they helped her even though she wasn't sure she wanted to be saved. They worked hard to save her. They kept her alive. She lived. She got better, or somewhat better. In the hospital, the NPI, the fourth level, then the sixth level. On medication, she "stabilized." She returned home, still on one of the two meds she'd recently overdosed on. Two years later, after we moved to Massachusetts, she tried again. She didn't try overdosing again. Or cutting herself. That time she succeeded.

In this cold, confusing hospital medical report, I feel like I found Momma, some part of her. And when I found her, I also found part of myself. A part I didn't realize I lost. A child, too young to understand what was happening. Who wasn't told what was happening, was protected from knowing, by Dad, by Nana. We barely talked about any of this later though, not even when I was grown up. Except those few times Dad abruptly divulged some undigested bits of his story. My memory minimized those months when my mother was missing to a time when she was away for a couple of weeks. In a hospital. In my mind, that time turned into something I rarely thought about.

In 1965, my mother made a serious attempt to end her life. She nearly died. She was in a mental hospital for three and a half months. It was a major event. In her life, in the life of our family, in my life as a child. Before that, Momma made two increasingly serious attempts to end her life. The silence surrounding my mother's story swallowed part of me. Helped turn me into a quiet person with a soft voice. Like her.

From reading these medical records, it's clearer to me now that my mother was on a definite trajectory toward dying by suicide, a path that began before she married and became a mother. A path that probably started with the suicide of her father. Seeing that she was already on that path, I feel released. What she did had almost nothing to do with me. The story of her ending wasn't about our family.

I can picture her there in the hospital. Smoking a cigarette, delivering an acerbic comment to chilly Dr. D. Super-quietly pursuing her ceramics projects, along with those other unusual craft projects she brought home as gifts for me and Sydney.

Empty jewelry boxes. A handwoven rug made of rags. A mosaic hot plate. I can see her. She is there in the hospital, the place they saved her, temporarily. Half revived her with drugs. She was never the same person again. I remember Dad telling me that once. When she came home and dyed her hair black.

• • •

Momma, what you did, I can see better now, those repeated suicide attempts that eventually hit home. Why, I think I even understand that more. You came out of the hospital more broken. All I can think to say is sorry. Even though I wasn't responsible for what happened, I'm sorry.

One more thing I can see, too, is how hard you were trying to stay. Like with those horseback riding lessons in Amherst. That note in your hospital record said you didn't even like sports. Were you trying to enjoy the horseback riding?

CHAPTER 34

Ghost Stream Waters

Mother of Two Dies Sunday,
Monday, February 26, 1968

> The wife of an assistant professor at the School of Business, University of Massachusetts, was found dead by her husband Sunday. Medical Examiner Dr. Papp today ruled the death a suicide… according to Lt. Grover of the district attorney's office. She died from "strangulation by ligature," according to Dr. Papp. Police said the woman was found with two plastic bags over her head, tied at the neck with a cord.

The rest of the article contains the same information as Momma's other obituary. The facts of her life condensed into a single paragraph. I don't remember exactly when I first saw this newspaper clipping that Dad saved. I still have all those other obituaries stuffed in my folder of family papers.

• • •

Sunday. I was outside with Sydney and the neighborhood kids. Bossy Peggy, Nick, the guardian. Deb of the flaming hair, my closest friend in the group. Tiny, tough Frances. Her tinier brothers weren't with us that afternoon. Not Angela because she couldn't climb. Instead, Peggy's brothers, the two older ones who usually avoided us, were there. We all ended up in the backyard of a house on Nutting. The retired couple who lived there had two girls in college who sometimes babysat for Syd and me. A worn playhouse stood at the far end of their backyard, a skeleton of tall wooden poles.

Calling down from the roof of the playhouse, Peggy's brothers dared the rest of us to climb up and join them, giant apes with lanky limbs and buzz-short haircuts. Peggy, Nick, Deb, Frances, Sydney, everyone started to scramble up, with me following, not wanting to be left out. By shimmying my body up one of the scratchy poles, I managed to reach the roof.

"Whoever's afraid to jump is a chicken!" one of Peg's brothers yelled. As I clung to one of the poles at the top of the playhouse, peering through the open grid at the dirt ground far below, a strange feeling rippled through me. The whole world rocked back and forth. I was a tiny creature inside a glass, and someone picked up the container of the earth and tilted it side to side, once, twice, with me clinging to one pole with its scratchy bark. Something was wrong at home. I saw Sydney's face as she clutched a nearby pole. She looked alarmed, staring at the distant ground. I didn't know if she felt the same earth tremor. I didn't wait to explain. Without a word to her or the others, I dropped down and hit the dirt hard, running toward home, not stopping for Syd, who raced after me.

• • •

When I think back to that day over fifty years ago, I don't know how I could have known something was wrong from a block away. My memory of that earth tremor may be a layer added by hindsight, but the feeling remains as vivid as if I still clung to the rough bark of that pole at the top of the playhouse.

Something is off about this memory though. When I look up the weather in Amherst for that Sunday afternoon, I see that it was cold and windy, even snowing a bit. I don't remember freezing temperatures or snow. I picture myself in a light jacket, no mittens or gloves, climbing up, then dropping from those rough poles with my bare hands.

At home, the kitchen was quiet. I found Dad in the living room, watching a Sunday afternoon movie: Tarzan on some silly adventure: climbing, running, canoeing, swinging through branches in the jungle. The sight of Dad seated on our couch reassured me. I tucked myself in beside him, while Sydney settled on his other side. Soon I noticed a strange noise.

"What's that?" I asked. I heard something behind the movie soundtrack coming from our small black-and-white TV across the room. It sounded like something heavy dragging across the floor overhead.

"It's nothing." Dad sounded calm, certain. I believed him, allowed myself to be reassured; simultaneously, the anxious feeling that something was wrong seeped into my thoughts.

"Where's Momma?" I pressed Dad.

"Upstairs, taking a nap." He kept watching the movie on the TV across the room.

With the distant calmness of watching a movie, next, I found myself in our upstairs bathroom, taking a bath. I hadn't turned on the light, and as the water cooled and the daylight dimmed, I saw the shimmering reflections from the bathwater on the wallpaper by the tub, a pattern of silvery seagulls with pastel pink-and-blue seashells.

Outside in the hall, Dad knocked on the door of the bedroom he and Momma shared: "Ann! Ann!" he called with increasing urgency.

"Call the fire department!" I heard him yell, his voice loud, sharp, like he never sounded in real life. He shouted for Sydney.

I heard pounding on the door to my parents' room, running feet in the hall.

Next scene: I'm wearing a red flannel nightgown, sitting on my familiar bed in the bedroom I share with my sister at the opposite end of the hall from our parents' room. Sydney, in her matching blue flannel nightgown, sits quietly beside me. We're waiting for something, I'm not sure what. With one hand, I sail a toy metal cup from my sister's tea set back and forth in front of our faces, pretending it's a flying saucer. I turn to Sydney and say a thought that pops with level certainty into my head: "Momma is dead."

Sydney's mouth drops open, but she says nothing as her blond curls float around her baby face. I feel as surprised as she looks. For once I know something before she does.

The last scene that day: Dad, Sydney and I sit together on Sydney's double bed. This is our new family grouping, although I don't realize that yet. No mother. Dad sits cross-legged on the bed between me and Sydney, one arm around each of us. Protecting and comforting us but also leaning on me slightly. A fourth person stands inside the closed bedroom door. A man dressed in black, a black satchel hanging from his hand.

"Who's that?" I whisper.

"The doctor. From up the street," Dad tells me quietly.

I feel exposed, watched.

Dad speaks again. "Momma is dead." His words break off, his chest and shoulders heave. Tears run down his face. The doctor watches.

Across from me, Sydney is crying too. I'm surprised that she can feel anything. I hover slightly above my body, observing the three of us, the doctor waiting at the door. I know I'm supposed to cry so I force myself to make the sounds of crying.

• • •

Something else Dad once told me about that Sunday afternoon. The detail didn't come out until I was older, one of the other times I got him to retell that story, probably during one of his summer visits when we sat talking in the kitchen of my house in Brooklyn, a home he helped me buy.

When the fire department arrived, the police came, too, Dad said. The part that still made him angry years later: a police detective questioned him. Took him downstairs to the kitchen, sat him at the table. Right then. Questions you ask a murder suspect. Immediately after he found his wife dead in their bedroom. With me and Sydney waiting in our upstairs bedroom.

I never asked Dad how he found Momma. In the eaves, that dark, narrow crawl space under the front roof? Did he first see her lying in the dark, plastic bag over her head, rope around her neck? Did he have to drag her out of the eaves into the middle of the bedroom? Or did someone else do that? One of the firemen?

Dad said he telephoned the couple he and Momma were supposed to see a movie with later. They came right over. The mom, whom I barely knew, fixed soup for Sydney and me, got us ready for bed. I have no memory of that.

The next morning, Monday, Dad drove me to school. We were taken by my teacher into a quiet office at the back of the church where I went to kindergarten. I sat beside Dad in an adult-sized chair, conscious of being a child because my feet didn't reach the floor.

Across a large wooden desk, Mrs. West looked at me intently. Usually friendly and motherly, she spoke in a serious voice. "You can always come to me if you need anything."

I nodded without answering, hoping to escape as soon as possible from her probing gaze.

After school, as if this were a typical day, I was dropped off on the sidewalk on the corner of Nutting, climbing out of a car full of children, driven by one of the carpool mothers.

A group of people were gathered on the sidewalk across from my house, in front of the three-story white house full of apartments where Nick lived. Usually, no grown-ups lingered outside in the middle of the day. I hovered near the group, not recognizing anyone. They spoke in hushed voices so I couldn't understand what they were saying. The next minute, Nick appeared at my shoulder, whispering in my ear. "They're talking about your mother."

I felt he was being kind, trying to explain what was happening. Standing at my side while the grown-ups gossiped about my mother, not seeing me or purposely ignoring me. My house across the street looked familiar but far away.

I have a nagging worry about this part of my memory though. Normally, I got out of kindergarten just before lunchtime. What was Nick doing there, whispering helpful words in my ear? He was in the same grade as Sydney and didn't normally get home until midafternoon.

As if this is a reminder that these parts don't quite fit together, next in my memory, Sydney appears, striding toward us along the sidewalk from the direction of town. Her head hangs down, metal Cinderella lunchbox in one hand, eyes and nose red and wet. Without stopping to speak, she dashes across the street, disappears into our house through the side door to our kitchen.

At my shoulder, Nick apologetically announces, "Some kids teased her in school today."

Looking back on this scene from the distance of my comfortable Brooklyn bedroom-office decades later, I recall the obituary in our small-town newspaper, the one that revealed the details of my mother's death. Those details which may have been so titillating to the neighbors that no one could remember to cross the street and offer a consoling casserole to my bereft father, or to Nana who soon arrived for her daughter's funeral.

If that obituary appeared the next day, on Monday, could details about Momma's suicide have circulated that quickly through our town, passing from parents to children, who took their ill will into school and used it to make my sister miserable? Possibly, or maybe my memory has mixed up the timing of these events, which could have happened a day or two later.

• • •

At the bottom of the basement stairs with Sydney, I stared at the lines in the wall, tracing my finger along the indents between the bricks. We liked playing in the basement, where it was cool and quiet. I looked at the pattern, imagining roads leading to far-away towns that I didn't know about. I imagined Momma going somewhere else to live. Maybe she slipped away on a bus at night without telling us. Maybe she was still alive somewhere else, living with a different family. If she left in the night with only one suitcase. If these lines were streets that led to other places.

I knew she was dead. I knew those words: Momma is dead. I had been told that, and I knew it was true. I was trying to understand what death meant. I knew that my story about streets leading to another town where Momma could be living with a different family was something I imagined. Through the closed door at the top of the stairs came a muffled sound.

"What's that noise?" I asked.

"It's Nana. She's crying."

I didn't turn to look at my sister, but I felt her next to me. I knew she enjoyed getting to be the one to tell me things. Nana was upstairs in the kitchen, making that crying sound that went on and on. I heard the water in the kitchen sink running to cover up the sound of her crying.

By the tone of Sydney's voice, the slight change in her breathing, the sniff she made as she spoke, telling me that Momma's funeral was today, I knew she was trying to make the most of this tiny escape route available to her. The width of one of those cement lines. A scrap of superiority she asserted over me. The slightest thing more that she knew. If that was her escape route, then mine would be through these roads between the bricks, through my thoughts, by whatever I could imagine.

> Protests Obituary:
>
> Dear Sir,
>
> I would like to protest the manner in which your newspaper handled the notice of the death of Mrs. Ann P. The detailed account of the circumstances of her death was in no way information to which the public's right-to-know applied. You did not mention the cause of death of any of the other eight persons whose obituary notices were in the same issue of your paper. Why did you find it necessary to do so in this case? You have clearly invaded the privacy of this family in the interests of sensationalism. That may make your paper sell better, but it does you no credit as a responsible journalist nor as a sensitive human being.
>
> Because of your reporting, two little girls, who had been told that their mother's death was suicide, but had not been told all the details, must now carry a mental picture of the exact manner of her death for the rest of their lives. Because of your reporting, they will be subject to the thoughtless and often cruel remarks of other

> children, who need not and should not have known any details.
>
> I hope that in the future you will have some compassion for the families of suicide victims and save them from the suffering you have caused this family.
>
> Mrs. West (Hilary's Teacher)

When Dad handed over that newspaper clipping he'd saved, I was probably in high school, around the time he gave me his letters from Momma. I was glad Mrs. West defended our family with her letter to the local paper. At the same time, I cringed when I read her words: "two little girls." They reminded me of her probing stare.

• • •

Crossing the open room of my kindergarten another day, a child said something to me. I didn't know her name. I was about to hop across one of the play mats spread on the floor when the girl's words stopped me. "Is your mother dead?"

This was a direct, unavoidable question of exactly the type I'd received explicit instructions never to answer. Probably it was Dad who warned me, maybe also Nana. "Don't tell anyone what happened. Don't talk about what happened to Momma."

The girl's question pinned me to the spot.

"Yes," I finally answered, feeling uneasy, as though even that was more than I should say.

• • •

Strangulation by ligature. Two plastic bags over her head, tied at the neck with a cord. Not one bag, but two. Momma wasn't taking any chances; she was determined to end her life. A shocking way to die, not that there are any wonderful ways. But strangulation by ligature sounds painful and lonely. She must have made a plan at some point. That day, or days or weeks earlier. Gathering the objects she needed. Plastic bags, a rope. Waiting for a chance, or for something to set her off. Or planning it for that day all along. When she and Dad had plans for an evening movie date with another couple. A Sunday. The same day her father died. And her fight with Dad that day was incidental. She must have felt hopeless, trapped. Maybe angry.

• • •

I followed Sydney and some of our friends to school. Not all of the neighborhood kids went to the same school. It was the fall after Momma died. I was in first grade. Every day I walked with Sydney to the elementary school near the center of town. Halfway there, seized with a moment of panic, without planning it in advance, I threw my brown paper lunch bag in the weeds beside the sidewalk.

"I forgot my lunch," I announced, not stopping to hear Sydney's objections. I had to see Dad again, just for a minute. Even if I got in trouble for being late to school.

I raced back in the direction we came from, alone. Running along the shortcut in reverse. Between the blond brick phone company and the fraternity, rotting couch in the yard. Along the narrow path into the shady woods full of ferns. Running as fast as I could past the haunted-looking, deserted stone house. Popping out in our backyard that looked unrecognizable on that quiet morning when I should have already been in school. I ran past the shed with its dark windows, up the sloping, grassy yard, around the side of the garage, bursting in through the unlocked kitchen door.

There, in his suit, briefcase in hand, about to go out the door, stood Dad. An oasis of safety, bending down, a look of surprised concern on his face, asking, "What are you doing here?" His arms circled me, reassuring me, but just for a minute. "I have to go to work," he announced.

He drove me to school, hugged me goodbye quickly on the sidewalk. An unknown woman escorted me to my classroom. Faint voices came from inside each classroom as I passed along the first-floor hall. I remembered Sydney's classroom was somewhere above me on the second floor. We reached the last door on the left, my first-grade classroom. Faint voices came from inside. The woman beside me exhaled impatiently, ready to be done with depositing me. The class finished reciting the Pledge of Allegiance, followed immediately by muffled singing: "From California to the New York island…" The familiar rise and fall of voices. The words blending together, floating in the air. "From the redwood forest to the ghost stream waters…"

I knew the words were actually "Gulf Stream waters." But what I heard was "ghost stream." I enjoyed letting the words run together in my mind, letting the meaning blur into something else. The woman at my side missed the tiny pause between the Pledge and the song. In she marched anyway. My class was enthusiastically belting out, "This land was made for you and me!"

I followed my escort, terrified of standing out, of being stared at for being late. But no one stopped singing or turned to notice me as I slid into my seat in the middle of the second row.

• • •

Dad started planning an extension on our house. The addition, he called it. Those rooms he wanted to add onto the ground floor at the back of the house. Two new bedrooms, one for me, one for Sydney, across from each other. Plus a new bathroom. A dining room big enough to hold a dining room table with chairs. A sitting room with a couch and chairs. Another room just for watching television. Dad could have found a new house, moved our family somewhere else, made a fresh start, even in the same town. Instead, he decided to change the place we already lived, to stay where we were. The addition was the way he invented to keep going.

He hired an architect, a builder. Some of the work he did himself. That year, 1969, all winter, if I went into the room off the kitchen that he made into his bedroom, looking for him after dinner to talk, I always found him at his desk. He was always surrounded by piles of books and papers, stacks of exams he was grading. That winter, even more piles of papers surrounded him. Sheets of special, large paper covered with thin blue-and-red lines. Drawings for the new part of the house.

When spring arrived, bulldozers appeared in the yard. Mountains of dirt sprang up. Overnight, behind our old house, a gaping hole opened in the grassy yard. A framework of beams rose. The wooden skeleton was soon filled in with sheets of plywood. The smell of sawdust and freshly cut wood filled the air. Sheetrock and paint were layered onto the metal and wood frame. Like a picture from one of our childhood coloring books being filled in with crayon, the blank spaces inside the frames quickly turned into rooms.

A last magic trick: Dad got the builder to save our old porch. In one day, the whole porch was moved from its original spot at the back of our old house to its new spot at the far end of the addition. I had to walk through the new rooms: dining room, sitting room, TV room. Exit out the back door into—voila, the same back porch. Dad, who hated waste, avoided throwing anything out, even reused the same porch door. The door I went through with Sydney to feed our kittens on the porch for the first time. The door with the glass window that Momma must have peered through to see us stealing pablum from the kittens' dish after dinner on that cold, distant night.

In my new bedroom, sometimes I couldn't fall asleep, surrounded by unfamiliar smells. New wall-to-wall carpeting with a swirly pattern like ocean water. New polyester curtains with a matching aqua design. Fresh white paint. Sometimes a panicky feeling seized me: what if Dad was dead? What if he died suddenly? I got out of bed and walked through the dark, unfamiliar rooms to the old part of the house, to Dad's room beside the kitchen. If he was awake, hunched over his desk piles, he'd stop what he was doing and lead me back to bed.

If his light was out, I stood next to his bed, watching his chest rising and falling in the dark. He always slept on his back, hands folded across his chest. No pillow, a habit he picked up in the Navy. He always sensed me standing there. Wordlessly, he got up, walked me back through those rooms to my new bedroom, watched as I got into bed, the antique wooden rope bed I'd acquired from Sydney.

At night as an adult, I still sometimes struggle with falling asleep or staying asleep. Sometimes during a bout of insomnia, I revisit that scene with Dad. I watch as he leads me through those unfamiliar rooms of the addition. He always takes me back to my room on the other side of the house. In my memory, it's perpetually winter. I always wear a flannel nightgown, one of Nana's Christmas gifts. Dad, bare legs below a knee-length, cotton nightshirt, scuffs along in leather slippers that are always old because he never wanted to waste money on new ones. The slippers were his annual Christmas gift from Momma, he once confided. With a gruff hug, barely any words, he always leads me back to bed in my new, swirly aqua-patterned room.

Watching the two of us in that perpetually bleak winter world, it's Dad I feel sorry for, more than the motherless girl who was me. At that time, suicide survivor support groups didn't exist, not that Dad would have agreed to go to one, grouchy, independent man that he was, reared on white Protestant myths, especially prevalent for males, fantasies designed for boys involving the necessity of never letting down your guard, never requiring help, never admitting defeat. All I needed to hear, a few simple, impossible words: "I promise I will never die."

• • •

I saw Dad in our yard, bent over, spreading out some things on the grass, the tall, narrow windows of the addition glinting in the sunlight behind him.

"What's that?" I asked, running up to him.

"Momma's clothes," he answered, looking tired, his back hunched, mumbling something about the basement flooding, needing to get her clothes to dry. It was over a year since Momma died. I was eight already by then. Dad rarely mentioned her.

"I'm saving these, for you and Sydney," he explained, "in case you want them when you get older." He sounded irritated. About the flooded basement. About the extra work of needing to dry out her clothes. About needing to remember her at all.

CHAPTER 35

Momma

Hey, you two, Momma and Grandfather, your photos sit on the shelf above my desk today. This last message is for you, Momma. You can stand there silently next to her, Grandfather, listening, providing support.

I was really young when you died, Momma. I didn't have complex adult judgments about you yet, like whether you were responsible for what you did; let alone understand why you died by suicide. After your death, I was surprised that other people always had unspoken opinions about you, usually negative; people who barely knew you or our family. No one ever came out and said: suicide is a terrible act, a crime even. Therefore, anyone who kills themself is bad, evil even, or at least, without question, worse than everyone else. They didn't have to say it. The air was always so crowded with other people's feelings and judgments, it was hard to make room for my own thoughts about how you died.

• • •

I get on a Coney Island-bound Brooklyn bus, ride all the way to the edge of land, the ocean. Why? Sometimes it's too easy to lose hold of the edge of something. I walk up and down along the edge of the ocean. The wind is brutally cold, a weekend day, maybe a Sunday. Gray, the kind of day when she died; and before her, my grandfather Henry who was unknown to me. A late winter day. I walk up and down along the nearly deserted boardwalk beside the steel-cut ocean. The water and the air are both nearly freezing, and I'm freezing too. This is not the kind of day or place that reminds anyone of reasons why it's good to remain alive.

I walk until I'm too tired to walk anymore. Then I drag myself back from that edge, go to the subway, catch a train home, get myself to sleep. From there I can haul myself back so that when I wake up the next morning, I'm most of the way back. The feeling of contemplating death—wishing a certain miserable feeling would cease, fantasizing about killing myself, wrestling myself out of the grip of that feeling—has receded, and I can remember I'm glad to be alive. I've been to that edge before. I wish I never felt like that.

I'm not like my mother. I know that's true: I'm not her. I wish I came away from the story of what happened to her untouched, that I came out clean and undamaged, that none of her death wish rubbed off on me. I am safe. I made it. I still have to remind myself of that sometimes.

• • •

January 2023. Jacksonville, Florida. Visiting my mother-in-law. In the grassy yard of the house we're renting this week, a short walk from the beach. Me, my husband, our two children, my mother-in-law. A single-story bungalow with pool, patio, firepit. Bess lives in a nearby retirement community. We visit her every year for a week or two. Sometimes my husband's sisters join us. We've never stayed in this rental before. We don't usually have a firepit. I really want to use it.

We didn't build a fire or sit outside on New Year's Eve. My husband and I were too tired; we went to sleep early. We don't usually stay up until midnight anymore. Now it's a few days into the new year, and we're already leaving tomorrow after a peaceful week of everyone cooking and eating together, sitting around the pool, walks on the beach a few blocks away, after-dinner drives to ice cream places, even a trip to a pool hall for our teenage son. Still no bonfire. I really wanted the bonfire.

My husband and son drive to the store for whatever you can buy to burn in Florida. I collect dried palm fronds and bark from the yard. One bulky log sits in the firepit, left by the Airbnb hosts.

Dusk. We light the fire. Even my son makes a brief appearance, then returns inside to his screens. In the sudden darkness, the rest of us sit in beach chairs on the gravel around the firepit in shorts, sweatshirts. Stars, clear sky, no bugs. The air is gentle and still like bathwater. The fire is bright, centering. We're quiet together. Bess, my husband, my daughter, too, but after a while, she also drifts inside, after telling Bess about her new job doing HR for a small NYC company; her first full-time, post-college job. She already told Bess a little about her job earlier this week.

Then it's me talking to Bess, my husband listening. Bess likes to talk, so I decide to outtalk her tonight. I tell her about my writing project, my mother's papers, exploring the story of her suicide. I've known Bess for decades; she knows my mother died by suicide, but I've never talked to her about my mother's story before.

On three sides of this fenced-in yard, other houses hosted private fireworks displays on New Year's Eve. We slept through most of it. Tonight, it's mostly quiet; a few startling pops send lights shooting into the dark sky. I think of my wish for a bonfire, a marker of something. Cleansing, change. Finality, rage, hope. Fire: a chemical reaction, releasing energy.

Soon I'm turning a year older. I'll be sixty-one. If Momma were alive, she'd turn ninety-one this year. The age Dad was when he died, close to Bess's age. Suddenly, I'm crying, talking to Bess about my writing, about my mother, telling her what I'm still trying to figure out. My crying surprises me. Bess wants to turn the conversation to writing as a type of therapy.

"I don't want to reduce my project to that," I tell her.

Instead, I shift the topic to how relieved I felt when our children returned safely from their car trip today. They took our car out on their own for the first time. They both agreed on a short trip to a nearby pizza place, their early dinner out alone together. We have our own car from home here, not a rental. My husband and son drove from New York to northern Florida, while my daughter and I took an airplane together. My son got tons more practice driving, which thrills him. Still, he never drove our car without a parent before, never with just his sister.

Unannounced, after their solo dinner, our children took the car to one of the ice cream places we went to earlier in the week; the best place that was farthest away. They didn't return when expected. My husband and I could watch their location on our phones. The dots on my phone screen kept moving as they drove; they weren't dead. Still, I worried. They did return, just an hour later than expected. An hour that felt like a century for a parent like me who knows too much about death. The reality of sudden, unexpected death.

Earlier in the afternoon, when I sat out here by the pool with my daughter, woodpeckers were drilling into the palm trees that arched overhead. Now sitting with my husband and mother-in-law around the firepit, the children safely tucked into their rooms inside, both probably watching shows on their screens, it's dark, quiet. A few more jarring pops explode in neighboring yards. The fire burns down. Behind us, darkness reflects in the sliding glass doors to the house. Time for bed, for sleep.

Tomorrow, travel. I brought no papers with me; I have nothing of Momma's to burn.

Lately, I'm thinking of keeping all of her papers, the ones I still have, even though there are so many. Even the ones I don't like: the obituaries. Even that last bitter pill: the printout of Momma's mental hospital record. What's changed in my relationship to Momma's papers? I love them more now. They're a record of my own life too. I don't want to get rid of anything.

• • •

Back at home in Brooklyn, I start to plan a celebration—no, that's the wrong word. A commemoration. Of the anniversary of Momma's suicide. I want to invent some kind of belated, but possibly annual, goodbye and moving-on ritual. I talk over the plan with my husband while we're out walking through our neighborhood one weekend afternoon.

I don't want to burn any of her papers, I explain. I've come around to deciding to keep everything I still have. Even the musty Denison yearbook. For the ritual, I need somewhere to burn a slip of paper. My husband suggests the decorative stone tabletop firepit we acquired after moving into our new place but haven't used much. It could probably be used to burn not armfuls of paper, but certainly a single, small piece. Enough for what I have in mind.

Like Nana, I begin to plan the meal that will accompany the event, my new ritual for saying goodbye to my mother's family suicide pattern and the silence surrounding it. Too many words. I'll have to come up with a better name for my ritual. Tofu teriyaki, that's what I'll cook, because everyone in our family likes it, as long as we don't have it too often. I don't think Nana ever tasted tofu; certainly Grandfather Henry didn't. I'm not sure about Momma, but probably not.

I wanted to write a story that explained my mother's suicide, that told her story. I wanted my writing to semi-magically recreate my mother, so I could bring her to life in my mind, even briefly, but I didn't want to include much about myself. I wanted to keep myself and all the messy, private parts of myself out of view. But my mother is still alive through me. We are separate. I'm a different, distinct person, complete without her. Yet in me is where parts of her continue to live. In my memories of her. Not only in the papers about her. In the parts of me that are like her. I look like her. I sound like her. Years ago, Reid told me that. For years I wore her clothes. As I grew up, most of her clothes fit me, and I liked wearing most of them. The blue suede jacket and gloves. The flowered cotton blouses. The Pepto Bismol-pink cardigan. I was her and I wasn't her, like her and not like her.

Why Momma died by suicide. A mix of many different negative factors. Her father who also died by suicide when she was a child, when he was her closest parent. That father, Henry, who might have been diagnosed as bipolar, if he'd lived in a later decade. Nana, a mother who covered up her husband's suicide, who never talked with Momma about what happened. There are still more reasons on the list of whys. The stress of motherhood; Momma's mixed feelings about being a mother. The loss of her friendship with Jean. The dragging on of winter. The violent Tet Offensive in the news and that low point in the war in Vietnam, with her connection to that place. Her recent move to a small New England town where she was a stranger.

• • •

I'm with some people. First, I'm with friends, people I know. Then they drift away and I'm with strangers, in the evening, walking toward the edge of a crowded road that I need to get across. From somewhere behind me, someone comes racing toward me out of the crowd, passing me, annoyingly jostling me as she passes. It's a woman, I see as she runs by. I only glimpse the back of her as she passes. I don't know who she is; not myself, not my mother, just a woman, a stranger. She runs toward the busy road in a rush to cross.

At the edge of the traffic, there's a dip in the pavement, but she moves fast, doesn't notice the dip, rushing to get somewhere. I hear a resounding bang; I almost see her go down, but it happens so fast; she disappears, smashing face downward behind the crowd of people as the bang echoes in the air.

I run forward to find her, thinking: I should help that woman. Now it's darker, the crowd has thinned out. I get to the spot where I think the woman went down, the dip before the road. I'm almost alone here in the dark. Even the traffic whizzing past is gone. No one comes to help. I find her, a woman lying on the concrete, but it's only her head and neck, her face turned toward me, her body missing. I almost recognize her as my mother; still, I feel I don't know this stranger. I'm not sure if she's dead, but she must be: the noise of her crashing down was so loud, her head must have fallen off. White skin, short dark hair, faded red lipstick. Her face turned sideways toward me, eyes closed.

It's a dream, just a bad dream, I'm telling myself by this point. When I wake up, it will go away and not be real. One of those dreams you're so glad is only a bad dream; pulling yourself back from it; glad you get to return from sleep to the waking world. So real, that image of a woman's head separated from her body. Her body missing, vanished.

Is this dream a fragment of a memory of my mother? Something I was looking for in my mind, and now my mind has given me this: a horrible dream, something I'd rather forget again. Like the statue of shiny black wood, the tall, thin sculpture of a woman that Momma brought back from her travels, then broke in one of her fights with Dad. The one I remembered when they were yelling at each other and I heard something crashing and breaking behind their closed bedroom door; later, Dad glued the statue back together. Just like what cold Dr. D. wrote in her "Admission Note" about Momma's history of stormy behavior at home, taken out on herself by breaking one of her valuable possessions. I have done that too. Lost my temper and thrown things, destroyed objects, not often but sometimes. Another thing I didn't want to include.

I don't want my dreams to send me any more messages like that woman's severed head. It's a message from myself that I wish I could send back, that I don't want to know. But I do want to know; I'm still trying to understand who Momma was. What happened to her. All the W's.

Who: White woman. Mother of two.

What: Suicide.

Where: Her own bedroom.

When: Sunday, February 25, 1968. Late winter. Vietnam War grinding on in the background. Same time of year and day of week that her father also died by suicide.

Probably that's all the "why" I'm going to get.

I write down that little story on a slip of paper. Those W's. That's the story of my mother's suicide. I've got it written on one piece of paper now.

On the back side, I pick one more word to write. There are a lot of different words I could choose from. Sadness. Anger. Loss. For now, I start with one: "shame."

• • •

When the evening in question arrives, my husband and children are home in our Brooklyn apartment, and I'm ready. Before dinner, I get out our tabletop firepit, fill the stone bowl with rubbing alcohol. The high alcohol content kind that burns longer. This firepit is too small for a major bonfire, but it should do the trick. While I do these last-minute preparations for my goodbye ritual, I have another short, silent talk with Momma.

I'm still working my way through your reading list, I tell her. I don't love everything. A lot of those books I don't even like and force myself to finish, but I'm trying. I've got about a dozen titles to go, if I tackle all that Faulkner. I even watched all the films you mentioned.

I know you were a big cat lover. I like cats, but I'm allergic to them. You didn't stick around long enough to learn that about me. Soon, Momma, by this summer, we're getting a puppy. A hypoallergenic one because I'm allergic to dogs too. The puppy is for my son; he really wants a dog.

I gather everyone for dinner. This night when everyone is home falls on my daughter's night to cook. I give her a break, let her set the table and fill everyone's water glasses. She's still jet-lagged from a week with her boyfriend in Spain, the first big trip she saved and paid for herself, returning days ago to her full-time job.

I didn't have time to prepare the planned tofu teriyaki for tonight. Instead, with a hand from my husband, I made soup using long-lasting potatoes from our cupboard, along with dill from the garden of our neighbors whose plants I've been watering while they're away. That's what inspires my best meals, using what's available, not wasting food, a lesson I learned from Dad, the Depression-era survivor.

I've told my family about what I have planned for tonight, this goodbye ritual. At first, while we eat, we discuss other topics. My daughter's recent Spain trip. A yearlong job in that country that she's considering, teaching English like a friend of hers. The puppy our family's getting soon.

Today is not the 25th of February, not the real anniversary of Momma's suicide, or even of Henry's. Today is not even the 25th of the current month, which is May. The soonest month after February that I'm ready to do this thing. Maybe if I repeat this ritual next year, or in coming years, I'll finally be ready on time, on the anniversary of her actual death. This year, this watered-down dose of remembering Momma's suicide is what I'm ready for. I don't tell my family all of this. Instead, when we finish eating, I say, "This isn't the real anniversary of my mother's death. But this is as close as I could get this year."

With a deep breath, I add, "This is my ritual for saying goodbye to the bad parts of my family suicides, of saying goodbye to my mother."

My daughter is into this, as long as it doesn't take too long. In Brooklyn, May is a sweet, lovely month, a contrast to the armpit of winter. May is also the month she was born. Right before she went to Spain, at her request, we all celebrated her birthday, ordering Indian takeout, eating dinner together at home.

I thought about telling one small story tonight, something pleasant about Momma. Ahead of time, I planned a few possibilities. Her reading to me. Or her cutting my hair. Or maybe a different one. Her exercising on the kitchen floor in Amherst. I found her that way once, lying on her side on the fake brick linoleum. Bumping her hip up and down so her lower side slammed repeatedly against the floor.

"What are you doing?" I asked, feeling confused by this activity I never witnessed before.

"Exercising," she answered, looking like she wasn't enjoying herself but didn't want to be interrupted. Even at whatever age I was, four or five, maybe within months of her final act, which of course I didn't know was coming, I sensed that something about her answer didn't make sense. When I was an adult and I recalled that memory, I wondered if something as useless and possibly self-harming as jamming her hip repeatedly against the floor was something she believed was a helpful exercise. Was this an activity that other women at the time were told to perform to improve their appearance or fitness? That Momma anecdote was too mixed with elements of self-injury to qualify as pleasant though. I figured that in the moment on the evening of my ritual, I'd pick which good Momma memory to share.

In the end, there isn't time to tell even one Momma story. My son isn't into this whole Momma ritual. No sooner do I give my short explanation, feeling awkward and embarrassed even in front of my closest people, than my son is already standing up from the table, unapologetically mumbling that he's got an online gaming session planned with a friend. Before he vanishes to his basement den of computer equipment, I manage to get him to take part in one thing of the kind he loves.

"Will you help light the fire?"

Of course he nods. Passing him the black culinary torch, I show him how to flick the metal notch with his thumb. A tiny, white-hot tongue jumps out. He touches the flame to the bowl of clear alcohol. The jet of fire seizes the vaporous liquid. A blue-green halo hovers over the colorless pool, leaps high in a burst of yellow, orange, and white in the darkened room. Like the rest of a magic trick, my son disappears. Drifts silently and effortlessly downstairs to his lair, and that's fine. My husband cracks open a window so any smoke can escape.

My daughter and husband remain at the table, which I stand beside. My husband sits silently, patiently—well, sort of patiently. Soon, despite our son's gaming date, my husband needs to help our son with some homework. My daughter stares at her phone, typing something, probably texting her boyfriend. My ritual feels silly, but I persist. Beside my elbow is a familiar, plain white business envelope, a place of safekeeping for Momma and Henry when they haven't been helping with my book.

"Here's my picture of Momma as a girl. Here's my grandfather too." I take them out, prop them on the windowsill by our dining room table.

From my pocket, I pull out a slip of paper. In my hand it appears large, too big to burn in the tabletop stone dish. My daughter and husband call out suggestions: "Fold it…tear it."

I end up folding the paper and ripping it in half. Now I'm holding two folded bits of paper. Will this ritual end up like a magic trick where the destroyed evidence is reincarnated as a fresh, whole sheet of paper? No, the story produces no such impossible result. I don't even read my husband and daughter my mini story about Momma and her suicide, all the W's. Just the single word before I rip it in half.

"This is the part I want to get rid of first," I say.

My daughter's dark eyes glitter as she listens. My husband's face is also full of emotion as I force myself to look at them both.

"Goodbye shame," they each repeat after me softly, quiet voices in the quiet room.

In my right hand, I grasp both folded bits of paper, hold them over the blaze, feed them together into the flames, watch the heat grab them. The paper burns fast, the words disappearing.

The fire eats the paper, devours the words. I let the flame swallow the last of the paper, even that one small word, the shame. I drop the vanishing blackened paper onto a white dinner plate my husband hands me. In a second, the paper is almost gone, all the words consumed. What remains on the plate is a lump of pale ash in the shape of a dead mouse, something to be deposited in our trash after it's cooled. I know doing this doesn't clear out all the unhappiness, but that's it. I'm done.

Except maybe I'll never be done. I'll take as long as I need. For as long as I need to keep doing this. To keep saying goodbye to her. Good riddance, to the worst parts.

Miss you, Momma. Goodbye.

Notes

CHAPTER 8:

1. Bowles, Chester. *Ambassador's Report.* Harper & Brothers, 1954.
2. *The Red Shoes.* Directed by Michael Powell and Emeric Pressburger. Eagle-Lion Films, October 22, 1948 (USA).
3. Gibbon, Edward. *The Portable Gibbon: The Decline and Fall of the Roman Empire.* Viking, 1952.

CHAPTER 9:

4. Shor, Jean Bowie. *After You, Marco Polo.* McGraw-Hill, 1955.

CHAPTER 15:

5. Greene, Graham. *The Quiet American.* Heinemann, 1955.
6. Williams, Tennessee. *Camino Real.* New Directions, 1953.
7. Greene, Graham. *The Living Room.* Viking, 1953.
8. Greene, Graham. *The Power and the Glory.* Heinemann, 1940.

CHAPTER 18:

9. Faulkner, William. *The Town.* Random House, 1957.
10. Faulkner, William. *The Unvanquished.* Random House, 1938.
11. Faulkner, William. *Intruder in the Dust.* Random House, 1948.
12. Faulkner, William. *Big Woods.* Random House, 1955.
13. Faulkner, William. *Sartoris.* Harcourt Brace, 1929.
14. Howe, Irving. *William Faulkner: A Critical Study.* Vintage Books, 1942. (Possibly this was the pre-1957 book about Faulkner mentioned.)
15. Faulkner, William. *Knight's Gambit.* Random House, 1949.
16. Faulkner, William. *A Fable.* Random House, 1954.
17. Saroyan, William. *Rock Wagram.* Doubleday, 1951.
18. Salinger, J. D. "Zooey," *The New Yorker.* May 4, 1957, p. 32-139.

19. Salinger, J. D. "Raise High the Roof Beam, Carpenters," *The New Yorker.* November 19, 1955, p. 51-116.
20. Dostoevsky, Fyodor. *The Idiot.* Penguin, 1955.
21. Joyce, James. *Dubliners.* Grant Richards, 1914.
22. Bernanos, Georges. *The Diary of a Country Priest.* Macmillan, 1937.
23. Eliot, T. S. *Selected Essays, 1917-1932.* Faber & Faber, 1932.
24. O'Casey, Sean. *Collected Plays: Volume I.* St. Martins, 1957.
25. Sibelius, Jean. Symphony No. 1–E Minor, conducted by Sir Thomas Beecham.
26. Saroyan, William. *The Human Comedy.* Harcourt, 1943.
27. Steinbeck, John. *The Pastures of Heaven.* Ballou, 1932.
28. Gide, Andre. *The Fruits of the Earth.* Knopf, 1949.

CHAPTER 19:

29. Ciardi, John. *As If: Poems New and Selected.* Rutgers University Press, 1955.
30. Eliot, T. S. "The Love Song of J. Alfred Prufrock," *Poetry: A Magazine of Verse.* June 1915, pp. 130-135.
31. Eliot, T. S. "Burnt Norton," *Four Quartets.* Harcourt, 1943.
32. Vanderbilt, Amy. *Amy Vanderbilt's Complete Book of Etiquette: A Guide to Gracious Living.* Doubleday, 1958.
33. Ustinov, Peter. "The Aftertaste," *The Atlantic.* May 1959, pp. 55-61.

CHAPTER 22:

34. Stein, Gertrude. *Alphabets and Birthdays.* Yale University Press, 1957.
35. Brinnin, John Malcolm. "Gertrude Stein in Paris," *The Atlantic.* September 1959, pp. 34-40; or "Gertrude Stein in America," *The Atlantic.* October 1959, pp. 98-106.
36. *Wild Strawberries.* Directed by Ingmar Bergman. SF Studios, June 22, 1959 (USA).
37. *The Seventh Seal.* Directed by Ingmar Bergman. SF Studios, October 13, 1958 (USA).
38. Chase, Edna and Ilka. *Always in Vogue.* Doubleday, 1954.
39. Thurber, James. *A Thurber Carnival.* Directed by Burgess Meredith, Hartman Theatre, January 7, 1960, Columbus, Ohio.
40. MacLeish, Archibald. *J.B.* Directed by Elia Kazan, Hartman Theatre, January 19, 1960, Columbus, Ohio.
41. Holbrook, Hal. *Mark Twain Tonight!* First performed in 1954.
42. *The Fugitive Kind.* Directed by Sidney Lumet. United Artists, April 14, 1960.
43. Harris, Mark. *Wake Up, Stupid.* Vintage Books, 1959.

CHAPTER 24:

44. *La Dolce Vita.* Directed by Federico Fellini. American International Pictures, April 19, 1961 (USA).

CHAPTER 25:

45. White, T. H. *The Once and Future King.* Collins, 1958.
46. Styron, William. *Set This House on Fire.* Random House, 1960. (Based on the time of the letter, this is probably the Styron book mentioned.)
47. Hayakawa, S. I., "How to Be Sane Though Negro," *Contact 1.* January 1958, pp 5-20.
48. Hayakawa, S. I. *Language in Thought and Action.* Harcourt, 1949.
49. Kerouac, Jack. *On the Road.* Viking Press, 1957.
50. Forster, E. M. *A Passage to India.* Grosset & Dunlap, 1924. (Possibly this was the Forster book that she read.)
51. *Breakfast at Tiffany's.* Directed by Blake Edwards. Paramount Pictures, October 5, 1961.
52. *The Night Before Christmas.* Directed by Aleksandr Rou, Gorky Film Studio, December 1961; based on the story by Gogol, Nilolai, "Christmas Eve," *Evenings on a Farm Near Dikanka.* Knopf, 1926.
53. Beerhohm, Max. *Portrait of Max: An Intimate Memoir of Sir Max Beerbohm.* Random House, 1960.
54. Thurber, James. *The Years with Ross.* HarperCollins, 1957.
55. Swados, Harvey. *False Coin.* Little, Brown, 1959.
56. Durrell, Lawrence. *The Black Book.* E. P. Dutton & Co., 1959.
57. Nabokov, Vladimir. *Invitation to a Beheading.* Putnam, 1959.
58. O'Faolain, Sean. *The Finest Short Stories of Sean O'Faolain.* Bantam, 1959.
59. Behan, Brendan. *The Hostage.* Methuen, 1959; or *Borstal Boy.* Nonpareil Books, 1958. (Based on the dates, one of these was probably the book she read by this author.)
60. Vidal, Gore. *The City and the Pillar.* E. P. Dutton & Co., 1948.
61. Shaw, George Bernard. "Don Juan in Hell." *Man and Superman.* Cambridge University Press, 1903. Recording with Charles Boyer, Charles Laughton, and Sir Cedric Hardwick. Columbia Records, 1952.
62. Seeger, Pete. "John Brown's Body." *American Favorite Ballads, Vol. 3.* Folkways Records, 1959.

CHAPTER 27:

63. Vidal, Gore. *Three.* Signet, 1962.
64. Porter, Katherine Anne. *Pale Horse, Pale Rider.* HarperCollins, 1939.
65. Stafford, Jean. *The Mountain Lion.* Harcourt Brace Jovanovich, 1947.

CHAPTER 28:

66. Porter, Katherine Anne. *Ship of Fools.* Little, Brown, 1962.
67. *My Name is Ivan.* Directed by Andrei Tarkovsky. Mosfilm, June 27, 1963 (USA).

Acknowledgments

Many thanks to Apprentice House Press for giving this book a home and for working with me through the publication process. Thank you especially to Marcia Trahan who helped me with careful, thoughtful editing near the end of this writing project. I have also been fortunate to receive the encouragement and guidance of several generous and gifted writing teachers to whom I will always be grateful. Finally, I could never have written this book without the loving support of my family and friends.

About the Author

Hilary Plattner has an MFA in fiction writing from Columbia University and has taught writing at The New School. Previously, she founded and directed Brooklyn Writers, a community-based writing program. Her fiction and poetry have been published in numerous literary journals, including *Allegro, Cider Press Review, Fence, GSU Review, Gulf Coast, Synkroniciti* and *The Ledge*. She lives in Brooklyn, New York, with her family.

Apprentice House Press is the country's only campus-based, student-staffed book publishing company. Directed by professors and industry professionals, it is a nonprofit activity of the Communication Department at Loyola University Maryland.

Using state-of-the-art technology and an experiential learning model of education, Apprentice House publishes books in untraditional ways. This dual responsibility as publishers and educators creates an unprecedented collaborative environment among faculty and students, while teaching tomorrow's editors, designers, and marketers.

Eclectic and provocative, Apprentice House titles intend to entertain as well as spark dialogue on a variety of topics. Financial contributions to sustain the press's work are welcomed. Contributions are tax deductible to the fullest extent allowed by the IRS.

To learn more about Apprentice House books or to obtain submission guidelines, please visit www.apprenticehouse.com.

Apprentice House Press
Communication Department
Loyola University Maryland
4501 N. Charles Street
Baltimore, MD 21210
Ph: 410-617-5265
info@apprenticehouse.com • www.apprenticehouse.com

www.ingramcontent.com/pod-product-compliance
Lightning Source LLC
LaVergne TN
LVHW010600100826
845148LV00014B/2791

* 9 7 8 1 6 2 7 2 0 6 5 4 9 *